AT RISK OF HOMELESSNESS

AT RISK OF HOMELESSNESS

The Roles of Income and Rent

Karin Ringheim

New York
Westport, Connecticut
London

Library of Congress Cataloging-in-Publication Data

Ringheim, Karin.
    At risk of homelessness : the roles of income and rent / Karin
    Ringheim.
        p.   cm.
    Includes bibliographical references (p.).
    ISBN 0-275-93582-5
    1. Poor—Housing—United States.   2. Rental housing—United
States.   3. Income—United States.   4. Cost and standard of living—
United States.   5. Homeless persons—United States.   I. Title.
HD7287.96.U6R56   1990
362.5'0973—dc20   90-34290

British Library Cataloguing-in-Publication Data is available.

Library of Congress Catalog Card Number: 90-34290
ISBN: 0-275-93582-5

First published in 1990

Praeger Publishers, One Madison Avenue, New York, NY 10010
An imprint of Greenwood Publishing Group, Inc.

Printed in the United States of America

The paper used in this book complies with the
Permanent Paper Standard issued by the National
Information Standards Organization   (Z39.48-1984).

10   9   8   7 6   5   4   3   2   1

To my parents and children

Contents

Tables and Figures

TABLES

FIGURES

Preface

"In many ways, the relationship between housing and homelessness seems self-evident. The homeless are by definition, without a permanent home. Yet the vast majority of the literature on the homeless concerns the personal and behavioral characteristics of the homeless." Undoubtedly this is related in part to the difficulty of finding or collecting appropriate data with which to investigate the structural determinants of homelessness.

Given these limitations, the approach presented in this book, to examine the incomes and rents of those who are at risk of, rather than literally homeless, tries to do more than make the best of a bad situation. I hope to make a convincing case that the extent of homelessness in individual metropolitan areas is not simply related to the extent of poverty in those areas. In fact, there have been dramatic changes over the brief 8-year period of study in the circumstances of renters, but both the cause and the extent of these changes vary considerably across metropolitan areas. This, I argue, is why we see variation in the extent of homelessness. While this approach is hampered by the ability to make only an associational rather than a causal argument, and because estimates of the homeless prior to 1983 were either nonexistant or too unreliable to be used, the parallels between these changes and the growth of homelessness as a significant social problem are hard to ignore. I hope this book will contribute to an understanding of and elimination of homelessness.

The research on which this monograph is based was completed at the University of Michigan. I am indebted to Professors Barbara Anderson, Reynolds Farley, Sheldon Danziger, and John Knodel, to the computing staff of the Population Studies Center, Dr. Albert H.

Anderson, Fran Heitz, and Michael Coble, and to the dear friends who helped keep me going. For financial support I am grateful to the National Institute of Child Health and Development, the National Institute on Aging, and the Center for the Continuing Education of Women at the University of Michigan.

More recently, I have been affiliated with the Institute for Research on Poverty and the Center for Demography and Ecology at the University of Wisconsin. While the timing of events did not allow the book to benefit from the valuable input of my colleagues here, I appreciate their helpful suggestions from which to build on this research.

It is my good fortune to have delightful parents and amazing children, all in good health and with roofs over their heads. I have depended on their affection, support, and good humor, and for these no thanks would be sufficient.

Finally, thank you to the shelter operators, transitional housing specialists, tenants organizers, volunteers with the homeless, public officials, and other researchers who have shared their time and insights with me. My appreciation goes to Katherine Nelson of HUD, to Elliot Liebow, who has had a long avocation as a volunteer at a shelter for homeless women, and to Cushing Dolbeare, who has tirelessly worked for affordable housing for the poor. May we see the day when there is a "decent home and suitable living environment for every American."

AT RISK OF HOMELESSNESS

Introduction

While the majority of Americans have moved into what has been called a post-shelter society (Sternlieb, 1981), in which housing is more significantly an investment and tax shelter than a protection from the elements, increasing numbers of persons are literally out in the cold and searching for the most basic of shelter. Across the nation, cities, small towns, and rural areas have reported a sharply increasing demand for emergency food and shelter over the last decade (Roth et al., 1985; U.S. Conference of Mayors, 1986, 1987), even as many Americans have enjoyed greater prosperity.

As one journalist quipped, "It's impossible to say whether The Question of the 1980's is 'Who is buying all those Mercedes?' or 'Who are all those street people?'" (Blonston, 1989). That there may be a connection between the two phenomena is worthy of speculation. A recent study investigating the "declining middle-class theory" finds that a greater proportion of those exiting from the middle class are entering the upper rather than the lower tiers of the income distribution, but that the lowest income quintile, while relatively stable in proportional size, is indisputably receiving a smaller share of total aggregate income (Harrigan and Haugen, 1988). The bottom 20 percent of the population now share only 4.6 percent of aggregate income, the lowest in 35 years, while the wealthiest 20 percent receive 44 percent, the largest share ever recorded. The 13.1 percent of all Americans who were poor in 1988 was not significantly different from the percentage who were poor in 1980, but the income of the average poor family in 1988 was nearly $5,000 below the poverty line, further below than at any time since 1960 (Center on Budget and Policy Priorities, 1989). This is convincing evidence that the poor are getting poorer and that the benefits of the economic recovery of the last five years have primarily accrued to those who were already well off. An increasingly visible segment of the profoundly poor has now become homeless, a critical situation that demands our concern and attention.

The population of homeless persons has not only grown larger during the past decade, but has also become increasingly diverse demographically. The "new homeless" are so called to distinguish them from the predominantly middle-aged and elderly single white male and alcoholic population of homeless persons in the past. [1] Increasingly, the homeless are composed of women, children, and minorities who are younger than their counterparts of several decades ago. A recent Urban Institute study describes the new homeless population as 54 percent black, 9 percent Hispanic, and 19 percent female, with more than 50 percent between the ages of 31 and 50 (Cohen and Burt, 1989). The proportion of shelter users who are members of intact families, primarily headed by women, is reported to be as high as 52 percent in some individual metropolitan areas.[2] On any given night, at least 100,000 children are without a home, according to a National Academy of Sciences panel, and this sad statistic prompted the majority of panel members to independently express "our sense of shame and anger" over the "outrage" and "national scandal" that is homelessness.[3]

Although there is little doubt that the numbers of homeless have increased, the absolute size of the homeless population remains in considerable dispute. Planners and policymakers would benefit from knowing how many homeless there are, but the sometimes contentious debate over the number of homeless persons has often overridden the importance of understanding why the population of homeless women, children, and minorities is increasing in both number and percentage. What forces are driving the change? Is homelessness primarily a result of a shortage of affordable housing (Carliner, 1987; Clay, 1987; Wright and Lam, 1987), of income (First, Roth, and Arewa, 1988; Redburn and Buss, 1987; Roistacher, 1987), of federal policies as they affect both income and housing, of demographic changes, or of exogenous changes such as deinstitutionalization of the mentally ill and the increasing affordability of illicit drugs? What is the likelihood that the homeless population will continue to grow and change, and what are the appropriate policy responses, given regional variations in homelessness, housing, and income?

Much controversy also surrounds the role that behavioral deviance may play in causing people to become homeless.[4] Most studies that have examined the issue report that a high proportion, but less than a majority of the homeless, have serious personal problems, primarily substance abuse and a history of mental illness.[5] These studies have generally not addressed the extent to which such conditions have been caused or aggravated by persistent poverty rather than the reverse.[6]

By focusing on the personal characteristics or failings of the homeless, social attention to structural changes that have negatively influenced the lives of the poor are more easily overlooked or ignored. The present study is premised on the assumption that the homeless, for all of their diversity and personal problems, are united by a common need. They are, by definition, without a permanent home.[7] Whether or not the event of homelessness appears to be precipitated by mental illness, substance abuse, interpersonal conflict, or destruction of the home, homelessness is hypothesized to result from a mismatch between incomes and the cost of housing. That homelessness has increased, I would argue, is a direct and perhaps inevitable outgrowth of structural changes that have influenced both the necessity for, and the ability of the low-income population to obtain, affordable housing on the open market.

Several studies of the homeless have suggested that housing-related problems dominate as the direct precursors to homelessness.[8] In spite of this, an association between the extent of homelessness, which varies considerably across metropolitan areas, and the factors of income and rent within those areas has not been clearly established. Primarily this may be the result of a lack of data with which to test the hypothesized relationship. A study of the determinants of homelessness would ideally utilize good retrospective data on the living environments, incomes, and rents of those who have become homeless or would prospectively follow a high-risk population as some members become homeless over time. But statistically, homelessness remains a rare event, and there has yet to be a prospective study in which individuals who become homeless are not lost to follow-up. Studies of the homeless that have collected retrospective data on incomes and living situations prior to homelessness are necessarily small, generally nonrandomly selected samples.

As an alternative, one can make the assumption that those who have become homeless have previously been housed. If the proposed predictors of homelessness are incomes and rents, it is justifiable to utilize the good quality data that exists on housing and to examine the incomes and rents of a population that is at risk of becoming homeless.

ESTIMATING A POPULATION AT RISK OF HOMELESSNESS

This study seeks to determine what accounts for the increase in number and the change in composition of the homeless population by examining the population of renters who may be considered at risk of homelessness because of low incomes, very high rent-to-income ratios, and lack of alternative low-cost rental housing within the metropolitan area (Standard Metropolitan Statistical Area, or SMSA) of residence. The study is based on the hypothesis that the increase in the population of homeless persons is related to changes in both the supply of rental housing[9] that is affordable to low-income households and in the demand by these households for low-cost rental housing, fueled by their increasing concentration at very low levels of income. A population of renters who are vulnerable to homelessness can be identified. The severity of the housing squeeze and the demographic characteristics of those most vulnerable to housing loss are hypothesized to be related to the extent and nature of homelessness in individual metropolitan areas.

Changing demographic composition of the renter poverty population is expected to contribute to the disproportionate representation of blacks and Hispanics and the increasing proportion of women and children among those who become homeless. Discrimination, which may prevent minorities from fully competing in the housing market and may exact a premium from households with children, is predicted to exacerbate these trends.

It is also hypothesized that both the supply of low-cost rental housing and the demand for it have been adversely affected by changes in federal policy. During the 1980s, subsidized housing programs received among the largest cuts of any social program, while private investment in low-cost housing was made less advantageous through the tax system. Cuts in income support for the poor contributed to a decline in the ability of the poor to afford market-rate housing. These factors contributed to the housing squeeze, forcing some individuals, who had exhausted the resources of family and friends or had nowhere else to turn, into homelessness.

The study utilizes the American (formerly Annual) Housing Survey of Metropolitan areas for four of the largest cities in the U.S., to estimate a population at risk of becoming homeless in each of three time periods, based on the number of renter households that have incomes of less than 125 percent of the poverty line and that pay in excess of 45 percent of income to rent.

This book has six main objectives:

1. to describe the mismatch between the available rental housing stock and what would be "affordable" to the low-income population within individual metropolitan housing markets;
2. to examine the characteristics of rental housing in terms of cost, quality, and overcrowdedness, as well as changes in these dimensions over time;

3. to identify a population whose income and rent burden place it at risk of being shut out of the housing market;
4. to describe the demographic characteristics of this vulnerable population and relate them to the limited available data on characteristics of the homeless as identified in these areas;
5. to determine if increases in the cost of rental housing are attributable to increases in the quality of the housing stock; and
6. to examine policy alternatives and directions for future research.

The proposed relationship between the extent of homelessness and the population at risk is as follows:

$$\frac{\text{Homeless}}{\text{Total Pop.}} = \frac{\text{Renters}}{\text{Total Pop.}} \times \frac{\text{Low-Inc. Renters}}{\text{All Renters}} \times \frac{\text{Vulnerable}}{\text{Low-Inc. Renters}} \times \frac{\text{Homeless}}{\text{Vulnerable}}$$

The per capita rate of homelessness is hypothesized to be a function of the proportion of the population who are vulnerable (low-income, highly cost-burdened) renters. The proportion of the population who are renters is thought to vary with the cost of homeownership in individual metropolitan areas (Gilderbloom and Appelbaum, 1987). The proportion of renters may also be affected by the extent to which otherwise qualified minorities are prevented from becoming homeowners by discrimination in residential mortgage financing (Shlay, 1985, 1987 a & b). Therefore, the extent of home ownership is proposed to be an important indicator of how extensive homelessness will be within an individual metropolitan area or central city. The size and makeup of the vulnerable population, while not an indication of who may become homeless, is hypothesized to provide a forecast of how the homeless population is likely to grow and change.

The remainder of this chapter provides a background on previous attempts to estimate the numbers of homeless and on the structural factors that are hypothesized here to play a role in the growing problem of homelessness. The second chapter proposes a theory of structural change and discusses the two most prominent competing theories of homelessness. In the third chapter a set of metropolitan areas for which the necessary data has been collected are identified, and a subset of these areas is selected for analysis. The fourth chapter describes the data and methodology used in this study. The fifth through eighth chapters report on the findings for metropolitan areas individually. In the ninth chapter, the relationship between quality and price of rental housing is examined through hedonic regressions of gross rent on the characteristics of housing in all four metropolitan areas. The final chapter summarizes the findings and discusses some of their policy implications.

Previous Estimates of the Homeless Population

Rising numbers of homeless have prompted numerous, primarily local, efforts to document the size of the homeless population, but methodological problems abound, including the potential to both double count and undercount the homeless. Many of the homeless may not want to be found, while others may appear with different identities in the same survey.

The U.S. Conference of Mayors' (1986, 1987) Task Force on Hunger and Homelessness has published several reports based on responses to questionnaires mailed to mayoral offices of major cities, which purport to document the substantial increased demand for shelter being placed on government and private social service agencies and the increasing representation of women and children among those seeking shelter. The Task Force surveys, unfortunately, do not offer base estimates on the numbers of existing homeless to which these new figures are being added.

The 1990 census attempted to count the entire undomiciled population in a systematic way, expanding on its efforts for 1980 through an "S-night" enumeration of pre-identified shelter and street locations nationwide.[10] The results of this survey are unlikely to be published for at least a year. Until then, only scattered state or local studies, some of which attempt to project to national populations, as well as a few national surveys based on mailed instruments or telephone interviews with government officials, shelter providers, and other key informants, are available.

In 1984, the U.S. Department of Housing and Urban Development (HUD) released estimates of the national homeless population derived from four sources: previously published figures, interviews with local experts in 60 cities, interviews with shelter operators, and an estimation extracted from street and shelter counts conducted in three cities. HUD concluded that as of January 1984, there were between 192,000 and 586,000 homeless in the United States, with the "most reliable range," according to HUD, being from 250,000 to 350,000. HUD estimates did not include women and children living on vouchers in welfare hotels as being homeless (U.S. Department of Housing and Urban Development, 1984), whereas most other studies have included this population among the homeless.

The HUD report was widely criticized for its methodological shortcomings and for being a hurried "in-house job," attempting to minimize the problem of homelessness (Hartman, 1988). It also failed to address growth and change in the population of the homeless, the very factors that precipitated the study. Even HUD's high figure of nearly 600,000 in 1984 stands in sharp contrast to the 2 to 3 million homeless estimated from a 25-city survey of agencies and organizations serving the homeless conducted by the Washington-based Community for Creative Nonviolence in 1980.[11] The latter figures have been criticized as resulting more from advocacy than from science, but they remain in wide circulation.

In partial support of the HUD figures were the findings of Freeman and Hall (1987), who developed a street-to-shelter ratio on the basis of a convenience sample of 500 homeless in New York City. The observed ratio of street dwellers to shelter users was then applied to the estimate of the numbers sheltered nationally in 1983 to obtain an estimate of total homeless. From this technique, Freeman and Hall concluded that HUD's figures were fairly accurate. They did, however, dispute HUD's decision to exclude women and children who received vouchers to live in welfare hotels. The authors felt that this exclusion underestimated the number of families who were legitimately homeless, even though such shelter arrangements may have been relatively long-term.

Utilizing estimates of increased shelter usage between 1983 and 1985, Freeman and Hall proposed that the homeless population of 1985 was 23 to 30 percent larger than it had been two years earlier, a substantial increase by any standard and one that corresponds quite closely to that found by the U.S. Conference of Mayors (1987) between 1985 and 1987. The range they defined, from 343,000 to 363,000 persons, corresponds to the higher "most reliable " estimate by HUD for 1984. HUD projected that the population of homeless would reach 400,000 by 1990 (U.S. Bureau of the Census, 1988d), a figure that would assume considerably slower growth in the future than would the figure found by Freeman and Hall between 1983 and 1985. More recently, HUD has announced that the population seeking shelter has doubled since its earlier survey. Perhaps in response to the criticisms of its 1984 report, HUD representatives were unwilling to cite a new national estimate (*National Coalition for the Homeless Newsletter*, April 1989). The most reliable current estimate, made by The Urban Institute, is that approximately 600,000 were homeless nationwide in 1989 (Burt and Cohen, 1989).

The number of homeless within individual metropolitan areas is also controversial. A study of Chicago homeless (Rossi, Fisher, and Willis, 1986) was, by Rossi's claim, the first "reasonably rigorous study that embraced all the homeless in any city" (Rossi, 1987). When his estimate fell far short of that used by the Chicago homeless advocacy constituents, Rossi contended that he was accused of doing a disservice to the cause of homeless people by diminishing the size of the problem, in spite of his own efforts to direct attention to the composition rather than the number of homeless.

DEFINITION OF HOMELESSNESS

The "homeless population" has never been consistently defined, and this lack of consensus has aggravated the problem of enumeration. It may be helpful as a first step to define *housing unit* and *home*. The U.S. Census Bureau identifies a housing unit as living quarters in a structure intended for residential use, such as a house, apartment, group of rooms, single room, mobile home, or hotel or motel in which the occupants live and eat separately from other persons in the building and that has direct access from the outside or from a common hall. This concept excludes facilities such as institutions, nursing homes, and group homes (U.S. Bureau of the Census, *Annual Housing Survey*, 1975). A home should be a place where a person's basic needs can be met, where there is a legal right to stay for a definite period of time, providing a sense of permanence, where protection from the elements is assured, where safety from personal or physical danger is afforded, and where mail can be received.[12]

A homeless person is one who does not occupy a housing unit as defined by the Census Bureau, or who does not have the legal right to stay for a defined period. For the purpose of this study, the definition provided in section 103 of the McKinney Homeless Assistance Act (PL 100-77) will be assumed when referring to the homeless population in general. A homeless person is defined as "an individual who lacks a fixed, regular, and adequate nighttime residence; and an individual who has a primary nighttime residence that is: a supervised publicly or privately operated shelter designed to provide temporary living accommodations (including welfare hotels, congregate shelters, and transitional housing for the mentally ill); an institution that provides a temporary residence for individuals intended to be institutionalized; or a public or private place not designed for, or ordinarily used as, a regular sleeping accommodation for human beings" (cited in the Resource Group, 1989). Where studies have defined the homeless population differently, such definitions will be noted.

Not usually counted among the homeless are families and individuals who are "doubled up" with friends or relatives, a situation that, as recent empirical work indicates, often precedes homelessness. Those who become homeless have typically exhausted the resources that were available to them in terms of staying with family

and friends (Piliavin, Sosin, and Westerfelt, 1987).[13] A study by Mc-
Chesney in Los Angeles found that doubling up had been the first line
of defense used by families to prevent homelessness, but as they ran
out of friends or family with whom they could stay, there began brief
and then more extended episodes of homelessness. McChesney concluded that doubling up could be an indication that the family is
vulnerable to becoming homeless (cited in U.S. Conference of Mayors,
1987). A study of the District of Columbia (Office of the Special Assistant for Human Resource Development, 1989) recently found that one
of every five household residents and one-third of all children in the
District live in a doubled-up household.

Doubling up is a severe problem among the poor occupants of
public housing. The head of the Chicago Housing Authority, Vincent
Lane, estimates that 50,000 to 100,000 additional tenants live illegally
in the 40,000 units under his jurisdiction (Schmidt, 1988). John Simon,
the General Manager of the New York City Housing Authority, cited
the extreme conditions associated with doubling up in New York's
76,000 single-family public housing units in testimony before the
House Subcommittee on Housing and Community Development in
1984. "Just imagine what this kind of overcrowding does to elevator
service, maintenance, janitorial conditions, utility and hot water consumption, not to mention the deterioration of quality of life it causes
and the dangerous social pressures which result" (Simon, 1984).

To enforce the occupancy regulations prohibiting more than one
family per unit would, according to Simon's testimony, only exacerbate the problem the city has in providing emergency shelter to its
estimated 50,000 homeless persons. The doubling and tripling up
of families in public housing projects put tremendous strain on
operating budgets at a time when federal allocations for both increasing the supply of public and subsidized housing and providing operating expenses for existing units were drastically cut.
During the 1981-86 fiscal year period, New York City's federally
allotted new budget authority for public housing was cut by 98
percent, more than any other program for the poor.[14] These cuts in
the face of increased demand illustrate the growing disparity between the supply of, and demand for, low-cost rental housing, a
disparity that may be driving families and individuals to double up
or to become homeless.

THE DEMOGRAPHIC CHARACTERISTICS OF THE HOMELESS

Increasingly, those becoming homeless include families with children. In November 1987, the city of New York provided shelter to

more than 17,000 children and their parents. This figure represents a quadrupling in the number of families, mostly single mothers with children, sheltered by New York City since 1982. In this same time period, the number of individual homeless persons, mostly single men, who were provided shelter nearly tripled, to more than 10,000.[15] The entrance of women and children into the ranks of the homeless, which had historically been dominated by single men, corresponds to the increasing proportion of the poor who are children, female heads of families, and/or female elderly (U.S. Bureau of the Census, 1987).

The disproportionate representation of black and Hispanic minorities among the homeless has also been found in a number of surveys (First, Roth, and Arewa, 1988; Hirschl, 1988; Cohen and Burt, 1989). The increasingly well-documented existence of a predominantly minority, profoundly poor "underclass" (Wilson, 1987), whose members may fall into homelessness, converges with this finding.

The majority of black, Hispanic and female-headed households are renters rather than owners.[16] A number of studies that have found that blacks pay more than whites for housing of comparable size and quality[17] may indicate that minorities are more prone to homelessness because of racial discrimination in housing and because they occupy older, more dilapidated housing (Furstenburg, Harrison, and Horowitz, 1974), which is at increased risk of being condemned or demolished. Some variation in ethnic or cultural tolerance for social pressure and crowded space has also been noted. Recent immigrants from Asian countries, for example, are rarely found among the homeless of New York City, but tremendous overcrowding of Asian families is found to occur in public housing.[18]

THE CONCENTRATION OF POVERTY

The perceived increase in the homeless population has been associated with a growing income shortfall of the very poor, relative to the poverty line. Current Population Survey data indicate that, although the poverty rate for the nation as a whole has fallen from a recent high of 15.2 percent in 1983 to 13.1 percent in 1988, the number of poor at the lowest level of poverty, below 50 percent and below 75 percent of the poverty line, has increased (U.S. Congress, 1988). Thus there is a concentration of the poor at the lowest levels of income. Two of every five poor persons had incomes below half of the poverty line in 1988 (Center on Budget and Policy Priorities, 1989). Concomitantly, the size of the income deficit, or that dollar amount that would be required to raise a family or individual to the poverty line, has steadily grown for many subgroups of the poor, particularly female heads of households, children, and blacks. In constant 1986 dollars, the mean income deficit was $1000 greater in 1988 than in 1979. For female-headed households overall, the median deficit was $1000 higher for black families than for whites (U.S. Bureau of the Census, 1988b).

The total number of families and unrelated individuals with income deficits greater than $5,000 was 2,768,000 in 1986, more than half of which (1,554,000) were female heads of households with children under the age of 18 years. Households with a deficit of this magnitude constituted 38 percent of the 7.3 million households below the poverty line (ibid). The latter figure represents an increase of 2 million since 1979 in the numbers of households living in poverty. Growth in the income deficit is another indication that the poor are indeed becoming poorer. The total poverty gap, or that amount that would be necessary to bring incomes up to the poverty line, was $47.5 billion in 1985, even after the inclusion of cash transfers (Danziger, 1988).

Increasing Female Headship

A growing proportion of poor families are headed by women, but this is not due to a decline in median income of female-headed families. Rather, the feminization of poverty is about equally attributable to an increase in the prevalence of female-headed families and to the economic stagnation of single-mother families, particularly relative to decreasing poverty among the elderly married and male-headed households (Garfinkel and McLanahan, 1985). Between 1979 and 1986, poverty rates increased for both single-parent and two-parent households, but 46 percent of all female-headed families were poor in 1986, whereas the figure for two-parent households was 7 percent (U.S. Congress, 1988). This discrepancy is due both the greater earnings of married men[19] and to the ability of married couples to be joint earners.

The increasing prevalence of female-headed families has led to a rise of nearly 5 percent since 1978 in the percent of children who live in poverty. More than 21 percent of all children under the age of 15 were in poverty in 1986. The figure for black children was twice as high (U.S. Bureau of the Census, 1987).

The poverty of female heads of households and their children has been exacerbated by changes in Aid to Families with Dependent Children (AFDC), which reduced both real benefits relative to inflation and the numbers eligible for benefits. Only three states maintained real benefit levels by fully indexing for inflation between 1970 and 1986. In ten states real maximum benefits for a four-person family fell by at least 40 percent, and in half the states by 25 percent (U.S. Congress 1988:51).

Following on the heels of inflation losses, tightened federal eligibility criteria eliminated between 400,000 and 500,000 AFDC families and nearly a million potential food stamp recipients during the early 1980s (Palmer and Sawhill, 1984). McLanahan, Garfinkel, and Watson (1988) estimated that single mothers who worked absorbed about two-thirds of the cuts and inflation losses in AFDC that occurred between 1975 and 1985. "The evidence suggests that the budget cuts increased the poverty of mother-only families by nontrivial amounts in return for small to trivial reductions in dependence and prevalence."

Structural Economic Changes

The economic expansion in the private sector during the 1980s has not offered great opportunity to entry-level workers or those leaving public assistance. Many service-sector jobs paying at or near the minimum wage would place a family of two below the poverty line.[20] Overall, the median family income in the United States in constant 1986 dollars had not been restored to its level of 1973 (U.S. Bureau of the Census, 1987).

Unemployment soared in the early 1980s, and though it has since fallen to lower levels, the proportion of out-of-work individuals who are receiving unemployment compensation is at a 30-year low of less than 25 percent (*New York Times*, Nov. 13, 1987). The shrinking middle class, it now appears, has been dispersed into both the uppermost quintile and the lowest quintile of the income distribution. The gap between rich and poor has grown wider, after remaining relatively stable for decades.[21] Much of the movement is due to the earnings difference between single- and dual-earner families.

RELATIVE VS. ABSOLUTE STANDARDS OF POVERTY

The figures on the poverty gap confirm that the average poor family, defined as one with an income below the poverty line for a given year, is in fact far below the poverty line. If we consider that the poverty line itself has fallen dramatically, from a level of about half of median income to about one-third, holding family size constant,[22] we can see that not only is a growing segment of the poverty population becoming increasingly concentrated at very low levels of income, but also that the poor are set further apart from the living standards available to the median income American.[23]

Heilbrun's (1974:179) comment, made in the economic growth years of the early 1970s, that "as the years pass, the standard [of poverty] is bound to appear increasingly unrealistic, and sooner or later it will be revised upward" seems unduly optimistic in retrospect. Such adjustment appears most unlikely for the present, when stagnation in median income[24] over the past decade has led to a stalemate in the war on poverty and when the reduction of poverty is no longer, for the most part, an aim of the welfare reform agenda (Danziger, 1988).

Nevertheless, deprivation is measured by all of us relative to the standards that prevail in our own society.[25] The increasing evidence of a two- or perhaps three-tiered society has prompted some to call for a relative rather than absolute measure of poverty (Townsend, 1974; Rodgers, 1986). A common proposal is that a realistic poverty standard should provide 50 percent of median family income. This is the standard that has prevailed in eligibility for subsidized housing programs since 1983.[26]

In spite of its shortcomings, Wilson (1987) and many others maintain that the current measure of poverty is acceptable and useful, in that the official poverty line accurately reflects gross changes over time and is widely recognized and understood. Furthermore, the use of a relative index of poverty would only increase the size of the population we have thus far failed to serve. As a matter of public policy, however, it seems critical to point out that the poverty problem is both larger and more severe than simply the numbers of persons who fall below a rather arbitrarily chosen point, particularly when even an income "at the line" may not be sufficient to purchase the basic necessities of life, such as housing.

FEDERAL HOUSING POLICY

When Congress declared in the Housing Act of 1949 that "the general welfare and security of the Nation, and the health and living standards of its people require . . . the realization as soon as feasible of the goal of a decent home and suitable living environment for every American family" (cited in Heilbrun, 1974), it acknowledged that shelter is a basic necessity of life, the absence of which can do unmeasurable damage to individuals and to society as a whole. It further implicitly agreed that such provision should be the obligation, where necessary, of the state. However, the ambition of universally available, accessible, and affordable housing has historically been undermined by political, economic, and racial motives (Hayes, 1985; Hartman, 1975; Sternlieb and Listokin, 1987). Housing for the poor has been perhaps the most neglected aspect of U.S. social welfare policy, with interest waxing and waning too quickly to make real progress toward the goal set in 1949.

Unlike most of the industrialized West, federal housing assistance in the United States has never been an entitlement program. Rather, housing assistance has been likened to a lottery in which "any eligible family has only a small chance of winning at all and, like all lotteries, the prizes vary enormously in value" (Salins, 1987). In recent years, the low-income renter has been increasingly forced to compete in the unsubsidized market as the numbers of households needing assistance outpaced growth in the availability of federal subsidies.

Whether or not one shares Paul Peterson's (1986) view that housing as a public issue has suffered because of a lack of professionally based expertise and advocacy, it is true that under the Reagan administration, redistributive housing programs were disproportionately targeted for reduced spending. Budget authorization for all low-income housing programs fell from $33 billion in 1981 to under $8 billion in 1987 (Dreier, 1987). These are drastic cuts to nonentitlement programs, which have even at their height benefited only a small percentage of the estimated 29 million poor needing housing assistance.[27]

At the end of 1980, the beginning of the Reagan years, there were 3 million HUD-assisted renter households, 1.2 million each in public and subsidized rental units and the rest in Section 8 new construction and rehabilitation units.[28] By 1988, there were 4.3 million, most of the growth due to previously authorized budget authority. More than a third of these households are not poor (Salins, 1987). Before the eligibility criteria were lowered in 1986, households with incomes up to 80 percent, rather than the current 50 percent, of local median income could qualify for assistance. The proportion of recipients who were elderly rose dramatically during the years of the Reagan administration, benefiting the elderly at a time when their social security incomes were not subjected to the same erosion by inflation as those of welfare recipients.

During his eight-year administration, Reagan requested a total of only $23 billion to house the poor. Congress authorized three times that much, but the housing budget remained among the most drastically cut of all social programs (Rep. Henry Gonzales, 1988). The focus of the Reagan administration away from social programs and toward defense is noted in the fact that by 1988, the United States was spending 42 times as much on defense as on housing, while in 1981, the ratio had been 7 to 1 (Gilderbloom and Appelbaum, 1987:77). A comparison of federal budgets reveals that while combined social housing programs were allotted about 1/100 of the federal budget in 1950 and in 1970, by 1986 this share was only 1/1000.[29] Had housing appropriations remained at the 1980 level, 1.5 million more families would have received housing assistance (Gonzales, 1989). Sadly, it has now come to light that at least $2 billion of the already bare-bones HUD budget was diverted from the poor through extravagant consulting fees, political patronage, and nepotism.[30]

Most major cities have long since stopped taking applications for assisted housing. One hundred thousand are already on the list in Chicago,[31] and the New York City waiting list is estimated to be 20 years long (Simon, 1984).

For the small percentage of households who qualify for housing assistance, estimated to be one in five of low-income renters, or 11 percent of all renters (Apgar and Brown, 1988), disposable income was reduced in 1983 when the maximum rent-to-income ratio was raised across the board from 25 to 30 percent of income, regardless of how deficient income might be. Originally, households assisted through the federal Section 8 housing program paid between 15 and 25 percent of income to rent, with the poorest households paying the least (Struyk, Mayer, and Tuccillo 1983:14). The new policy clearly ignores whether residual income remaining after rent is adequate to meet nonhousing needs and sets the United States apart from most of the Western industrialized world, both in the level and the uniformity of the rent burden it expects subsidized renters to pay (Gilderbloom and Appelbaum, 1987). It has been argued that Western European countries demand a smaller percentage of income in rent (generally 20 percent or less) largely because rental units are smaller and have fewer amenities. While this may have been true in the past, Sweden for one has improved both size and equality of access to space and other amenities among all income groups for a maximum of 20 percent of income among virtually its entire population (Gilderbloom and Appelbaum, 1987:170).

The bias of federal housing benefits toward owners through the tax system has been well documented (Slitor, 1985; Kain and Quigley, 1975). According to an estimate by the U.S. Senate Subcommittee on Children, Youth and Families (1984), "the cost of housing subsidies through the tax system in 1980 alone was more than the entire cumulative amount that the federal government has ever spent for providing housing assistance for low-income people" (U.S. Senate, 1984:87). Sixty percent of housing tax benefits accrue to taxpayers in the top 10 percent of the income distribution (Dolbeare, 1983).

Low-income rental units have been destroyed by federally financed urban renewal and lost through tax benefits favoring gentrification, including historic preservation. Changes in federal subsidies and tax laws that favor conversion, and expiration of federally assisted housing contracts, are expected to further reduce the supply of low-cost housing. For example, nearly half of the 1.9 million privately owned but federally subsidized low-income rental units in the United States could be converted to market rate units by 1995 as their 15-to-20-year commitments to below-market rents expire (Clay, 1987:11).

Another source of loss to the low-income rental housing stock is the sale of publicly owned units to private owners. HUD is currently engaged in a demonstration project to test the feasibility of this concept (Clay, 1987:16), an indication perhaps of HUD's desire to rid itself of responsibility for public housing. Such a policy would benefit the higher-income poor but would reduce the total public housing stock to the detriment of the most severely poor.

LOW COST RENTAL HOUSING AND THE RENT BURDEN

In view of the declining federal role in providing access to low-cost housing and of the inclining demand related to the concentration of poverty, it should come as no surprise that we see an increase in the population that can no longer afford housing at all. The growth in the number of female-headed households as a percentage of all households and in the percentage of all households who are renters has contributed to this trend.

"Poverty deepening," as it might be called, can be expected to produce intense competition for housing of very low cost, perhaps of a cost so low that it cannot be reasonably marketed without a subsidy. In such a market, what appears to be reasonably priced rental housing may be plentiful, yet beyond the reach of the poor.

Redburn and Buss (1987), for example, conclude that for Ohio, which has some of the most comprehensive statewide data on homelessness available, the vacancy rates and relatively low rents would indicate that homelessness results from lack of income rather than from a shortage of low-cost housing.

If low-cost housing can be profitably built by the private sector, increased demand will be expected to generate increased supply. If, however, the market for low-cost housing provides too few profit incentives, we can expect that supply will remain static or actually decline, while prices increase. Increase in the cost of housing can also be triggered by the demand of high-income renters for gentrification or by the conversion of rental units to owned units. Regardless of the cause of increasing rents, or decreasing stock, those at the lowest end of the income scale must compete with those who are better off for the same housing. The poorest renters do so by devoting an increasing proportion of their income to rent, often for housing of very poor quality. While the nation's children are increasingly being raised in rental housing, the growing rent burden indicates that low-income families have less actual disposable or residual income with which to feed and clothe them. Consistently, those with the least ability to afford them—female heads, minorities, and female elderly—have higher rent burdens than male-headed families (Stegman, 1982).

Many families may, in fact, be too poor to afford to pay anything for housing. If "affordable" housing is defined as a residual between total household income and all essential nonhousing expenses, large numbers of families cannot afford even 5 or 10 percent of income for housing.[32] "Shelter poverty" is what results, according to Stone, when high expenditure for housing by the poor leads to deprivation in the nonshelter necessities. Using Stone's framework and Bureau of Labor statistics for a lower living standard (125 percent of poverty), Stegman (1982) found that as early as 1981, nearly one-half million renter households in New York City, or 30 percent of the city's renters, were too poor to afford any amount of rent. This figure does not include the hundreds of thousands of renter households whose income exceeded this level but who could not afford the full cost of adequate housing. We can anticipate that many renters with high rent burden and little or no residual in their household income may be at considerable risk of becoming homeless. If shelter poverty becomes severe enough to compete with a minimal diet, the income that rent consumes cannot be sustained in light of the more pressing demand for food and other absolute necessities. The individual or family may then be forced to double up with relatives or friends or become homeless.

Rent control has frequently been cited as both a cause of housing shortage and a solution to maintaining the availability of low-cost housing, yet rent regulation in New York City has not succeeded in preventing nearly 60 percent of all renters from spending more than 25 percent of income for rent. Although this figure is related to the underrepresentation of low-income families in rent-controlled units, Stegman (1982) concludes that incomes, and not the unresponsiveness of rent regulations to the actual cost of doing business, might be "the more serious challenge to creating and maintaining a healthy rental market."

VACANCY RATES

While national and many metropolitan rental vacancy rates would seem to indicate an adequate rental housing stock, there is disagreement about how reliable the vacancy rate is as an indicator of housing availability. A HUD internal report, for example, concluded on the basis of rental vacancy rates, market absorption rates for new apartments, and demand estimated by the rate of new household formation, that the supply of rental housing was sufficient to support a housing voucher program.[33] It would be risky, however, to assume from national vacancy rates that there is a supply of standard quality (not inadequate) housing that would be affordable to low-income renters in a given metropolitan market. The national vacancy rate was 7.5 percent in 1987, but because vacancies typically rise monotonically with increasing rent, very few units may be available below the median rent, which itself usually exceeds the "affordable" rent burden of the poor. For example, the median rent nationally for vacant units in 1987 was $333. This would represent 30 percent of an income of $13,320. As we have seen, millions of households have far less income than this with which to compete in the housing market. Nationally, only 9 percent of vacancies would be affordable to an individual or family earning $7,000 and paying 30 percent of income in rent, the current standard for "affordable" rent burden (U.S. Bureau of the Census, 1986).

Milgram and Bury (1987) found in a study of 25 SMSAs that none of the areas surveyed, regardless of vacancy rate, had a supply of rental units of an acceptable quality and size sufficient to rehouse all families that were currently unsatisfactorily housed, that is, living in housing that was substandard or overcrowded, or both. The percentage of renters who could potentially be rehoused at levels below 30 percent of income varied across SMSAs from 20 to 71 percent and across central cities from 10 to 68 percent. The great majority of those who could not have been properly accommodated were households of five or more persons, indicating a shortage of larger dwelling units.

The large variations by metropolitan area that Milgram and Bury found in the availability of rental housing, in the proportion of households unsatisfactorily housed, and in the relevance of the vacancy rates within areas for those households, illustrate the importance of examining metropolitan areas separately. Most empirical work has used national data that would tend to obliterate the variability of metropolitan housing markets. While it is recognized that the poverty population is not stable and that individuals may fall into and leave poverty within a relatively short period (Bane and Ellwood, 1986), the use of Annual Housing Survey data from three time periods should reveal trends in the size and characteristics of the renter poverty population.

The composition of the poverty population, as well as the availability of low-cost housing, can be expected to vary from city to city. It is anticipated that the problem of being at risk of homelessness is neither exclusively related to income nor to housing, but to both, and that the strength of these two factors will vary by city. In the following chapter a theory as to how changes in these factors have developed is discussed and is compared with other prominent theories of homelessness.

NOTES

1. Donald Bogue (1963) documented that the homeless inhabitants of Chicago's skid row of the late 1950s were 95 percent white males who were disproportionately physically or mentally disabled pensioners and alcoholics.

2. A March 1989 study released by the U.S. Department of Housing and Urban Development reports that the number of families seeking shelter had doubled since its earlier 1984 report (cited in the *National Coalition for the Homeless Newsletter*, vol. 8, no. 4, April 1989).

3. The statement was issued independently from the official report (Associated Press, *St. Paul Pioneer Press Dispatch*, September 20, 1988, p. 3-A).

4. A sizable proportion of the homeless, according to most studies, could be identified as behaviorally deviant in that they have spent time in prisons and mental institutions or are long-term welfare recipients or have alcohol and drug problems. (See Rossi, 1988, and Piliavin, Sosin, and Westerfelt, 1987). However, such indicators are far from universal among the homeless. Wright (1988) found in a large study of the health of the homeless that in the approximately 22 percent of the total homeless population who were members of intact families, incidence of substance abuse and mental illness were far less in evidence than among lone individuals.

5. The Urban Institute study of 1,704 randomly selected adult users of soup kitchens and shelters in 20 cities with populations over 100,000 found that 19 percent had been previously hospitalized in a mental institution, 33 percent had been treated for chemical dependency, and 43 percent had either or both history (B. Cohen and M. Burt, 1989).

6. An exception is the study by M. Sosin, P. Colson, and S. Grossman (1988), who found that among the 20 percent of the homeless who had been institutionalized, a third had first been hospitalized since becoming homeless. Hospitalization may have been precipitated by a breakdown or, they speculate, might have been an opportunity to obtain temporary shelter.

7. A commonly used definition is one employed by the state of New York, which defines a homeless person as "an undomiciled person who is unable to secure permanent and stable housing without special assistance" (Gover-

nor Mario Cuomo, as cited in the United Community Services of Metropolitan Detroit, 1984).

8. Sosin et al. (1988). Based on a sample of 137, 17 percent were found to have become homeless as a result of a housing condemnation, demolition, or fire. Half had been evicted from their last residence or were unable to pay bills, and 23 percent lost their homes because of an argument or abuse.

9. As will be discussed, the majority of the poor are renters rather than owners, and the homeless have rarely come directly from homeownership to homelessness.

10. U.S. Bureau of Census Memorandum No. 44. The S-night enumeration was held March 20, 1990, two weeks before the 1990 census day, and was to include all hotels and motels that cost $12.00 per night or less, as well as any hotels and motels identified by a city that are used partially by the homeless, regardless of price. The Census Bureau hired persons who live or work in shelters as enumerators, to conduct the survey of those living in shelters or on the street. Enumerators worked in teams and were not accompanied by police officers. However, the enumeration appeared subject to widespread noncooperation (*New York Times*, March 22, 1990).

11. Mary Ellen Hombs and Mitch Snyder, 1982. The figure of 2 million was used at the time the above book was published. More recently, CCNV has publicly used the figure of 3 million (Harold Moss interview, CCNV, March 1989.) While this organization lacks scientifically gathered evidence on which to base such an estimate, the figures it generates have gained such widespread use that it seems important to mention them as an upper bound of the estimates that are in current use.

12. Suggestions on the requirements for a home by the United Community Services of Metropolitan Detroit staff report: *Homeless Persons in the Metropolitan Detroit Area*, May 1984.

13. New York State Department of Social Services (1984) also discusses a population at risk of homelessness. The report estimated that 143,000 families in the state were doubled up, while another 4000 were tripled up.

14. Simon's (1984) estimate of 220,000 families living in 76,000 units, or nearly three families residing in each public unit, may seem improbable. The estimate is based on water and utility consumption, maintenance requirements, and elevator usage.

15. *New York Times*, Nov. 23, 1987. The average size of families receiving shelter in 1987 was 3.7 persons.

16. U.S. Bureau of Census, Census of Housing, 1980, HC80-1-A1, table 7, cited in R. Farley and W. Allen (1987). Fifty-six percent of black households were renters, as opposed to 36 percent of all households.

17. J. Kain and J. Quigley (1975:3) speculate that "many bundles of housing services may be altogether unavailable to black households. That is, the price black households must pay for these bundles or the information, search, and psychic costs they must be prepared to incur to acquire them may be so high that such bundles are practically never consumed by black households." Robert Schafer (1979) found that blacks "nearly always pay more than whites for the same bundle of housing attributes at the same location."

18. Frank Bardy, New York Housing Authority, 1988, personal communication. Bardy speculates that cultural values will not allow Asian families to put a relative out of the house, regardless of the level of overcrowding.

19. Single mothers earn only 30 to 40 percent of the earnings of married men (S. McLanahan, I. Garfinkel, and D. Watson, 1988:103).

20. B. Bluestone and B. Harrison (1986) found that although there was growth in new jobs, more than half of the 8 million new jobs created between 1979 and 1984 paid less than $7,000 per year.

21. James Heilbrun (1974) cites figures showing stable income distributions through 1970.

22. Harrigan and Haugen (1988:11) point out that according to Bureau of Census figures, the poverty level income for a three-person family in 1986 was $8,737, or 28 percent of median family income for a three-person family in that year, while the figures for a family of four were $11,203, or 32 percent of the median for a family of that size. The average family size in 1986 was 3.2 persons. If family size is not held constant, the poverty line for a family of four is about 40 percent of the overall median family income.

23. U.S. Congress (1988:13-16) states that median family income of all families in 1986, adjusted for inflation using the CPI-XI, as it is in this study, was just over three times the adjusted poverty threshold, "the highest level attained since detailed income data became available in the late 1960's." Nonelderly childless couples had incomes nearly five times as high as the adjusted poverty threshold.

24. S. McLanahan, I. Garfinkel, and D. Watson (1988:132-33) conclude that "over the long run, the real wage level has been the principal determinant of the average level of living and of benefits to the poor."

25. The consideration of relative versus absolute poverty standards seems relevant to the discussion of housing and homelessness, because housing represents the most expensive and visible of consumable assets. It is the one item most likely to be "overconsumed," relative to need, by those with large disposable incomes, as well as to be absent altogether for the homeless.

26. According to the Housing Authority of Ann Arbor, Michigan, the federal eligibility guideline for the "235" subsidized housing program was narrowed from 80 percent of median income to 50 percent in 1983 to more effectively target subsidies to the poor. However, new applications have not been accepted since 1987, since there have been no new monies to allocate and a substantial waiting list already exists.

27. U.S. Senate (1984:71). This figure included 11 million children and 4 million elderly. The latter need may have been reduced by the targeting of subsidized housing for the elderly in the 1980s.

28. Ray Struyk, Neil Mayer, and John Tuccillo (1983:16-17). The Section 8 programs either subsidize renters directly or provide tax incentives to suppliers to provide below-market rate rents to low- and moderate-income tenants.

29. Calculated from OMB federal budget expenditures provided in Robert Haveman (1988).

30. *New York Times* (June 10, 1989) reported that James Watt, former secretary of the interior, received $420,000 in consulting fees from HUD. New

scandals of mismanagement, nepotism, and abuse were surfacing almost daily in June and July 1989. On July 11, Secretary of HUD Jack Kemp estimated that waste and fraud at HUD amounted to $2 billion (*New York Times*, July 12, 1989).

31. Schmidt (1989). Yet one in six public units is vacant. The vacancy rate is even higher in some cities, such as Detroit and Houston.

32. Stone (1989) calculates that a Boston family of four with an income of $23,500 in 1985 could not afford to spend 25 percent of income on rent, and a family with an income of $16,000 could afford nothing for rent in that city without being driven into shelter poverty.

33. D. McGough and C. Casey (1986) concede that for very low income renters and in some housing markets, there may be shortages, especially of large units.

2

Theories of Homelessness

A theory of the development of homelessness as a social problem must address other current investigations into the causes of homelessness. Empirical work, as has been previously pointed out, is in short supply. This chapter will first discuss and criticize two of the most widely publicized competing theories—that homelessness has resulted primarily from the deinstitutionalization of the mentally ill and that it has resulted from increased addiction to drugs or alcohol. I will then develop the theoretical arguments on which the present research is based.

MENTAL ILLNESS AND DEINSTITUTIONALIZATION

A common criticism of the proposed relationship between lack of affordable housing and homelessness is one expressed by Salins, a conservative housing expert: "To speak of a housing crisis is not only hyperbolic, it is downright untrue. Much of the case of the crisis-mongers rests on the increasingly publicized plight of the 'homeless.' Homelessness, however, is far more symptomatic of the growing number of uncared-for mentally and socially dysfunctional people to be found in our central cities than it is of a housing emergency" (Salins, 1987). A leading theory is that homelessness as a social problem emerged primarily as a result of deinstitutionalization of the mentally ill,[1] a process begun in the mid-1950s that was made possible through the development of powerful new tranquilizers. These drugs stabilized psychiatric patients sufficiently to enable them to function without continuous medical supervision and ideally allowed them to be able to live with greater freedom and dignity in the community. Subsequently, the institutionalized population of mentally ill in the United States fell from 558,922 in 1955 to 125,200 in 1982 (Freeman and Hall, 1987).

That many of the "uncared-for" mentally ill, those without social support or income adequate to afford housing, did become homeless is not in dispute. What can be disputed is the extent to which this is attributable to deinstitutionalization itself or the extent to which it resulted from the loss of affordable housing in the 1970s and 1980s for those who had previously been released. The role of mental illness in creating the social problem of homelessness has been challenged (Snow, Anderson, and Baker, 1986), and there is no evidence that the per capita incidence of mental illness is greater today than in the past. Numerous studies of the homeless have found that as many as 30 percent of the homeless have histories of mental illness (Bassuk, 1986; Roth et al., 1985; Hope and Young, 1988), although a smaller percentage of homeless have been institutionalized (Cohen and Burt, 1989). Wright's (1985) review of the medical records of more than 6,000 homeless shelter users found that the incidence of confirmed mental illness was 16 percent. While he concluded that this underestimated the true prevalence of mental impairment, this finding nevertheless supports the contention that the great majority of the homeless are not mentally ill.[2]

The process of deinstitutionalization was to have been accompanied by the construction of a nationwide network of community mental health centers. President Kennedy signed the Mental Retardation Facilities and Community Health Centers Construction Act of 1963, authorizing one such center for each 100,000 persons in the United States.

According to Daniel Patrick Moynihan, a member of the task force that devised the plan, "it was explicitly understood that there would be 3,000 such centers by the year 2000. That would translate into some 2,400 today. But we have built only 768. In New York City, where the ratio would call for 73, we have only 14" (Moynihan, 1989). How serious would the problem of homelessness be if institutionalization had continued at the same rate in the 1980s as it had in the 1950s? Freeman and Hall (1987) estimated that about 14 percent of the 657,000 who, on the basis of previous rates and population growth, would have been institutionalized in the past have become homeless. By this calculation at least 100,000 persons nationwide, or about one-fifth of the lowest current estimate of the homeless, have become homeless as a direct result of failure to institutionalize the mentally ill. Although this is a large share of the homeless population, deinstitutionalization alone cannot account for the extent of homelessness, nor for the fact that it has continued to increase after the process of release has largely run its course.

There are also at least two flaws in the assumptions that generated this estimate. First, Freeman and Hall assume, on the basis of previous research, that one-third of the homeless are mentally ill and that all of these would have been institutionalized. Neither now nor in the past has institutionalization been necessary for all forms of mental illness.[3] Second, the finding by Sosin, Colson, and Grossman (1988) that one-third of institutionalizations among the Chicago homeless population were subsequent to rather than prior to the first episode of homelessness indicates that for a substantial proportion of homeless, the trauma of homelessness itself precipitated mental illness. This reversal in the direction of causation illustrates the importance of preventing homelessness as a primary strategy in averting mental illness.

LOSS OF SINGLE ROOM OCCUPANCY HOTELS

In addition to the failure of Public Law 88-164, authorizing the community mental health centers, to be fully enacted, the mentally impaired were also severely affected by the widespread demolition of the traditional home of the marginally functional—the single-room occupancy, or SRO hotel. As a perhaps well intentioned consequence of urban renewal in some areas, and of rising land values in others, the elimination of the SROs has been widespread throughout the nation's central cities. It was most severe in New York City, where the numbers of homeless mentally ill are greatest. Further destruction without replacement of SROs in New York City was halted in 1985, but by this time, many thousands of units, which once had offered at least a measure of privacy not available in shelters for the homeless, had been lost (*New York Times*, March 6, 1989). The New York State Court of Appeals recently ruled that requiring landlords to preserve SROs amounts to "property-taking" and can no longer be enforced (*New York Times*, July 7, 1989). Thus the moratorium imposed by the lower court is invalidated and demolition of SROs in New York City can resume.

The loss of single-room residencies has been documented in studies throughout the country. In Chicago, 18,000 SRO units, or nearly half of its urban stock of SROs, were lost between 1973 and 1984, and in the much smaller urban area of Seattle, 15,000 SROs were eliminated between 1960 and 1981. Hoch and Slayton (1989) argue that this loss was the major factor in the rise of homelessness among single persons in urban areas. It is ironic that the demolishment of these shabby and decrepit units has created such a vacuum in "affordable" housing. That this may be indicative of declining societal expectations for the quality of life to which the poor and mentally ill are entitled will be discussed later in this chapter.

In sorting out the relative weight that these two factors, deinstitutionalization and elimination of single-room occupancies, may have had in precipitating homelessness, it is important to remember that the majority of community mental health centers were not intended to be residential, but to provide day treatment and services to the mentally ill, who would live in the community. The primary purpose of deinstitutionalization was to save the state the cost of permanent residential care. Moynihan (1989) points out that in the 1950s, the expense of building state hospitals was prohibitive—requiring "bond issue after bond issue."

The failure to provide adequate community treatment and supportive services has jeopardized the ability of the mentally ill to live independently. The fact that community-based centers were not built to the extent intended does not tell us what proportion of the mentally ill homeless have become so as a direct consequence of their illness, that is, through an inability to manage their affairs sufficiently to maintain an independent home, and what proportion might have continued to eke out an albeit less than desirable existence had the only housing they could afford on a disability grant[4] not been taken away. Throughout the 1970s, the mentally ill who had been released from state facilities continued to occupy the SROs. Homelessness did not emerge as a widespread social problem until the early 1980s (*New York Times*, March 6, 1989).

I assume that even among the mentally ill, the state of homelessness cannot be divorced from the factors of income and rent. Like AFDC grants, non–social security disability transfer payments have not kept pace with realistic shelter costs. The SRO or efficiency apartment may be in short supply at any price.

To make this argument does not imply that homelessness is exclusively a function of housing and/or of income. But if the plight of the mentally ill homeless will not be solved only by securing for all a decent home, neither would it be solved were all the community mental health centers authorized in 1963 suddenly built, in the absence of affordable housing. Undoubtedly, subpopulations among the homeless need service-based or supervised living situations. But experts in the field state that with appropriate mental health outpatient services and affordable housing, most of the currently homeless mentally ill could successfully live in their communities (Health and Welfare Council of Central Maryland, 1986).[5]

HOMELESSNESS AS A RESULT OF SUBSTANCE ABUSE

A second popular theory about the origin of homelessness is that it has grown in relation to the increasing drug abuse problem in this country. The association between drugs and homelessness has been hypothesized by some, particularly in the media, to be causal. For example, the New York Times recently reported that "the major role that drugs or alcohol abuse plays in causing homelessness has emerged in recent comments by advocates for the homeless" (Kolata, 1989a). The author quotes several advocates and shelter operators in a context that suggests that the extent to which addiction causes homelessness has not previously been acknowledged and in fact has been deliberately downplayed for fear that the "nasty little secret"[6] of drug and alcohol abuse will decrease public sympathy for the homeless. While noting that affordable housing was still an important issue contributing to homelessness, several case studies are cited by the author in which homelessness, for a previously employed, housed, and ostensibly "normal" individual, had been directly precipitated by addiction to crack cocaine. The implication is that in the absence of such an addiction, these individuals would not have become homeless.

Most studies that have investigated this issue have documented the persistent marginal existence of those who have eventually become homeless (Rossi, 1988; Sosin, Colson, and Grossman, 1988). Although a substantial percentage of the homeless are employed in low-wage jobs, the incidence of formerly middle-class persons becoming homeless, either as a result of drug addiction (as in the case studies discussed in these articles) or through another economic crisis, is rare.[7]

While there are personal characteristics that may predispose a poor person to addiction and/or homelessness, I would argue that structural changes affecting the lives of the poor are more important in explaining rising levels of both homelessness and addiction. Increased housing costs and stagnating or falling incomes erode the living standards of those who can least afford it. The frustration and despair that must accompany the powerless situation of deepening poverty would predictably lead to an increase in all forms of social deviance—theft, child abuse, battering, alcoholism, and drug abuse.

The drug epidemic has been attributed to the sheer economic accessibility that has occurred.[8] Undoubtedly the availability and low price of drugs in recent years has contributed to widespread experimentation to achieve the short-term escape from physical and emotional pain that these drugs offer. But the structural relationships between poverty, despair, and addiction are overlooked when we attempt to identify the personal shortcomings that have led an individual to homelessness or addiction.[9] Drug use is also endemic in physical environments conducive to hopelessness and despair. Some of the most drug-infested areas of New York have been described as "blocks of desolation . . . cluttered with debris. . . . Crack and cocaine are being sold by desperate-looking men against a backdrop of bombed-out devastation. . . . There is little left of the area beyond the dark and crumbling apartment buildings" (Marriott, 1989). Chicago public housing, where drug use is rampant, is pictured as "spare and forboding, smeared with graffiti and garbage, and surrounded by desolate expanses of concrete (Schmidt, 1989). The imagery evoked by these passages suggests to me that homelessness and addiction arise from the same conditions of increasing poverty, powerlessness, and despair. The homeless are not more apt to be substance abusers than the domiciled poor.[10]

Only for a very small percentage of the homeless, I would argue, is addiction a precipitating rather than a concomitant factor in becoming homeless. Addiction, like homelessness, is an outcome, the likelihood of which might be predicted from structural changes that have occurred in recent years. This relationship, while not a focus of the present study, will be further discussed later.

The Housing Act of 1949 specified not only a decent home, but "a suitable living environment for every American." In the case of the homeless who are mentally ill, retarded, disabled, substance abusers, or have AIDS, housing alone is clearly not enough. But many shelter operators and transitional housing experts maintain that efforts to treat, rehabilitate, and employ the homeless must be preceded by a stabilized home environment. The trauma of being homeless and living in the stressful environment of a group shelter presents, for many, too great an obstacle to learning new skills or coping mechanisms.[11]

A STRUCTURAL MODEL

Although identifying the policy of deinstitutionalization as a cause of homelessness might be viewed as a structural argument, in practice both leading competing theories of homelessness focus on the personal failing or impairment of the homeless. The homeless are distinguished from the nonhomeless by the personal characteristics of mental illness or addiction. The condition of homelessness in either case is only subsequently exacerbated and extended by the lack of affordable housing.

In making the argument that the widely recognized increase in levels of homelessness is largely attributed to the severity of a housing squeeze across metropolitan areas, I theorize that a causal link exists between deepening poverty of renters, rising rents and homelessness. Empirically, I hope to demonstrate an association between the changes that occurred in these factors over the 1975 to 1983 period and the extent of homelessness found in individual metropolitan areas in the 1984 HUD study as well as in subsequent local studies.

My theoretical assumptions do not challenge that the use of drugs has reached epidemic proportions or that a high proportion of the homeless are mentally ill or addicted to alcohol and drugs. The model proposed indicates that both homelessness and addiction—and, to a lesser extent, increased family dysfunction and mental illness[12] —have the same structural proximate determinants.

In this model, redistributive policies have led to a widening gap between rich and poor. The phenomenon of a decreasing share of total aggregate income going to the most disadvantaged population and the largest increase in wealth to the already wealthy is hypothesized to have created the climate for both increasing levels of homelessness and higher housing costs. The former occurs as a result of cuts in the redistributive income and housing benefits targeted to the poor. The latter is proposed to occur through the increasing concentration of rental property owner-ship in fewer hands. This process was made possible through the tax system, which augmented the disposable income of those who occupy the top 20 to 30 percent of the income distribution. The concentration and professionalization of rental property ownership has been found to be related to higher rents (Gilderbloom and Appelbaum, 1987). This will be dealt with more fully in a later section.

REDISTRIBUTION OF INCOME

Peter Townsend (1979) has observed that one of the enigmas of our societal collective consciousness is that "throughout a given period of history, there may be no change whatever in the actual inequalities of wealth and of income, and yet social perceptions of those inequalities and of any change in them may become keener. Alternatively, substan-tial changes in the structure of incomes in society may occur without the corresponding perception that such changes are taking place." That this is true may be evidenced by the growing societal awareness of, and response to, poverty in the 1960s and early 1970s, a period when the proportional share of income held by the lowest quintile had been relatively stable for decades (Heilbrun, 1974). The growing ine-quality of the income distribution in the last decade, on the contrary, occurred in a climate of social inattention to poverty. It may well be the increasing visibility of the homeless that has once again spurred concern for the poor. The homeless are assumed in this study to be one of the casualties of increasingly regressive redistributions of income.

That some redistribution to the poor, elderly, ill, and ill-fated must take place has generally been accepted, but how much and in what spirit it is given is seen by some as an ethical issue and by others as a largely manipulative response to economic circumstances (Piven and Cloward, 1971). Harvey (1973) argues convincingly that exactly how much redistribution of income should occur is the "central ethical judgment which has to be made in the formulation of any social policy with respect to a city system."

Income of the poor in this decade has of course been affected by a number of demographic and structural factors: growth in the total proportion of households that are headed by females, alteration of the economy from high-wage manufacturing to low-wage service sector jobs, stagnation in the minimum wage, and growth in the minority population historically subjected to job discrimination. The unusually large size of the baby-boom birth cohort is hypothesized to have lessened the fortunes of this generation relative to those of its parents by increasing the labor pool, heightening competition for jobs, and depressing wages (Easterlin, 1980).[13] All of these factors increase the need for redistributive policies toward the poor, but we have instead seen a tightening of eligibility for transfer payments and unemployment benefits and failure to index welfare payments to inflation.

The benefits that those who fall below the poverty line are thought entitled to receive is subject to cyclical fluctuations. Piven and Cloward argue that the historical pattern of relief has been that long periods of restrictive criteria on who qualifies and for how much are punctuated by shorter periods of liberalization in benefits and eligibility. The English Poor Law of 1834 established a principle of "less eligibility," which mandated that relief for the poor be kept below the wages of the lowest paid laborer (1971:35). This principle has remained a foundation of our welfare system, gaining greater strength in times of economic stagnation, such as we have experienced for the past 15 years, when many of the poor are in fact full-time workers.

DECLINING SOCIETAL STANDARDS FOR THE POOR

During such times, according to Piven and Cloward's theory, societal expectations of acceptable living standards for the poor are likely to be scaled down. The poverty programs of the Great Society, instituted in a time of relative prosperity, did have measurable success, particularly in alleviating the poverty of the elderly (Danziger, 1988). But stagnating incomes and compositional changes in households increased the size of both the working and nonworking poor populations, making welfare programs vulnerable to charges that they were ineffective in reducing poverty (Murray, 1984; Mead,1986).

Townsend's argument in favor of a relative poverty standard is founded in the belief that those who lack the resources to live in even a minimal facsimile of the customary lifestyle are excluded from participation in society. Such exclusion is characteristic and perhaps formative of the underclass. The growing disparity between the "truly disadvantaged," as Wilson calls them, and the working and middle class may indicate that we are once again socially redefining what it means to be poor. As a society we may tolerate greater deprivation and be less inclined to believe that the state is responsible to provide remedies for poverty.

The heterogeneity of the "new homeless" population in relation to the vagrant population of the depression era has been previously discussed. The entrance of women and especially children into the ranks of the homeless may be altering the widespread perception of homelessness, from that of a condition that may, in some sense, be considered voluntary or self-induced—that is, related to alcoholism or to a preference for an unorthodox lifestyle—to one that may be indicative of our failure as a nation to provide even a minimum standard of living to those who have had seriously unequal opportunities.

Yet even as our perceptions inform us that the homeless of today may be more clearly identifiable as victims of societal inequities than in the past, our remedies may be much more modest than might have been true in another era. For example, the skid row district that has been home to many marginal men was widely viewed as a blight on a city and less universally as a viable target for either housing reform or the rehabilitation of individuals. In his classic account of skid row, Donald Bogue (1963:405) called for an end to the degrading conditions in which the Chicago inhabitants he surveyed lived.[14]

Twenty years later, in its disappearance, skid row, with its single-room occupancy or "welfare" hotels, soup kitchens, and thrift shops, has emerged as a "resource" worth saving. The skid row of the past offered services, housing, and social support far superior to what is available to the "new homeless." The efforts underway in many cities to save the SROs from demolition or conversion to more expensive housing, while necessary in the present context, further attest to our declining standards of acceptable living conditions for the poor. Whereas skid row used to represent the bottom of the housing hierarchy, its place has been now undermined by the homeless shelter.

To paraphrase a recent commentary, our goal used to be to get people out of low-quality housing. Now it is to get people back in. A recent New York Times headline declares: "Rats, Leaks, Crack and All, Apartments Beat Welfare Hotels" (Rimer, 1989). The story concerns a two-year resident of a New York welfare hotel who is thrilled to be returning to a decrepit but larger home for her family of four. According to Robert Hayes, director of the National Coalition for the Homeless, "These families are going back to grinding abject poverty, which is a tremendous improvement over welfare hotels" (ibid., 1989). We must question how and why our societal standards have become so quickly eroded.

FEDERAL RESPONSE TO HOMELESSNESS

Ellwood (1988) suggests that the basic shortcoming of welfare policy has been its focus on the symptoms rather than the causes of poverty. Such a symptomatic focus, I would argue, has characterized the federal response to dealing with homelessness. While it is questionable whether a sizable portion of homeless persons, either now or in the past, have had a preference for living on the street (Hoch, 1987), it is equally questionable whether the current societal response of providing emergency shelter to the homeless is in any sense a solution to the problem of homelessness. As an increasingly visible population of men, women, and children without food or shelter has emerged during this decade, there has not been a federal commitment to investigate and eradicate the root causes of homelessness. Rather, the lack of governmental initiative has forced responsibility onto communities often ill-equipped to take action. Some communities have attempted to rid themselves of the problem altogether by exporting their homeless elsewhere.

Fabricant (1987) contends that "the state's legitimating role is being reconstructed and translated into policies that reflect 19th-century structural and social relationships."[15] The major responsibility for feeding and sheltering the homeless, for example, has fallen to religious and charitable organizations,[16] much as it was before the advent of social welfare legislation. The federal role, as it belatedly evolved, has been to funnel money to communities and voluntary organizations and to remain aloof from any direct responsibility for providing permanent housing or income solutions. The focus on emergency rather than preventive policies is likely, according to Charles Hoch (1987), to "legitimize the social marginality of the homeless as a subgroup of the politically disenfranchised underclass," fostering the permanence of homelessness instead of seeking to eradicate it.

By the very nature of establishing "permanent" institutions, such as shelters for the homeless, we acknowledge the state of homelessness as a component, however undesirable, of our society. Institutions often perpetuate themselves through the dependencies they create, and emergency shelter, while necessary, offers no route out of homelessness. A problem-solving rather than problem-perpetuating approach would demand permanent housing, services, and income generation plans for the homeless and for low-income persons at risk of becoming homeless. But given the severity of the problem, this would require a major commitment to a more equitable redistribution of income and benefits—for example, through policies that would not punish the poor for their inability to become homeowners.

REDISTRIBUTION BROADLY DEFINED

Redistribution of real income is used here in the broad sense employed by Harvey to include both direct and hidden costs and benefits that accrue to various actors in a complex (usually urban) setting, the "market value of rights exercised in consumption."[17] Redistribution of income can be accomplished through changes in the location of jobs and housing, changes in the value of property rights, and through changes in the price that consumers pay for resources (Harvey, 1973:86). Harvey argues that changes in the value of property rights and in the availability and price of resources can have a "very substantial effect upon income distribution, and that their effects become disproportionately important as the size of an urban system increases." This scale factor becomes important when we consider why the per capita rate of homelessness is positively related to the size of urban areas. "'Fringe benefits . . . generated by changes in the urban system. . . are distributed unequally across the population." Thus, the "hidden mechanisms" of income redistribution in a complex city system usually increase inequalities rather than reduce them. Air and water pollution, crime, and litter are all examples of hidden costs that may be disproportionately borne by minorities and the poor.[18]

The cost and benefit of housing tenure are principal mechanisms by which income is redistributed, particularly in the United States. Tax benefits to property owners, for example, redistribute income away from renters and toward owners. Furthermore, once individuals become homeowners, their housing costs are stabilized, and thus typically consume less of a proportion of income over time. For those who rent and must compete monthly in the housing market, housing costs rarely stabilize for more than a year at a time. Additionally, while the percentage of income going to housing has been increasing for both renters and owners, the cost burden increase has been much more rapid for renters than owners, and greatest for very low income renters. As Table 2.1 illustrates, the median percentage of income being spent on housing by home owners with a mortgage advanced slowly from 18 percent in 1976 to 20 percent in 1983. Renters, on the other hand, experienced an increase in median gross rent as a percent of income from 20 percent in 1970 to 29 percent. Nearly 55 percent of all low-income renters were cost-burdened in 1983, paying more than

Table 2.1
Comparison of Costs and Incomes of Renters and Owners

Year	Housing Cost as % of Income		Number Paying > 35% Renter	Median Income	
	Renter	Owner		Renter	Owner
1970	20	na	5,209	$6,300	$9,700
1976	24	18	6,687	$8,200	$14,400
1980	27	19	8,482	$10,500	$19,800
1983	29	20	10,236	$12,400	$24,400

Source: Annual Housing National Survey Published Tabulations.

30 percent of income to rent (U.S. Bureau of the Census Annual Housing Survey national files, 1973-1983).

The median income of renters in 1983 was only about half that of owners, whereas in 1970, it had been about two-thirds, and the absolute numbers of renters paying more than 35 percent of income to rent has nearly doubled to more than 10 million.

In terms of direct redistribution, the amount of mortgage interest and property taxes that is deductible for owners is unlimited and thus increases in value as these payments, which are highly correlated with income, grow larger. But in addition to the direct mechanisms, tenure implies hidden redistributive costs and benefits that might be thought of as social and emotional rather than financial. Renters, for example, have gone to court for the right to maintain pets, to have overnight visitors, or to paint or otherwise alter their apartments.[19] Owners have the freedom and autonomy to arrange their environments and conduct their affairs much as they choose.

The effect of hidden redistribution "has immediate implications for social policy in that it indicates the necessity for a policy of 'overkill' in direct redistribution if the general direction of hidden redistribution is to be counteracted" (Harvey, 1973:54). As an example, Harvey cites the prevalent dislocation between jobs and housing, which has a disproportionately negative effect on the poor. Kasarda (1988) has documented that poor inner-city minorities have been especially hard hit by structural transformation of urban areas. The main supply of low-cost housing is in the central city, although relative to its actual value, this housing may be quite expensive. Low-skilled jobs are increasingly concentrated outside the central city, but the thrust of transportation services is to transport highly skilled workers from the peripheral to the central city rather than from the central city to jobs in the suburbs. This leads to higher levels of unemployment among those who can afford to live only in the central city or who are confined by segregation to inner-city housing markets. The hidden redistribution further impoverishes the poor by denying access to jobs and by increasing transportation expense and time for those who do commute. The direct redistributive costs, if they are provided at all, must overcompensate by subsidizing the greater number of people who will be unemployed under these circumstances than would be if jobs and housing were colocated.

The rationale for defining redistribution more broadly will become clear as we examine factors such as racial discrimination in the price that is paid for housing services, a hidden redistribution that is hypothesized to increase the risk of homelessness for minorities. For the poor, who disproportionately occupy substandard housing, hidden costs are encountered to the extent that such housing is not discounted in the market and to the extent that defective housing increases health and social problems. The low quality of such housing also places the occupant at greater risk of eviction due to condemnation or demolition. The poor tenant has less ability to withstand the expense of relocation. These factors can and do precipitate homelessness as Sosin, Colson, and Grossman (1988) have shown.

Racial discrimination in housing and employment constrains minorities, more than comparable whites, from obtaining housing that may be closer to jobs,[20] from obtaining jobs, and from obtaining jobs that pay well. The hidden cost of racial discrimination thus can have a direct effect on reducing income for minorities. One-third of all blacks and 28 percent of Hispanics live in poverty, as compared with 11 percent of whites (New York Times, Sept. 1, 1988). The prevalence of poverty among minorities, coupled with housing discrimination and segregation, may be expected to produce greater vulnerability to homelessness for minorities than for whites.

In its simplest form, the structural model I propose would indicate that redistribution policies, both direct and hidden, have had the effect of increasing both poverty and rent. These, in turn, have increased both homelessness and addiction, as well as familial or social dysfunction, and, to a lesser extent, mental illness. While mental illness and addiction will not be addressed in this study, their inclusion in this model is intended to show that all of these outcomes are more likely to occur as a result of changing redistributive policies that work against the disadvantaged. The long-term consequences to society have not been fully considered in formulating such policies. As Harvey observes, "If we simply pursue efficiency and ignore the social cost [of redistributive policy], then those individuals or groups who bear the brunt of that cost are likely to be a source of long-run inefficiency either through a decline in those intangibles that motivate people to cooperate and participate in the social process of production, or through forms of anti-social behavior such as crime and drug addiction which will necessitate the diversion of productive investment towards their correction" (Harvey, 1973:97).

In the case of homelessness, the "overkill" to which Harvey refers would be that in allowing the poor to become homeless through both hidden and direct redistributive mechanisms, corrective social policy will require not only jobs and housing, but also rehabilitation to overcome the humiliation and demoralization of becoming homeless.[21] So detrimental are the consequent effects on an individual's ability to work, learn, or carry out independent tasks such as searching for housing, that those who work with the homeless stress the importance of preventing those at risk from falling into literal homelessness (interviews with Steinbruck, 1989; Posa, 1989; Liebow interview, 1989).

THE IMPACT OF REDISTRIBUTIVE CHANGES ON HOMELESSNESS

In this study I hypothesize that homelessness is causally linked to a mismatch in the availability of affordable housing and the demand by low-income renters for housing of low cost. While the extent of the mismatch is predicted to vary across metropolitan areas, a general theoretical assumption is that nationwide, homelessness has been exacerbated by a decrease in redistributive programs benefiting the poor, coupled with an increase in the cost of housing, which has exceeded the overall rate of inflation.[22] I theorize that these factors are not unrelated and that the increase in rent cannot be explained by an increase in quality. Rather, the effect of income transfers to the affluent has been to encourage a concentration of ownership of rental housing among fewer investors through increased availability of investment capital. This concentration fosters increases in rent.[23]

Gilderbloom and Appelbaum (1987) found that higher gross rent was positively related to the extent to which private rental housing has become "professionalized," with the concentration of a large number of units under the ownership of a single individual or firm.[24] This finding, the authors contend, lends support to their hypothesis that the "institutional structure of housing markets is a major (if neglected) factor in the determination of rents."[25] I argue that this institutional structure has been influenced by the redistributive policies of the last decade, policies that have benefited high-income investors with both the means and the incentive to increase their rental real estate holdings.

This professionalization has occurred in an environment in which rental housing, at least until 1986, remained relatively strong in comparison with other forms of investment.[26] Investors with large portfolios and growing amounts of cash to be put to work at the beginning of the decade were likely to diversify at least some of their assets into real estate because of the presumption that continued inflation in the housing market would expand equity even if rent profits faltered. Rental housing purchases could be heavily leveraged—purchased for a small down payment yet allowing a tax shelter, in the form of depreciation, on the full purchase price. These benefits to investors were enhanced in the 1981 Tax Act and although many were eliminated in the 1986 Tax Reform Act (Gilderbloom and Appelbaum, 1987:50), the growth of large corporations within the rental industry had firmly taken hold.

Why should this phenomenon be related to higher rents, even in the presence of high vacancies? Stegman (1982) suggests not only that widespread ownership of the rental housing stock fosters competition, but also that amateur landlords have quite different interests from those of professional landlords. For the latter, the highest rate of return in the shortest time period is the primary goal of investment, whereas for the amateur, social and personal considerations, including an interest in maintaining a property long term, have led generally to lower rents and better upkeep.[27]

Professionalization has been accompanied by a growing social organization that may be formal or informal. In major cities, private firms provide periodic rent and vacancy surveys, make rent forecasts, and analyze the strength of the market for future investment in additional building.[28] These firms largely take the guesswork out of investment in rental housing. It is clear that, in the absence of subsidies for doing so, there is no compatibility between maximizing profits and providing a high-quality unit (or perhaps any unit) at a price affordable to the poor.

Some publications of the rental trade suggest standard percentage rent increases to their landlord subscribers, encouraging across-the-board rent increases from which tenants will not be able to flee. For example, the Institute of Real Estate Management of the National Association of Realtors, "the largest and most influential landlord organization in the United States" (Gilderbloom and Appelbaum, 1987:61), publishes "How to Get Your Manager to Raise Rents." This reprint criticizes some owners for failure to raise rents sufficiently, thereby "harming the real estate industry as a whole."

Here's a tip: When you raise rents, send a notice to your competition. It's the best mail they'll get all day. Everyone is afraid to be the first to increase rents. Once your competition sees you doing it, they'll very likely follow suit, thus making the rent increase a fact of life for all tenants. The need to make rent adjustments to restore or safeguard the return on your investment should be very clear. Your goal is not occupancy levels, but money in the bank.[29]

Hypothetically, such advice, were it widely accepted within a geographic area, could lead to a cartel of apartment owners who were able to operate outside the "laws" of supply and demand. Based on Marx's analysis of rent, which although primarily directed to the rent of agricultural land, has application to urban and residential property, Harvey shows that scarcity is socially defined. Under some circumstances a monopoly rent can be established as producers (landlords) set up "cartel arrangements among themselves, as a single producer operates over many production points and as the various competitive practices among firms with distinctive territories are restricted or modified to prevent strong competition" (Harvey, 1973:183). Conceivably, the supply of "affordable" housing for low-income tenants could thus decline even in a city such as Houston, with a vacancy rate of 18 percent (in 1983), or where normally discounted substandard housing is plentiful. While Gilderbloom and Appelbaum state that they do not wish to imply that a system of monopoly rents has been established, they point out that the extent to which collusion occurs in the setting of rents is underestimated (1987).

When the stagnating or declining incomes of the poor are challenged by the rising rents of the market, I hypothesize that homelessness results for some. Those most at risk of homelessness will be those whose rent-to-income ratios make them most vulnerable to the vagaries of the market. This population is likely to be disproportionately one that also bears hidden redistributive costs such as racial discrimination and occupancy of the frail housing stock. The likelihood of homelessness occurring, however, is hypothesized to vary across metropolitan areas. In chapter 3 I examine a number of the largest metropolitan areas in the United States and compare their rates of homelessness, as estimated by HUD in 1983, with a number of indicators that may be related to homelessness.

NOTES

1. A *New York Times* CBS-TV poll (June 29, 1989) reports that, in overlapping categories, 60 percent of those polled thought deinstitutionalization was responsible for much of the homelessness problem, while 50 percent blamed

policies of the Reagan and Bush administrations, and 49 percent cited drug and alcohol abuse. Thirty-two percent blamed the homeless themselves for their failure to work.

2. It should also be kept in mind that 32 percent of all Americans, according to the National Institute of Mental Health, will experience mental illness or substance abuse at some time during their lives (*New York Times*, Nov. 7, 1988). Thus the extent to which these problems distinguish the homeless from the general population can be questioned.

3. The majority of those released from mental institutions who need supportive services have families who will care for them (Lamb, 1986). If there has been a decline in the willingness of families to provide long-term care for such members, these individuals may be increasingly forced to seek housing on the market.

4. In Seattle, for example, it is estimated that 93 percent of the average disability grant would be expended on the average rent (Seattle's 1989 Housing Assistance Plan, 1988).

5. A New York City program to get the homeless mentally ill off the streets, after hospitalizing 466 people against their will and stabilizing them with drugs, has been successful in placing "dozens" of formerly homeless in community residences or their own apartments. The program has been criticized, however, by Robert Hayes of the National Coalition for the Homeless, for being "a tiny drop in an ocean of need" (*New York Times*, July 18, 1989).

6. G. Kolata quoting Ernest Drucker, "Twins of the Street: Homelessness and Addiction," *New York Times*, May 23, 1989:1.

7. Cohen and Burt (1989) found that, while 27 percent of their sample received income from working, mean income per person was only $139 for the previous month and mean length of current joblessness was 40 months.

8. "Crack has so glutted the market [in New York] that the price of a vial has dropped to $3 to $5 [or] it is sold by a single draw on a pipe for pocket change," Michael Marriott, "The 12 Worst Drug Bazaars: New York's Continuing Blight," *New York Times*, June 1, 1989.

9. Even New York City's chief of police, Benjamin Ward, notes that "the drug problem is complicated—rooted in poverty and joblessness" (Marriott, 1989).

10. Sosin, Colson, and Grossman (1988) found that the incidence of binge drinking among a sample of homeless did not distinguish them from a comparable sample of poor.

11. This statement is based on interviews with shelter managers and transitional housing experts. Not all concur with this view. Some shelters have mandatory participation requirements for job readiness and substance abuse programs, but the majority of those I interviewed believe these efforts to be largely futile with the sheltered population and advocate such programs only after living situations are stabilized (Melvin, 1989; Steinbruck, 1989; Liebow, 1989).

12. The evidence suggests that the majority of mental illnesses may be biochemically rather than environmentally caused, but to the extent that mental illness may be either precipitated or aggravated by stress, extreme and worsening poverty provides such stress.

13. Easterlin proposed that declining incomes would lead to delayed marriage. This could result in both a delay in the formation of new households and in an increase in the proportion of households composed of single persons. If this occurred, it would raise demand for smaller rental units, which would drive up rents and contribute to the vulnerability of renters to homelessness. The Easterlin hypothesis is most viable for a city such as Seattle, which has a high proportion of single younger heads, a very low vacancy rate, and a rapid increase in rent.

14. But as Hoch and Slayton (1989:200) point out, "The residents of Skid Row . . . were not for the most part disaffiliated bums or immoral derelicts. They were poor single people using the modest resources of the Skid Row community to secure both a living and a modicum of independence."

15. Michael Fabricant (1987) argues that recipients of entitlements are being resocialized to less, just as the broader economic resocialization brings new low wages and wage rollbacks to the labor force.

16. "The thousand points of light," as President George Bush likes to refer to the voluntary sector.

17. David Harvey (1973), quoting R. M. Titmuss, *Income Distribution and Social Change* (London, 1962).

18. Joe Feagin (1988) documents the extent to which central city black neighborhoods in Houston have disproportionately borne the social costs of garbage landfills and incinerators, while failing to get the benefits of public services, paved streets, and lighting to the extent that white neighborhoods have received them.

19. Jeffrey Freedman, a journalist who writes the "Tenants" column for the *Toronto Star*, draws attention to the regulation that apartment dwellers face, such as the choice that renters must sometimes make between keeping an apartment or having a pet (Personal Communication, 1989).

20. Noting that the availability of housing loans can make or break a neighborhood, Anne Shlay (1987a) demonstrates that housing loans are heavily segmented by race and location. Blacks are prevented from purchasing housing by discrimination on the part of residential lending institutions.

21. Harvey's argument is similar to the once radical but now increasingly well accepted idea that what we fail to provide in social and educational benefits for children we will pay for several times over in maintaining prisons and in welfare benefits for adults inadequately prepared for a productive life.

22. As previously noted, it is recognized that factors such as job loss to foreign markets and the alteration of the economy from higher-paying manufacturing to lower-wage service jobs have contributed to the declining or stagnating incomes of renters. To the extent that redistributive policies not only failed to compensate for these changes, but also cut social spending to those most severely affected by them, I would argue that the policies have contributed to impoverishment and homelessness. On a broader scale, it could be argued that laissez-faire government economic policies have allowed the export of jobs and the transformation of the economy to take place.

23. An increasing concentration of capital is taking place throughout our economic system, as corporate takeovers, mergers, and

buyouts attest, much as predicted by Marx (*Capital*, Vol. 3, 1909, p. 257) 1909. (See L. Brown and E. Rosengren, eds., *The Merger Boom*, proceedings of a conference sponsored by the Federal Reserve Bank, October 1987).

24. Among the studies documenting the concentrated ownership of rental property *cited by* Gilderbloom and Appelbaum (1987) are Linson (1978), who found that the entire multifamily housing stock of Santa Barbara, California, was owned by just 687 persons, 7 of whom owned one-fifth of the stock; Marcuse (1986) who reported that 975 owners, or 5 percent of all owners, held 56 percent of all rent-stabilized units in New York City, and Gilderbloom and Keating (1982), who discovered that 10 owners or companies held nearly one-third of the rental stock of Orange, New Jersey. The authors cite a steady growth in the construction of large as opposed to small apartment complexes, as reported in the U.S. Census of Housing reports, as indicative of increasing concentration of ownership in rental property. While the construction of large units is a more efficient technology in terms of land use and services, the savings that might be anticipated from such efficiency are not always passed onto the renter consumer.

25. Gilderbloom and Appelbaum (1987:101-3) use as a measure of professionalization the percentage of a city's rental stock that consists of either 10 or more or 50 or more units at one address. They find this positive relationship in separate equations with each of the two measures, although the relationship is twice as strong for 10-plus units as for 50-plus. However, in the equation containing 50-plus units, the percentage of the total housing stock that was lacking complete plumbing was also positive and significant. The authors speculate that in highly professionalized markets, a larger proportion of substandard units may only force tenants in higher-quality units to pay higher rents, rather than to reduce rents for lower-quality units. They cite an earlier study by Cronin (Market Structure and Price of Housing Services, *Urban Studies*, 20:365-75), in which rent differentials within a city were found to be correlated with the number of rental units in the neighborhood owned by a single landlord.

26. Real Estate Research Council report, "Housing Opportunities in Apartments," *Housing and Development Reporter*, 1986, showed that apartments were better investments than other forms of real estate in the 1980-85 period. Average total return in both income and appreciation totaled 17.4 percent between 1978 and 1984 (cited in Gilderbloom and Appelbaum, 1987:228).

27. Part of this interest may result from the lack of alternative investment strategies for the small-time landlord, as well as from long-term mortgages with low monthly payments, not requiring a large monthly cash flow (ibid., 100). It is conceivable that middle-income workers, who in the past may have supplemented their earnings with income from small rental property, may no longer find it necessary to do so.

28. For example, Cain and Scott of Seattle publish (for a $165 per year subscription) a quarterly apartment investment study of all 20-and-larger units in the three county area surrounding Seattle. Included are price per unit, price per square foot, expense ratios, capitalization rates, cash returns, and detailed operating expense analysis for 10,000 units. Addition-

ally, the Cain and Scott vacancy report ($155.00 per year) surveys 100,000 units, covering 48 submarkets in five counties. Rents and vacancies are broken out by neighborhood, type, and age of the structure (Cain and Scott, Inc., Income Property Specialists, Seattle, Washington).

29. E. N. Kelley, "How to Get Your Manager to Raise Rents," reprinted from *Journal of Property Management*, March/April 1975, by the Institute of Real Estate Management, Chicago, as cited in Gilderbloom and Appelbaum (1987:61).

3

Homelessness and Area-Specific Characteristics

What factors may be related to the risk of homelessness? Why do some cities appear to have a more extensive problem of homelessness than others? This study hypothesizes that homelessness is related to the availability and affordability of rental housing for the low-income population. These in turn may be influenced by other factors. Before looking at how rents and incomes vary across metropolitan areas, it may be useful to examine factors that appear to be related to estimated levels of homelessness in these areas.

The 18 SMSAs available for inclusion in the study are those among the 35 largest SMSAs that have had an Annual Housing Survey conducted as recently as 1983 or 1985. This chapter provides descriptive statistics on variables that are hypothesized to be related to the prevalence of homelessness in these metropolitan areas and their central cities. It concludes with a selection of SMSAs that are representative of the range of variation demonstrated by these statistics and that, it is hoped, can function as prototypes for metropolitan areas with similar attributes.

THE RANGE OF HOMELESSNESS IN METROPOLITAN AREAS

Because our concern is estimating a population at risk of becoming homeless, we first turn to the "point-in-time" estimates of homelessness in these 18 SMSAs in 1983, as generated by the U.S. Department of Housing and Urban Development (HUD). These are accompanied, where available, by estimates from other sources. Table 3.1 provides the low, high, and "most reliable range" estimates HUD obtained from one of the four previously identified sources, its interviews with local experts. Nationally, the HUD figures assume an overall rate of 13 homeless per 10,000 persons for cities over one million, and 6.5 per 10,000 for areas with populations less than 250,000. It found, however, that the rate for the largest SMSAs, based on the midpoint of the "most reliable range," varied from 3 per 10,000 for Baltimore to 43 per 10,000 for Los Angeles. The methodology HUD used to produce these estimates suffered from a number of shortcomings, but the estimates have been both criticized and defended (Appelbaum, 1988; Redburn and Buss,

Table 3.1

Estimates of Homeless Population in 18 Major Metropolitan Areas

RMA	Low est.[a]	High est.[a]	RMA 'Most Reliable Range'[a]	Homeless per 10,000	Other Estimates
Baltimore	450	750	630–750	3	1,200[b]
Boston	2,300	5,000	3,100–3,300	13	2,000–8,000[e]
Chicago	17,000	26,000	19,400–20,300	28	3,700–5,900[c]
Dallas	2,700	6,500	3,900[d]	d	
Denver	1,500	3,600	2,100[d]	d	1,500–5,000[e]
Detroit	3,000	9,000	7,200–7,900	17	2,000–8,000[e]
Houston	450	12,500	5,200–7,500	22	10,000[f]
Los Angeles	19,500	39,000	31,300–33,800	43	22,000–30,000[e]
Miami	1,000	10,000	5,100–6,800	37	8,000–10,000[g]
Minneapolis	700	1,150	870–1,150	5	900[e]
New York	12,000	50,000	28,000–30,000	33	45,000–63,000[h]
Philadelphia	450	8,050	2,200–5,000	8	8,000[e]
Phoenix	300	1,500	750–1,400	8	500–6,200[e]
Portland	600	2,700	1,400–1,700	12	1,000–2,000[e]
St. Louis	2,100	5,200	3,100[d]	d	
San Francisco	7,500	11,500	7,700–8,800	25	4,000–10,000[e]
Seattle	1,300	5,000	3,100–3,250	20	2,000–2,500[e]
Washington	3,000	10,500	3,000–6,400	15	4,350–7,150[j]

Sources:

[a] U.S. Department of Housing and Urban Development, 1984, estimates for Rand McNally Areas.

[b] Cowan, Breakey and Fischer, 1986, city of Baltimore.

[c] Rossi, Fisher and Wilis, 1986, city of Chicago.

[d] Based on HUD general estimates of 9–22/10,000, and 13/10,000 as a most reliable range.

[e] Reported by HUD from other published sources, 1984.

[f] McKinsey, Inc., 1989, Houston/Harris county.

[g] New York Times, 11/9/88, city of Miami.

[h] Hirschel, 1987, New York City.

[i] Seattle Human Services Strategic Planning Office, Seattle/King county, 1988.

[j] UDC Center for Applied Research and Urban Policy, 1985.

1987; Freeman and Hall, 1987). For our purposes, it will be assumed that the relative position of SMSAs with regard to the homeless population is accurate, even if the exact levels may not be.

As might be expected on the basis of population size alone, the 10 SMSAs with the largest homeless populations in the nation, as estimated by HUD, are included among this list of 18. However, only Los Angeles, New York, and Chicago are among the 10 metropolitan areas with the largest per capita estimates of homeless persons. The highest per capita rates of homelessness were found, according to HUD, in Tucson (61/10,000), El Paso (59/10,000), and Worcester, Massachusetts (47/10,000) (Redburn and Buss, 1987:24).

In an attempt to determine what factors may account for the wide variability in per capita rates, Redburn and Buss (1987:25,32) regressed HUD estimates for 71 metropolitan areas on five potential predictors of homelessness. Of these, only total population size and rate of population growth were significantly related to the estimates, and these explained only 15 percent of the variation in rates found across these areas. Climate, rent levels, and rental vacancy rates were all found to be statistically insignificant in explaining the rates of homelessness estimated by HUD.

There are flaws in this approach that should not allow us to accept the results without question. For example, we would expect that the relationship between heating degree days[1] and a point-in-time estimate of homelessness would only be significantly negative if the estimate were obtained at a time of seasonal climate variation across regions. In other words, the influx of homeless persons to Miami[2] during the winter months will not be apparent if the point estimate is made in the summer and will overstate average prevalence if made in the winter, assuming that some homeless individuals move with the season from the north to the south.

Average rent as a predictor of homelessness should only be considered in relationship to average income or rent affordability within a metropolitan area. However, Redburn and Buss may be quite correct in finding no association between the rental vacancy rate and incidence of homelessness. As previously noted, the number of vacancies generally rises monotonically with gross rent, and the vacancy rate at the level of rent affordable to the poor may be very low even when overall vacancy levels are considered "adequate."

VARIATION IN INDICATORS RELATED TO HOUSING

Table 3.2 identifies a number of housing parameters for the 18 SMSAs and illustrates the substantial variation in these indicators across metropolitan areas. The percent of the population who own their own homes, for example, varies from 42 percent in New York to 71 percent in Detroit. All but New York, Los Angeles (46 percent), and Dallas (46 percent in 1980) have in excess of 50 percent homeowners, but 13 of the 18 areas are below the U.S. average of 63.8 percent owners in 1986 (U.S. Bureau of the Census, 1988c, Table 60). Interestingly, New York and Los Angeles also have the lowest vacancy rates among the 18, 3.9 percent, or about half the U.S. average of 7.6 percent (U.S. Bureau of the Census, 1983). A majority of households who are renters may be indicative of a very tight rental market and one with a virtual absence of low-cost rental housing.

OVERCROWDING

The standard measure of housing density is the number of persons per room, with a ratio of more than one to one indicative of overcrowding. Column 3 in Table 3.2 indicates a considerable range, from about 2 percent of Minneapolis renters to 11 percent of Los Angeles renters, living in overcrowded conditions. Six of the ten metropolitan areas for which comparison data were available showed slight increases over time in the percentage of households with more than one person per room, while four showed a decline or no change. The changes in either direction were slight and are unlikely to be statistically significant.

Overcrowding has presumed detrimental effects, but empirical tests of its impact have generally failed to control for socioeconomic status and quality of housing.[3] In a large stratified probability sample of Chicago households, which did control for socioeconomic status and race, Gove and Hughes (1983) concluded that the number of persons per room was the best objective measure of crowdedness. Overcrowding was found to be strongly related to poor mental and physical health, inadequate child care, physical and psychological withdrawal from the home, and disrupted social relationships.

Crowdedness is a culture-bound concept, and one to which ethnic and racial groups react differently. The study revealed the extent to which persons per room as the objective measure of overcrowding interacts with culture, both in terms of ability to manage the environment to obtain privacy and in terms of emotional reactivity to high-density interaction. Blacks were the most successful at maximizing privacy, but also experienced more mental and physical distress due to crowded conditions than whites. Although Hispanics experienced the highest levels of crowding, they were least reactive to the stress of overcrowding of the three groups. The authors hypothesize that Hispanics historically have had a close-contact culture with less need for interpersonal space

Table 3.2
Housing Parameters of 18 Major Metropolitan Areas

SMSA	% Own	PPR>1	%35% + rent		Med %	Mort.% Inc		rentinc %own		%vac	%sub
	82–3	82–3	82–3	75–6	82–3	82–3	75–6	82–3	75–6	82–3	82–3
Column No.	2	3	4	5	6	7	8	9	10	11	12
Baltimore[a]	61.2	3.2	32.1	24.5	26	18	16	48.6	54.1	7.5	1.8
Chicago	57.4	6.1	35.0	26.4	28	19	18	45.1	54.1	7.6	2.0
Denver	61.2	3.0	36.2	19.0	30	19	18	45.6	47.5	8.4	.8
Houston	60.9	8.5	31.3	22.0	26	19	17	50.8	57.8	20.8	1.4
New York	41.5	7.4	36.8	33.7	28	20	22	41.2	48.2	3.9	1.0
Philadelphia	68.5	4.5	37.8	28.1	29	19	18	46.3	57.2	9.3	1.0
Portland	61.2	2.7	33.5	26.6	27	20	18	50.0	57.0	9.1	1.1
St. Louis	67.2	4.4	31.8	27.0	26	17	17	46.3	52.8	9.1	.5
San Fran.	52.5	4.8	36.0	28.8	29	19	19	48.8	52.7	4.2	2.0
Seattle	62.3	2.7	31.6	25.8	26	17	16	48.2	50.6	8.9	.9
Boston[b]	51.9	3.5	na[c]	na	na	na	na	48.4	na	4.8	na
Dallas	45.7	7.6						59.5		10.4	
Detroit	71.2	3.9								7.5	
Los Angeles	46.4	11.2						48.4		3.9	
Miami	54.6	8.8						48.7		5.4	
Minneapolis	64.7	1.6						47.5		4.2	
Phoenix	68.7	8.9						55.6		11.8	
Washington	54.3	6.5						48.7		5.4	

[a]Source: 1982–1983 Annual Housing Survey SMSA Characteristics

[b]Source: 1980 Census Characteristics of Housing and Detailed Characteristics of Housing by State

[c]not available

Column two: Percent of population who own homes.

Column three: Percent of renters with more than 1.0 persons per room.

Columns four-five: Percent of renters whose rent exceeds 35% of income.

Column six: Median percentage of income going to rent, 1982–3.

Columns seven-eight: Homeowner's mortgage as percent of income, for those with a mortgage.

Columns nine-ten: Renter's income as a percent of owner's income.

Column eleven: Rental vacancy rate.

Column twelve: Percent of renter households with related subfamilies.

than blacks and whites. In view of their very high level of crowding, however, the impact of crowding on Hispanics is quite substantial. These racial and ethnic variations in response to overcrowding may become important as we attempt to account for variation in rates of homelessness among whites and minorities.

The level and prevalence of overcrowding relates directly to estimating the population at risk of homelessness because of the evidence previously cited that links the onset of homelessness, for a high percentage of homeless persons, to eviction by friends or relatives. Having lost the independent living arrangements they once had, doubling up is, for many, the immediate precursor to living on the streets or entering a shelter.

The last column of Table 3.2 gives the percentage of renter households with related subfamilies in residence.

Nationally, the number of households with related subfamilies increased by 98 percent between 1980 and 1987, while those with unrelated subfamilies increased by 57 percent (U.S. Bureau of the Census, 1988c, Table 56). The combination of related and unrelated subfamilies represent nearly 3 million households who were doubled up in 1987. These levels have not been seen since the post–World War II housing shortage,[4] and are certainly suggestive of a crisis in housing availability, affordability, or both.[5] Blank and Rosen (1989) find that over the 1977 to 1987 decade, the poor especially have become less "housing independent," with more than half of all heads of poor families not heading their own households, but living with other heads.

HOUSING COSTS AND INCOME OF RENTERS AND OWNERS

Table 3.2 provides some of the information on housing costs for renters and owners in individual metropolitan areas that was given for the nation as a whole in Table 2.1. The *Annual Housing Survey* published reports use more than 35 percent of income spent on rent as a measure of housing distress (as opposed to the 30 percent of income used as the maximum "affordable" rent charged by the federal government for participants in its housing programs). Although mortgage companies have relaxed the conventional standard of 25 percent of cash income as a maximum allowable mortgage for home purchasers, 30 percent is still thought to represent the most that a potential home buyer should commit to housing costs. About one-third of all renters in these SMSAs paid 35 percent or more of income in rent in 1982-83 (Table 3.2, columns 4-5), a substantial increase from 1975-76 in all the SMSAs for which comparison data were available.

For owners, the sharp increase in housing prices and interest rates have not had a dramatic effect on the median mortgage-to-income ratio. As columns 7 and 8 indicate, not only have housing costs for those with a mortgage remained relatively stable over the 1975-83-year period, but also the median amount of owner income spent on housing costs is only 65 to 75 percent of the median percentage of renter income being spent on rent.

There is also a growing imbalance in the income distribution between renters and owners in these SMSAs. Columns 9 and 10 show a significant decline in the income of renters as a percentage of the income of owners. Renters, then, are increasingly less well off as compared with owners, and they spend a much larger and faster-growing percentage of income on rent. This may mean that today's renters are less able than renters in the past to move out of rental tenure, since they have less potential to save for a down payment and there are fewer federal programs to encourage home ownership among low- and moderate-income households.

The decline of an average of 6 percentage points in the income of renters relative to owners over this period may be due to a number of factors. A majority of the lowest-income groups in the population—blacks, Hispanics, and female heads—are renters, and the relative size of these groups within the population has increased over time. Fifty-nine percent of Hispanic households rent, while the comparable figures for black and female-headed households are 56 and 54 percent (U.S. Bureau of the Census, 1988c). We have already seen that the income of female heads has been adversely affected by cuts in social welfare spending. These segments of the population may have also been hard hit by loss of manufacturing jobs, high unemployment, and by sex and racial discrimination in a surplus labor market.

Owner incomes may have increased while renter incomes remained stable. Owner households have a greater potential for being two-earner families than do renter households, thus increasing owner income relative to renter. For example, 77 percent of married couples own their homes as compared with just 46 percent of nonfamily households. For the 80 percent of nonfamily households that consist of one person, there is no potential for dual earnings. The proportion of single-person households as a percentage of all households has increased, from about 17 percent in 1970 to nearly 24 percent in 1987 (U.S. Bureau of the Census, 1988c:43).

Another hypothesis is that selectivity takes place with regard to home-ownership in that higher-income renters have become owners (Farley, 1983). This is a process that has presumably always taken place but that may have escalated under the inflated housing markets of the 1970s. Any renters who could afford a mortgage were encouraged by this inflation to become owners, leaving behind a relatively poorer body of renters than in the past.

Household Composition and Increasing Rental Tenure

This hypothesis is not inconsistent with the falling median income of renters but does not fit well with the fact that a declining percentage of Americans have been able to become homeowners over the last several years. Presumably, high mortgage costs and inflated housing prices have instead forced an increase in the percentage of all households who are renters and have prevented all but the most highly qualified buyers from purchasing homes. Four of the ten cities for which comparisons can be made experienced a decline in owner tenure during the eight-year period.

The advantages to homeownership—exercise of personal autonomy, opportunity for wealth accumulation, and tax shelter—are presumed to make homeownership the preferred state of tenure. The goal of national housing policy has ostensibly been to provide an increasing proportion of the population with an opportunity for homeownership. The constraints to ownership are both income and a sufficient down payment to qualify for a loan. Racial discrimination in the ability to obtain financing plays an increasingly well documented role, at least in some housing markets, in who is able to become a homeowner. Controlling for income, blacks are seen to be significantly less able to obtain mortgage financing (Shlay, 1985, 1987 a, b).

The necessity of saving a sufficient down payment has typically made the progression from renter to owner a life-cycle transition. Only 20 percent of those under the age of 25 own their own homes, while about 80 percent of those over 55 are homeowners.[6] This is reflective not only of savings, but also of mobility. Young persons are perhaps not interested in being permanently settled or in assuming the responsibilities entailed by ownership. Nevertheless, the advantages to ownership are substantial and have grown as the cost of housing has inflated. Owners have seen their investment rising, while renters find that they are unable to stabilize their housing costs. Therefore, the advantages to ownership should compel those who are financially able to become owners. The proportion of the population who are renters thus may increasingly represent those who are financially unable to become owners rather than those who are young, transient, and renters by choice.

Although only a minority of the poor have been able to become homeowners, the proportion of the poor who are owners has fallen by more than 3 percent in the last 11 years. (Blank and Rosen, 1989). Overall, the proportion of the population who are renters rose from 35.4 percent in 1978 to 36.1 percent in 1985. Regionally, the percentage of renters varies from 33 percent in the Midwest to 41 percent in the West, but all regions experienced an increase in rental tenure between 1980 and 1985 (McGough and Casey, 1986).

The reversal of the long-standing trend toward increasing owner-ship is reflected in the increasing median age of renters and in the rising average age of first-time buyers. As the number of renter households increased by 33 percent between 1975 and 1987, the num-ber of renter households with children quadrupled.[7] This may be due to a number of factors in addition to the move toward rental tenure. The large cohort of the baby-boom generation remained in prime childbearing years, and an increasing proportion of families with children may not have been able to afford to purchase housing while more affluent singles were able to. The growth in the proportion of all families that are headed by females and in the proportion of children being raised in female-headed poor families undoubtedly contributed to the trend of children living in rented quarters as well.

.The 1980-83 period saw a decline in the number of renter households formed by those in the 20- to 24-year-old age bracket, the ages during which new renter households are typically formed. About 800,000 ex-pected new households, of which 80 to 90 percent would have been renters, were not formed (McGough and Casey, 1986). Speculatively, these potential new householders are still living with their families of origin, as high rents and/or low incomes prevent them from moving out on their own. This shortfall will gradually be made up, but the high cost of housing might be expected to keep new household formation lower than what would be anticipated on the basis of the age structure alone.

IDENTIFYING RELEVANT INDICATORS ACROSS SMSAs

Having discussed the variation in homelessness across metropoli-tan areas and in some parameters pertaining to the housing stock, we now turn to categorizing metropolitan areas along dimensions that are hypothesized to be related to housing supply and demand. This is an effort to define a set of SMSAs that are representative, along these dimensions, of a number of metropolitan areas with similar charac-teristics. The set of SMSAs will be the focus of this study and will be analyzed in depth.

Numerous attempts to rank order or categorize cities or metropoli-tan areas have been made. Berger and Blomquist (1988) ranked 24 SMSAs on a quality of life (QOL) index based on a number of economic indicators, including a hedonic housing expenditure equation. Sur-prisingly, the rankings are not tied to such indicators as the poverty or unemployment rate; thus, among the 11 cities with a positive QOL index are 4 cities with the largest homeless populations.

More relevant to the present study is a format that was used to develop housing policies for the urban poor. Struyk, Marshall, and Ozanne (1978) found that the great diversity in U.S. metropolitan areas and the accompanying broad range of housing market conditions demanded a mix of housing policies. Because it is expensive and impractical to develop policies for individual metropolitan areas, a rationale for categorizing SMSAs was necessary. Based on empirical evidence and theory, the authors determined that racial composition and the rate of growth of low- and moderate-income households had a strong influence on housing policy outcomes and were therefore appropriate benchmarks by which to subdivide metropolitan areas.

As the authors note, racial composition "may prevent an efficient match of households and dwellings," if discrimination is presumed to enter the sorting equation in which consumers attempt to maximize their benefit relative to cost (ibid., 1978). Courant (1978), for example, proposes a model in which discrimination, even by only some whites, can create an equilibrium in which blacks will be prevented indefinitely from exercising their housing preferences. More affluent blacks will thus remain in the black submarket, competing with lesser-income blacks for housing and raising the relative costs of housing for blacks overall. The predicted outcome of Courant's model runs counter to the argument that market forces will eventually enhance racial equality. Wilson (1979) shows that low-income blacks are the most severely affected by housing discrimination. Where this population is growing in size or where its poverty is deepening, competition created within the segregated housing market to which these renters are confined will drive up housing prices for those who can least afford it.

These factors are hypothesized to contribute to the increased vulnerability of minorities to homelessness. We have already seen that most minorities are renters rather than owners and that blacks have been prevented from becoming homeowners by discrimination in mortgage financing. If, in addition, minority renters are confined by racial discrimination to compete in limited submarkets and within those markets they pay higher housing costs, then, all else held constant, we would expect minorities to have higher rent-to-income ratios and consequently to be more at risk of homelessness than whites.

The growth of low- and moderate-income households is assumed by Struyk, Marshall, and Ozanne to be accompanied by a growing surplus of low-quality housing and by greater diversity in price per unit of housing services for this type of housing than for other units. Housing services are the space, quality, mechanical systems, and so on, that a housing unit provides and that, when divided by gross rent, yield a price per unit for these services. Growth in the percentage of all households that have low and moderate incomes can lead to competition for substandard units, allowing increased variability in the price per unit of service.[8]

On the basis of these considerations, Struyk et al. divided a random sample of SMSAs into four quadrants. These were based on whether the nonwhite population in 1970 and the growth rate between 1960 and 1970 of households with incomes under $10,000 in 1970 fell over or under the median for all SMSAs in that year. In 1970 the median nonwhite population was 12 percent, and the median growth of lower-income households was 4 percent. Metropolitan areas were thus classified as being high minority, rapid growth (of low- and moderate-income households); high minority, slow growth; low minority, rapid growth; and low minority, slow growth.

This format has been adapted to the present study and updated to the 1970 to 1980 decade. The 18 SMSAs are categorized according to whether the percentage of nonwhites exceeds that of the U.S. average of 16.6 percent in 1980 (high minority) and according to whether there was positive or negative growth in the percentage of households, regardless of household size, with incomes under $20,000 between 1970 to 1980. Table 3.3 lists the 1980 total population, the percentage that was white, the percentage of population with household incomes of less than $20,000 in constant 1980 dollars for 1980 and 1970, relative minority status (nonwhite), and growth of low- and moderate-income households as defined above.

RELATIVE STABILITY IN THE PERCENTAGE OF LOW- AND MODERATE-INCOME HOUSEHOLDS, 1970-1980

Table 3.4 then categorizes the SMSAs into four quadrants and compares the present category with that of Struyk, Marshall, and Ozanne. The 1970 categories are preserved with regard to nonwhite status, but not with regard to household income.[9] Among the high-minority areas, New York, Chicago, and Detroit had experienced a decline in the percentage of low- and moderate-income households in the 1960 to 1970 decade, but that trend was reversed in the 1970 to 1980 decade. On the other hand, a number of high-minority areas such as Houston, Dallas, and Washington, D.C., which had rapid growth in the percentage of low/moderate-income households in the 1960 to 1970 decade, were now experiencing negative growth in these households. Overall, 13 of the 18 areas had reversals in either direction, in the percentage of their lower-income households. In general, the rate of change in the percentage of households that had low to moderate incomes had slowed considerably. All except Houston are within five percentage

Table 3.3
SMSA Minority Population and Percent Change in Households with Incomes under $20,000

SMSA	1980 Pop.[b]	% White[b]	% HH Income <$20,000 1980[c]	% HH Income <$20,000 1970[d]	Relative Minority Population	Growth of Low/Mod. Households
Column No.	2	3	4	5	6	7
Baltimore	2,174,023	72.9	47.4	52.8	high	negative
Boston	2,763,357	91.5	52.3	49.9	low	positive
Chicago	7,103,624	73.8	46.5	46.1	high	positive
Dallas	2,974,805	80.1	51.3	54.0	high	negative
Denver	1,620,902	88.5	50.0	53.2	low	negative
Detroit	4,353,413	77.9	46.7	43.7	high	positive
Houston	2,905,353	72.6	46.1	54.9	high	negative
Los Angeles	7,477,503	68.7	50.8	54.0	high	negative
Miami	1,625,781	77.2	64.8	61.5	high	positive
Minneapolis	2,113,533	95.3	41.9	46.7	low	negative
New York	9,120,346	67.7	57.1	53.2	high	positive
Philadelphia	4,716,818	78.7	51.1	52.4	high	negative
Phoenix	1,509,052	87.5	56.2	57.4	low	negative
Portland	1,242,594	93.6	54.3	56.0	low	negative
St. Louis	2,356,460	81.8	49.8	54.2	high	negative
San Francisco	3,250,630	72.7	48.2	49.7	high	negative
Seattle	1,607,469	87.9	42.7	48.0	low	negative
Washington	3,060,922	68.1	37.3	42.3	high	negative

[a] In constant 1980 dollars as inflated by the CPI-XI, equivalent to 10,000 in 1970 dollars

[b] Source: U.S. Census, General Social and Economic Characteristics, 1980.

[c] Source: Table 244, U.S. Census, Detailed Population Characteristics by State, 1980

[d] Source: Table 206, U.S. Census, Detailed Population Characteristics by State, 1970

Column 2: Total 1980 population

Column 3: Percentage of population white

Column 4: Percent of households with incomes less than $20,000

Column 5: Equivalent households in 1970

Column 6: Minority status relative to U.S. average in 1980 of 16.5%

Column 7: Growth or decline in households with incomes less than $20,000

Table 3.4
Categories of SMSAs by Percent Change in Households with Incomes Under $20,000 and Relative Minority Status

SMSA	1980		1970		
	Percent Nonwhite[a]	% Change HH Income<$20,000[a]	Percent Nonwhite[a]	%Change HH Income <$20,000[a]	1970 Category[b]
1980 High Minority, Positive Growth in Low/Mod Income Households					
Column No.	2	3	4	5	6
Chicago	26	1	18	−1	high, slow
Detroit	22	3	19	−12	high, slow
Miami	23	3	15	19	high, rapid
New York	32	4	18	−2	high, slow
1980 Low Minority, Positive Growth in Low/Mod. Income Households					
Boston	9	2	5	−11	low, slow
1980 High Minority, Negative Growth in Low/Mod. Income Households					
Baltimore	27	−5	24	0	high, slow
Dallas	20	−3	17	11	high, rapid
Houston	27	−9	20	37	high, rapid
Los Angelos	31	−3	14	3	high, slow
Philadelphia	21	−1	18	−2	high, slow
St. Louis	18	−4	16	−3	high, slow
San Francisco	27	−5	17	5	high, rapid
Washington	32	−5	26	13	high, rapid
1980 Low Minority, Negative Growth in Low/Mod. Income Households					
Denver	11	−3	5	5	low, rapid
Minneapolis	5	−5	3	−3	low, slow
Phoenix	12	−1	5	35	low, rapid
Portland	6	−2	4	9	low, rapid
Seattle	12	−4	6	7	low, rapid

[a] Sources: 1980 U.S. Census, General Social and Economic Characteristics, and Detailed Population Characteristics by State, 1970 and 1980.

[b] Struyk, Marshall and Ozanne, 1978.

Column 2: Percentage of population nonwhite in 1980.

Column 3: Percentage change in low/moderate income population, 1970–1980.

Column 4: Percentage of population nonwhite, 1970.

Column 5: Percentage change in low/moderate income population, 1960–1970

Column 6: Category in 1970 according to Struyk et al., (1978).

points, positively or negatively, of the previous decade's percentage. Houston, which had a 37 percent increase in low/moderate-income households in the 1960 to 1970 decade, showed a decline of nine percentage points. I would argue that the relative stability of this measure over the 1970 to 1980 decade makes it less useful as a means to delineate variation in the present study than it was for Struyk, Marshall, and Ozanne.

INCREASE IN THE MINORITY POPULATION OF METROPOLITAN AREAS

The increases in minority populations are in most cases much more dramatic. All SMSAs experienced an increase, as might be expected from national trends. The increases ranged from 2 percentage points in Minneapolis and Portland to 17 percentage points in Los Angeles. A number of SMSAs doubled or nearly doubled their previous minority population.

The specification of relative minority status is problematic, because it does not include the proportion of the population of Spanish origin who are identified as white and yet may be subject to discrimination as minority. The proportion of the population that is of Spanish origin varies in this sample of SMSAs from less than 1 percent in Baltimore and St. Louis to nearly 36 percent in Miami, and of these, the proportion of Hispanics who are white varies from 40 percent in Philadelphia to 86 percent in Miami (U.S. Bureau of the Census, 1980). When whites of Spanish origin are included in Miami, for example, the minority population rises from 23 to 54 percent. While the additions of white Hispanics to the minority populations are not large enough to change the relative categories if the U.S. average minority population is calculated in the same way, it should be kept in mind that for cities such as Phoenix and Denver, which have 11 and 13 percent Hispanics respectively, "low" relative minority status relates specifically to the percentage of nonwhites only.

CHANGES IN THE CENTRAL CITY

It should also be noted that the figures for the SMSA as a whole may camouflage striking changes in the inner city. In just ten years, the minority population of central-city Detroit increased from 48 to 67 percent; that of Chicago, from 41 to 57 percent; New York, 36 to 48 percent; and Philadelphia, 36 to 45 percent (Kasarda, 1988). Bane and Jargowsky (1987) have identified these four cities as accounting for three-quarters of the increase in the urban "underclass." All four of these central cities experienced substantial restructuring of their populations, losing between 9 and 28 percent of total population between 1970 and 1984 (Dearborn, 1988). In all four cases, the exodus of non-Hispanic whites exceeded the total population lost, the difference being made up by increases in minority groups, whether by natural increase or by in-migration. While three of these four SMSAs are categorized, as one might expect, as having positive growth in low-to-moderate income households, the Philadelphia SMSA as a whole experienced a 1 percent decline in the percentage of such households.

Table 3.5 describes some of the characteristics of the central cities that may have a bearing on housing and homelessness. The percent of married couples in the population is an indication of potential two-earner families as well as of the level of homeownership, since married couples are far more likely to be owners than are singles or female heads. The percent of nonfamily households may be indicative of a young population and may be associated with a higher percentage of renters.

The poverty rates of the central city will in most cases exceed those for the SMSA as a whole. In general, we do not see as strong a relationship as might be expected between poverty and the unemployment rate. Miami, for example, with the highest level of persons below the poverty line in 1980, had an unemployment rate of 6.1 percent in 1980. The 1982 unemployment rate demonstrates the effect of the recession of that year on unemployment, and the 1987 rate is, in general, an indication of the recovery that has taken place. It can be seen that for Houston, Dallas, and St. Louis there has in fact been an increase in unemployment since the recession. For Houston, this is a 2.9 percentage point increase.

Detroit stands out almost across the board, but especially with regard to female headship, rate of poverty for these heads, and very high long-term and continuing unemployment. Given these circumstances, why does Detroit fail, according to the HUD estimates based on the records and opinions of local experts, to demonstrate the extremely high rates of homelessness seen in New York and Los Angeles? Similarly, why does Baltimore, which has nearly equivalent levels of female headship and poverty as Detroit, as well as high unemployment, have the lowest per capita rate of homelessness found among the 18 SMSAs in Table 3.1.

POPULATION CHANGE, EMPLOYMENT, AND CLIMATE

To explore this dilemma further, Table 3.6 presents characteristics ranging from population change in the 1970-84 period to the number

Table 3.5
Household Structure, Unemployment, and Poverty of Central Cities

City	Family Households		Nonfamily Households		Poverty		Unemployment		
	Married	Female Head	Total	One Per.	Persons	Female Heads	1980 Census	1982 BLS	1987
Column No.	2	3	4	5	6	7	8	9	10
Baltimore	40.5	21.5	33.3	28.0	22.9	39.8	10.8	11.4	8.7
Boston	33.6	16.2	47.7	36.8	20.2	37.1	6.1	9.1	2.5
Chicago	42.6	17.9	35.4	31.0	20.3	40.2	9.8	11.7	9.8
Dallas	47.7	12.4	37.1	30.7	14.2	29.0	3.4	6.2	6.9
Denver	42.7	10.4	44.3	36.0	13.7	30.2	5.0	7.0	5.6
Detroit	40.0	22.5	33.3	28.9	21.9	41.0	18.5	20.3	17.2
Houston	50.3	11.5	34.9	28.7	12.7	26.5	3.6	7.0	9.9
Los Angeles	44.3	12.8	38.9	31.5	16.4	29.4	6.8	10.4	5.9
Miami	44.9	15.6	35.2	29.8	24.5	37.0	6.1	12.3	5.0
Minneapolis	37.9	10.9	48.8	38.2	13.5	26.8	4.8	6.5	4.6
New York	43.1	16.6	37.0	32.7	20.0	41.0	7.7	9.6	4.9
Philadelphia	44.3	18.5	33.4	28.9	20.6	30.8	11.4	9.0	4.9
Phoenix	57.9	10.1	29.0	22.7	11.1	23.0	5.6	8.1	4.7
Portland	43.2	10.0	44.2	35.6	13.0	25.2	6.9	10.7	4.5
St. Louis	38.2	18.5	40.0	36.0	21.8	36.6	11.1	10.8	11.0
San Francisco	34.0	9.9	53.0	41.4	13.7	24.0	6.1	8.4	6.5
Seattle	40.3	9.1	48.0	38.1	11.2	20.7	5.9	10.9	5.2
Washington	29.5	19.3	47.2	39.5	18.6	28.5	6.8	10.6	5.7

Sources: 1983 City and County Data Book; Geographic Profile of Employment and Unemployment, 1987;

Column 2: Percentage of households headed by married couple.

Column 3: Percentage of households headed by a female.

Column 4: Percentage of all households that are nonfamily.

Column 5: Percentage single person households.

Column 6: Percentage of all persons below the poverty line.

Column 7: Percentage of female heads below the poverty line.

Column 8: Percentage unemployment – 1980 census.

Column 9: Percentage unemployment – 1982 Bureau of Labor Statistics.

Column 10: Percentage unemployed, 1987.

Table 3.6
Population Change, Fiscal Condition, Percent Manufacturing, Percent All Heads
Who Are Poor Females, Heat Degree Days, and Percent Families with No and 2
Earners in 18 Central Cities

City	Population Change[a]	Fiscal Condition[a]	Percent Manufacturing[b]	% Poor Female Head[b]	% Fam. with No Workers[b]	% Fam. with 2 Workers[b]	Heat Degree Days[b]
Column No.	2	3	4	5	6	7	8
Baltimore	−15.7	.7	18.8	8.7	18.9	46.5	4083
Boston	−11	−6.0	14.3	6.0	19.1	49.2	5593
Chicago	−11	−8.5	26.6	7.2	17.7	48.6	6455
Dallas	15.4	5.9	18.7	3.6	9.3	58.6	2301
Denver	−2.0	3.1	12.2	3.1	13.6	55.0	6014
Detroit	−27.9	−3.1	28.6	9.2	23.3	41.9	6563
Houston	38.4	3.7	16.9	3.0	7.3	58.6	1549
Los Angeles	10.0	3.1[c]	23.0	3.8	13.3	52.5	1204
Miami	na	na	18.6	5.8	16.7	49.5	199
Minneapolis	−17.4	14.4	17.7	2.9	14.8	56.8	8007
New York	−9.2	.1	17.4	6.8	20.5	43.4	4868
Philadelphia	−15.5	1.8	20.9	7.1	21.9	42.6	4947
Phoenix	46.7	4.4	18.0	2.3	10.5	56.4	1442
Portland	na	na	16.4	2.5	15.1	53.0	4691
St. Louis	−31.0	.8	21.6	6.8	19.1	46.2	4938
San Francisco	−.4	21.8	10.3	2.4	16.6	51.5	3161
Seattle	−8.0	12.3	16.4	1.9	14.9	53.0	4681
Washington	na	na	4.5	5.5	15.5	50.1	4083

Sources: [a] Dearborn, 1988.

[b] 1983 City and County Data Book, Table C.

[c] year=1981.

Column 2: Population change, 1970–1984.

Column 3: Fiscal condition balance or deficit, 1984.

Column 4: Percent of employment which is in manufacturing.

Column 5: Percent of all families headed by a poor female, excluding one-person households

Column 6: Percent families with no workers.

Column 7: Percent familes with two workers.

Column 8: Heating degree days per year.

of heating degree days. There was no consistent pattern in whether cities with a large or small percentage of minorities lost or gained substantial portions of their populations. Minneapolis, for example, with a minority population of only 5 percent, lost a greater percentage in the central city than did Boston or Philadelphia. The pattern of population loss and gain is consistent with the regional redistribution that took place in that decade.

The fiscal condition of the city, however, corresponds quite closely to the growth of low- and moderate-income households, as presented in Table 3.3. The SMSAs that experienced an increase in these lower-income households all had deficits in 1984, with the exception of New York, which had essentially a balanced budget.

The percentage of employment in manufacturing identifies the typical "steel cities" of the Northeast, which were hard hit by structural economic changes, but also shows that a large percentage of Los Angeles employment is in manufacturing. There is not a consistent relationship between the percentage of manufacturing and the growth of low- and moderate-income households, as might be expected if these industries were in decline everywhere during the 1970s.

Comparing metropolitan areas by the proportion of all family households headed by a poor female (the rate of female poverty multiplied by the percentage of female heads) gives a sense of the significance of female poverty within SMSAs.[10] There appears to be a fairly strong relationship between the fiscal condition of the city and the percentage of poor female heads, supportive of Wilson's hypothesis concerning the associaton between black male unemployment and rising female headship (1987).

Columns 6 and 7 give the percentage of families with no earners and those with two earners. The first is a measure of dependency, since these families may be retirees or recipients of welfare or unemployment insurance benefits. Detroit, Philadelphia, and New York have the highest percentage of families with no earners, as might be expected given the percentage in poverty. But Los Angeles, with the highest per capita rate of homelessness, has a surprisingly low percentage of nonearner families.

Two-earner families have a greater potential to escape poverty, to be above the median income, and to be homeowners. Most of the cities that have a high percentage of poor female heads, above 5 percent, also have fewer than 50 percent of families with two earners. The exception is Chicago. Minneapolis also stands out as a city that has a low percentage of married couples but a very high percentage of two earner families. The last column in Table 3.6 gives the number of heating degree days per city. Although Redman and Buss found no relationship between climate and homelessness, it may be that a climate threshold exists that influences the level of homelessness. It would be nearly impossible, for example, to survive in Minnesota out-of-doors in the winter. Minneapolis is therefore unlikely to attract nonnative homeless persons who do not wish to use a shelter in the winter, whereas Miami and other southern cities do report a winter influx of homeless persons. There is no obvious correspondence, however, in the levels of homelessness reported in Table 3.1 and this climate variable.

HOMEOWNERSHIP, RENTING, AND HOMELESSNESS

Thus far the search for a variable other than the growth of low- and moderate-income households with which to categorize metropolitan areas has not yielded a measure that corresponds closely to differing observed levels of homelessness among cities that have similar levels of minority population. Returning to the very low levels of home-ownership observed in New York and Los Angeles and noting that these areas also have among the highest rates as well as the highest actual numbers of homelessness, I hypothesize that there is a relationship between the percentage of the population who are renters and the per capita rate of homelessness. Gilderbloom and Appelbaum (1987:102) found that the cost of owning a home had a strong positive effect on rent, suggesting that "ownership acts as a lid on how much landlords can get for rents in a particular area." If we can assume that the extent of homeownership is inversely correlated with its price, then a higher percentage of renters will be predicted to be associated with a higher rate of homelessness within metropolitan areas.

In Table 3.7 I rank the 15 SMSAs for which HUD made official estimates according to the per capita rate of homelessness and to the percentage of households who are renters. I hypothesize that home-lessness is related not only to the availability and affordability of the rental stock, but also to the total percentage of households who are homeowners or, conversely, renters. Assuming that ownership is the tenure of choice, particularly as renting takes an increasing percentage of income, the level of rentership is proposed as a measure of vulnerability. Renters cannot control their housing costs over time in the same way that owners can. Metropolitan areas in which fewer than 60 percent of households are owners (the median for these 15 areas is 60.9 percent) may indicate keen competition in the rental market. Such competition may drive up rents, leading to a higher proportion of renters who are at risk of homelessness because of high rent-to-income ratios and doubling up or crowding.

Table 3.7
15 SMSAs Categorized by Relative Minority Status; Percent of Households Who Own Homes; Rate and Rank of Homelessness

SMSA	Percent Nonwhite[a]	Percent Homeowners[b]	Renter Rank	Homelessness[c] Rate /10,000	Rank
1980 High minority, Low percentage of Homeowners					
Chicago	26	57.4	7	28	4
Los Angeles	31	46.4	2	43	1
Miami	23	54.5	6	37	2
New York	32	41.5	1	33	3
San Francisco	27	52.5	4	25	5
Washington, DC	34	54.3	5	15	9
1980 Low Minority, Low Percentage of Homeowners					
Boston	9	51.9	3	13	10
1980 High Minority, High Percentage of Homeowners					
Baltimore	27	61.2	9	3	15
Detroit	22	71.2	15	17	8
Houston	27	60.9	8	22	6
Philadelphia	21	68.5	14	8	13
1980 Low Minority, High Percentage of Homeowners					
Minneapolis	5	64.7	12	5	14
Phoenix	12	68.7	13	8	12
Portland	6	61.2	9	12	11
Seattle	12	62.3	11	20	7

Sources: [a] U.S. Census General Social and Economic Characteristics, and Detailed Population Characteristics by State, 1980.

[b] 1983 Annual Housing Survey; 1980 Census (see Table 2).

[c] U.S. Dept. of Housing and Urban Development, 1984

Column 2: Percent of population that is nonwhite.

Column 3: Percent of households that are homeowners.

Column 4: Relative rank of percent of households that are renters.

Column 5: Homeless persons per 10,000 based on midpoint of HUD's most reliable range.

Column 6: Relative rank of per capita homelessness.

A Comparison with the Categorization by Growth in Percentage of Low- and Moderate-Income Households

Comparing Table 3.7 with Table 3.4, one sees that the two low-minority quadrants remain the same. Among the high-minority populations, however, the percentage of households who are renters correlates more closely with the estimated rate of homelessness than does the percentage growth in low- and moderate-income households. It is particularly interesting that the aging industrial cities of Baltimore, Detroit, and Philadelphia do not, on the basis of the HUD estimates, have rates of homelessness as high as might be expected. All of them have fairly high levels of homeownership, with Detroit and Philadelphia well above the national average. Thus it appears that the percentage of homeowners does a better job of predicting levels of homelessness than does the growth in the percentage of low- and moderate-income households. The rank order correlation coefficient for the relationship between homelessness and homeownership in Table 3.7 is .63, whereas the coefficient for Table 3.4 is .59.

Ultimately, the selection of the metropolitan areas to be analyzed was constrained by the late release of the 1985 data tapes by the Census Bureau. This eliminated Boston, the only metropolitan area with both a low rate of homeownership and a low rate of homelessness. New York was eliminated from consideration because of the unpredictable effect that rent control might have on the study. Chicago was selected from the first quadrant over Miami, both because it is less subject to seasonal influx of homeless persons and because more is known, for comparative purposes, about the homeless population of Chicago. Among the areas with a high rate of homeownership and a high percentage of minorities, only Baltimore and Houston had surveys completed in 1983. Houston is of particular interest because of its extremely high vacancy rate in 1983. It should be noted that these two areas also represent the high and low end of the per capita rate of homelessness in this category. Finally, Seattle was the only city among the low-minority high percentage of homeowners category for which data were currently available. Interestingly, it also had the highest rate of homelessness in its category.

In the final analysis, only about five percentage points separated the low homeownership SMSA (Chicago) from the others. As will be seen, however, when the central city is considered separately, Chicago has a significantly greater percentage of renters than do the other three cities.

NOTES

1. The number of heating degree days is the sum of the number of days during which heating is required times the number of degrees the temperature needs to be raised.

2. The annual winter influx of homeless persons to Miami is estimated to increase the homeless population from 8,000 to 10,000 (Jeffrey Schmalz, "Miami Police Want to Control Homeless by Arresting Them, *New York Times,* Nov. 9, 1988,p. 1).

3. W. Gove and M. Hughes, 1983. Early studies were often epidemiological, and while a relationship was established between housing and health conditions, it was generally not clear whether factors other than crowding might have been responsible for the observed relationships.

4. In 1950, there were 2,867,000 households with related and unrelated subfamilies, but this number had fallen to 1,280,000 by 1970 (U.S. Bureau of the Census, *Statistical Abstracts,* Table 60, 1982).

5. Shifting family structure could also play a role, if, for instance, cohabiting couples with children were counted as two families doubled up instead of as a single family unit.

6. U.S. Bureau of the Census, *Statistical Abstracts of the United States,* Table 728, 1988. Homeownership drops off somewhat after age 65, when 73 percent own their own homes.

7. The average age of first-time buyers has increased by nearly 3 years since 1976. First-time buyers were 28.1 years old in 1976 and 30.9 years old in 1986. The percentage of the population who were homeowners was 45.6 percent in 1920 and increased to 64.7 percent in 1976. It was 63.7 percent in 1987 (U.S. Bureau of the Census, 1988c). The median age of renters in family or nonfamily households increased from 32.9 in 1977 to 34.6 in 1987, while the median age of homeowners over this period fell from 54.7 to 48.6. Single-person households are excluded from these figures (U.S. Bureau of the Census, Current Population Reports, P-60 no. 163, *Poverty in the United States, 1987,* 1989, and P-60 no. 108, *Household Money Income in 1975 by Housing, Tenure and Residence for the U.S. Regions, Divisions and States,* 1977).

8. Struyk, Marshall, and Ozanne (1978:22). The assumption that growth of low-income households leads to an excess of low-quality housing would presume either that existing stock is allowed to deteriorate in response to the inelasticity of the low-income demand or that new low-quality units are constructed in response to the increased demand. Such predictions are unlikely to be borne out in every location, particularly where the income constraint of the very poor prevents any profit taking.

9. $10,000 in 1970, adjusted by the CPI-XI used in all inflators in this study, yields $19,947 in 1980, while the CPI adjusted income would be $21,221. Because statistics are generally provided for the percentage of households with incomes less than $20,000, it will be assumed that $19,947 rounds to this figure.

10. Note that this figure does not include poor single-person households headed by a female and is a percentage of all households, not just renter households, which have a much higher rate of female poverty.

11. Denver, Dallas, and St. Louis were not included among HUD's sample. The rates shown for these three SMSAs in Table 3.1 were calculated from HUD's average per capita estimate of 13 homeless per 10,000 for cities of over 1 million, rather than from official sources.

4

Data and Methodology

The data for this study come from the American (formerly annual) Housing Survey of Metropolitan Areas (AHS), which has been conducted by the Census Bureau in 60 metropolitan areas on a three-to-four year rotation since 1974. These 60 areas were nonrandomly selected as the largest and fastest growing in the country. The survey has been "undermined"[1] to the extent that it is a rich source of data on both housing units and occupants and provides the most thorough information available nationally about the quality of housing and yet has not been widely used. The time periods to be studied are 1976, 1979, and 1983 for Baltimore, Houston, and Seattle, and between 1975, 1979, and 1983 for Chicago.

HYPOTHESES TO BE TESTED

The following are the main hypotheses of the study:

1. There has been a decrease over time in the stock of low-cost rental housing.

2. There has been an increase over time in the demand by the low-income population for low-cost housing, as measured by "affordable rent" based on 30 percent of gross income in constant 1986 dollars.

3. These factors may be occurring simultaneously and at different rates, creating a housing squeeze that will vary across cities.

4. The extent of homelessness within individual metropolitan areas will be associated with the extent of the mismatch between incomes

of low-income renters and gross rent of the available rental housing stock.

5. The composition of the homeless population is affected by the changing demographics of the society as a whole, as well as by city-specific demographic changes. The changing characteristics of low-income vulnerable renters over time can be compared with what is known about the composition of the homeless population in individual cities. The analysis of these changes will lend strength to the argument that predictions about the size and makeup of the homeless population can be made from an analysis of the growth and change over time in the population of low-income renters who are experiencing housing problems.

6. Both the supply of and the demand for low-cost rental housing are affected by federal policies.

7. The effects of the aging of the population on the composition of those at risk of becoming homeless have been offset by disproportionate targeting of subsidized housing benefits to the elderly, as well as by the declining poverty of the elderly due to social security indexing and availability of private pensions. This should be reflected in a declining percentage of low-income renters at the older ages.

8. Increases in gross rent beyond the rate of inflation in the decade from 1974 to 1983 cannot be accounted for solely by an increase in the quality or size of housing consumed, particularly at the level of housing affordable to the poor.

RATIONALE FOR THE USE OF THE AHS

Ideally, a study of the structural determinants of homelessness would utilize good retrospective or prospective data on the homeless. Obviously, the unit of analysis in the AHS is neither the homeless nor households, but housing units. Why, then, use the AHS to estimate a population at risk of homelessness? In the absence of high-quality data on the homeless, I argue that utilizing the Annual Housing Survey represents a reasonable, and perhaps the best, means to assess structural change that may be associated with homelessness. The approach is limited by the lack of cross-sectional data on the homeless for a period comparable to that covered by the AHS. In previous research, Wright and Lam (1987) used AHS data for 12 SMSAs in two time periods to show that the stock of housing available to rent at 40 percent of poverty-level income was declining at the same time that the population at or below poverty was increasing. They concluded that this trend was contributing to the problem of homelessness.

The rationale for using the SMSA data of the AHS to determine the population at risk of homelessness in the current study is as follows:

1. The overriding consideration is the hypothesis that the precursors to homelessness are primarily housing and/or income shortfalls. The former can only be measured by examining the housing stock. The latter might be tested through Current Population Survey (CPS) or Survey of Income and Program Participation (SIPP) data. Like the AHS, the CPS and SIPP only collect household information on those currently housed. Individuals in longitudinal studies such as SIPP are lost to follow-up if they become homeless. Much of the household and income data available in the CPS is also available in the AHS, but the latter allows the comparison of characteristics of housing units as well as occupants.

The analysis of the housing stock and demand for low-cost rental housing can tell us a great deal about the potential for homelessness to occur and to increase.

2. Homelessness as a phenomenon appears to vary widely across regions. The hypothesized housing squeeze created by a drop in the availability of low-cost housing and/or an increase in demand for such housing driven by low incomes will vary by the economic forces at work in the SMSA, as well as by the response of the housing market to both the local economic conditions and to changes in federal housing policies that affect additions and losses to the local housing stock. Previous attempts to look at the availability of low-cost housing throughout the United States with national files of the AHS (Clay, 1987) did not address the extreme disparity of housing prices and the dislocation of availability of low-cost housing with the need for housing by the poor. Thus the abundance of low-cost rentals in the rural West, for example, will have little relevance for the majority of the poor who are concentrated in the central cities of our largest SMSAs. Using the AHS data, differences in the affordability and availability of housing within and between metropolitan regions can be compared.

3. The perceived rapid change in the composition of the homeless population over recent years indicates that a snapshot portrait of the homeless at a given point in time, through a survey of the actual population of shelter and street residents, may be quickly outdated. A major concern of the U.S. Conference of Mayors (1987) has been the unanticipated rapid increase in demand for emergency services for the homeless, particularly by families with children. The difficulty this has posed for planning, revenue generating, and long-term solutions is evident. Twenty-eight of the 29 cities comprising the Task Force on Hunger and Homelessness reported an increase, by an average of 31 percent, in the number of families requesting emergency services, between 1985 and

1987. If it is found that poor female and minority headed households are experiencing a disproportionate share of housing problems, we can anticipate that the percentage of total homeless who are women, children, and minorities will continue to increase. It is hoped that the selection of prototypical cities examined in this study will suggest policies that are generalizable to metropolitan areas with similar characteristics.

4. Surveys of the homeless that have addressed the issue have found that a majority of those who end up on the street or in shelters have been evicted, either by a landlord or by a primary tenant with whom they have been doubled up, or have left a condemned or substandard unit and do not have sufficient income to rent another. The rare study that has collected retrospective data on the most recent residence, rent, and income of those who have become homeless has not addressed changes in these circumstances over time (Sosin, Colson, and Grossman, 1988). Because homelessness remains a statistically rare event, interpretation of data is often hampered by small sample sizes and nonrandom selection. As an alternative, it is appropriate to use good-quality data to study the conditions that are direct precursors to homelessness.

5. Some housing experts, as well as former president Ronald Reagan, have claimed that rising rents and the decreasing availability of low-cost housing are the result of an increase in the quality and size of housing—that people are paying more because they are getting more (President's Commission on Housing, 1981:18-19). Aggregate national data have been used to show that the quality of housing stock has risen. Fewer units are without plumbing and heating and kitchen facilities. For example, K. Peroff, formerly with HUD, cites an 8 percent decrease between 1981 and 1983 in the percentage of very low income families and elderly paying more than 30 percent of income for rent who lived in severely inadequate housing.[2]

Other research indicates that the poor and minorities have not benefited proportionally from the overall improvement in the housing stock and that the quality of housing available to the very poor has actually declined. Female heads of households have been found to be particularly likely to occupy substandard dwellings (Birch, 1985). Milgram and Bury (1987) demonstrated that while on a national level the proportion of all housing that was substandard declined between 1975 and 1983, the absolute numbers of severely inadequate units remained quite constant. Furthermore, the number of crowded housing units has not diminished, despite the decline in average household size. When all housing problems are considered, the incidence of housing problems (cost-burden, crowding, and inadequacies) grew faster than the rate of new household formation.

Because a significant proportion of the homeless have become so through the demolition or condemnation of their home or because the unit was unlivable, the quality of housing occupied by the poor, as well as the price paid for substandard housing, should be of concern. Housing quality is examined in much greater depth in the AHS than in the decennial census (Irby, 1986), allowing a more thorough test of the relationship between rent, size, and quality of housing units and of the changes in these relationships over time than previously possible.

SURVEY DESIGN AND ERROR

The AHS is a stratified cluster sample of addresses drawn from the 1970 U.S. census. The same housing units are followed over time, with compensatory additions for new construction and housing lost to the stock through demolition, fire, and so forth. However, the sample was reduced considerably prior to the 1983 survey, so that the majority of units available for study in the first two surveys are no longer part of the sample in 1983.[3] This increases the size of sampling errors in the most recent year of the survey and limits the longitudinal uses of the survey.

Nonsampling errors in the AHS may be due to omissions from the sample (about 6 percent of all housing units). Omissions from the sample occur more frequently with new construction, with homes that were built without a permit in an area where a permit is required, and with households of illegal aliens. Thus nonsampling errors due to omissions would be more problematic in Houston, where there has been a great deal of recent residential construction, than in Chicago or Baltimore. A special Houston adjustment was done by the Census Bureau in the 1979 survey to obtain a better estimate of the growth that had occurred in non-permit-issuing areas outside the central city. Nonsampling errors may also be due to noninterviews (about 5 percent of housing units sampled) and to errors made by the interviewer, the respondent, or in processing.

The Census Bureau deals with noninterviews in the AHS by assuming that those who refused to be interviewed or could not be interviewed would have answered similarly to those who were interviewed. The weights of interviewed households are increased to compensate for those not interviewed. Because this assumption is probably not true, a nonsampling error of unknown magnitude is introduced.

Taken together, inaccuracy introduced by sampling and nonsampling errors will result in differences of at least plus or minus 2 percentage points between actual and reported percentages (Hadden and Leger, 1988:1-1). Considering the large samples on which the cross-tabulations reported here are generally based, errors larger than this are not anticipated. Sampling errors will vary across metropolitan areas, and, although it is not used in this study, a formula for calculating sampling errors specific to metropolises is provided in Hadden and Leger (1988).[4]

Weights

This study employs two weights per metropolitan area in calculating populations and in weighting regressions. The first, or population, weight, is the inverse of the probability of selection for each housing unit, adjusted for noninterviews, new construction (units built after April 1970), a special stratification adjustment, the previously mentioned adjustment for Houston in 1979, and a decennial census adjustment. These adjustments are discussed in the appendixes of the published volumes, as well as in Hadden and Leger (1988). The adjusted weights, when applied to the sample, are presumed to provide an accurate estimate of population size subject to the error discussed above.

The second weight is used in the regressions and is the population weight divided by the mean weight. It is a relative weight that produces a sample size equal to the real sample size. It allows the regressions to more accurately reflect the population that the sample represents, without inflating the significance tests for the model, as would be the case if the population weights alone were applied.[5] Separate weights are calculated for the central and suburban areas, as well as for the entire SMSA.

Income Data

The comprehensiveness of income data reported in the AHS has improved over time, but as a survey of housing rather than income, the AHS is not as thorough in collecting income data as the Current Population Survey (CPS). In 1974 and 1975, only total family income is reported. Beginning in 1976, information on the income of nonrelatives is gathered and can be added to family income to obtain total household income. Thereafter, total household income has been calculated. Thus income figures in 1975 will underrepresent total household income as is used in this study. Because median income declined in Chicago (the only SMSA included here that was surveyed first in 1975 rather than 1976), the effect of this will be to understate the size of the decline that occurred between 1975 and 1979. However, the income of nonrelatives was found to contribute relatively little to household income in the following year.

Total household income can also assume a negative value if there was a net reported loss in self-employment or farm income. These negative incomes are treated as missing values. There are relatively few renters who are self-employed.

Total money income reported in the AHS is estimated to be 94 percent of that gathered through the Current Population Survey. The CPS itself does not fully capture total household income.[6] The AHS income data as a percentage of an independent estimate of income, according to the Census Bureau, is 86 percent. If it is assumed that underreporting of income has been stable over the eight-year period of this study, the fact that the study focuses on changes in median income over time, rather than on absolute income, should mean that underreporting of income does not seriously affect the results. As will be discussed in the methodology section, the use of a conservative measure of low income (125 percent of the poverty line as calculated from the CPI-XI), should compensate to some extent for this underreporting.

For some variables, omissions that occur in the survey due to nonresponse are allocated values by the Census Bureau, while others are coded as "not answered." Missing data categories are not included in this analysis, and none of the variables included in the study is among those most frequently allocated by the Census Bureau.[7]

METHODOLOGY

The study examines units that were rented in any one of the three years of each survey. Vacant units are analyzed separately. It will be recalled that the selection of the metropolitan areas to be studied was related in part to the rate of home ownership or inversely to the rate of rentership within the area. As the U.S. Federal Housing Administration has noted, "The rate of home ownership is perhaps the single most meaningful statistic that can be used to sum up the overall housing conditions under which families live. Home ownership, as opposed to rental status, is generally associated with more amenities, both within the dwelling unit and its environment, more room, pride of ownership, and a certain degree of social status."[8]

Although a majority of Americans own their own homes, among those with incomes below the poverty line, 63 percent lived in rental housing in 1986 and nearly 25 percent of all renters were poor.[9] Since the majority of poor are renters, this study will only analyze rental housing. The rationale for including only renters in this study is that the homeless are much more likely to have been renters rather than owners. Studies that have looked at the proximate determinants of homelessness find them most often to be eviction from a rental unit due to nonpayment of rent, personal conflict, or condemnation, and eviction from a doubled-up arrangement in which the homeless individual or family was not the primary tenant. The latter arrangement often occurs in response to previous loss of a rental unit. Secondly, owners are unlikely to become homeless without first passing through a period of rental tenure. One study has reported that only 0.3 percent of its homeless sample had been the victims of a foreclosure on an owned home (Health and Welfare Council of Central Maryland, 1985).

The effect of looking only at renters will be to underestimate the percentage of those at risk who are elderly, since, as has been pointed out, the elderly are much more likely to be owners rather than renters. Elderly renters are predicted, however, to be less at risk in recent years because social security benefits have been indexed to the rate of inflation and because public housing has been increasingly targeted toward those over 62 years of age. While just 3 percent of the public housing units were occupied by the elderly in 1960, this percentage had grown to 27% in 1980 and has remained at this level. Two-thirds of the units under construction in 1986 were specified for elderly or disabled tenants (U.S. Bureau of the Census, 1988d, Table 1234), in spite of the small percentage of elderly who are competing in the rental market. This phenomenon may be tied to the greater social acceptability of providing public housing to the elderly rather than to female-headed households, minorities, or welfare recipients.

Use of the CPI-XI to Adjust for Inflation

Income and gross rents in this study were adjusted to constant 1986 dollars using the Consumer Price Index Experimental Measure I (re-based), known as the CPI-XI. This allows a direct comparison of rents and incomes over time, not possible with the information in the published volumes of the AHS. The incomes by household size of renters are compared with 125 percent of this poverty threshold. Dummy variables identify households that have low incomes.

While most studies continue to use the Bureau of Labor Statistic's Consumer Price Index (CPI) to adjust for inflation, the CPI-XI is an appropriate inflation index to use in a study of renters. The method used to construct the CPI was altered in 1983 when it was recognized that housing prices for homeowners have both a consumption component and an investment component, the latter of which was unduly inflating prices. The new methodology used in calculating the CPI is called the "rental equivalency method." It retains only the consumption aspect of homeownership, thus putting renting and owning on a more even par. The post-1983 CPI is not, therefore, a continuous series with regard to its method of calculation.

The CPI-XI was developed for research purposes to retroactively treat the period prior to 1983 consistently with the new CPI by eliminating the investment portion of homeownership from the onset, thus leading to a lower rate of inflation than that implied by the CPI.

The CPI-XI and the standard consumer price index were equivalent in 1967, but by 1981, the ratio of the CPI-XI to the CPI was only .91 (U.S Congress, 1988), and it has remained at this level since. The two indexes are compared in the appendixes. Use of the CPI-XI will provide a conservative estimate of the low-income population and should counteract some, if not all, of the effects of the omission of in-kind income and the failure to fully capture other income that occur in the AHS.[10] Although the CPI-XI is appropriate for a study of this kind, I do not advocate, as some have, the use of the CPI-XI to recalculate the percentage of persons in poverty. As I argued in the discussion of relative versus absolute measures of poverty, the fall in the poverty line relative to median income has already led to an underestimation of those who live in great relative deprivation.

STUDY DESIGN

Four metropolitan areas were chosen for analysis based on variation in the extent of homelessness and homeownership, in region, and in the percentage of minorities in the population.

Definitions

Demand for low-cost housing = the number of units needed in order to be affordable at 30 percent of income for households at or below 125% of the poverty line.

Supply of low-cost housing = distribution of the number of units available at rents that are affordable at 30 percent of gross income by the low-income population, generally those units renting for less than $350 per month.

Housing squeeze = mismatch between supply and demand.

Low Income Renter Households = those below 125 percent of the poverty line as adjusted for inflation by the CPI-XI.

Population at risk of homelessness = low-income renters who are highly cost-burdened—who pay more than 45 percent of income to rent. This population is referred to as vulnerable. Two more stringent definitions are employed:

The very vulnerable are low-income renters who pay in excess of 60 percent of income to rent.

The severely vulnerable are low-income renters who have less than $50 per person remaining in residual income after paying rent.

Lastly, the less vulnerable are those low-income renters who pay less than 45 percent of income to rent.

In the Annual Housing Survey, the unit of analysis is the housing unit or dwelling. Hotels and motels are counted as housing units only when the occupant considers the unit his or her usual residence or has no usual residence. Vacant rooms in such hotels and motels are counted as a housing unit only if more than 75 percent of the occupants are permanent residents. Ostensibly, then, occupants of welfare hotels who by the definition of homelessness discussed earlier would be considered homeless may be included as renters in this study.

Households with incomes below 125 percent of the poverty line meet the commonly used "lower living standard" that has been the qualifying level for a number of federal programs. This standard is used in this study rather than the poverty line to more realistically reflect the size of the population that is at risk of being unable to maintain independent housing. As noted earlier, the majority of poor family heads no longer live independently (Blank and Rosen, 1989). Furthermore, the residual incomes remaining after rent for those with incomes from 100 to 125 percent of the poverty line frequently leave these households in a state of de facto poverty because of excessive rent burden.

A 45 percent rent-to-income ratio is 15 percentage points above that of the official level for "affordability," a level that was adjusted upward in 1981 from 25 percent. Although a somewhat arbitrary cutoff, a 45 percent rent burden for a low-income household clearly represents a hardship and one that may force a dissavings. Over time, a household may be less and less able to sustain a rent burden of this magnitude. It may ultimately have utilities cut off or be evicted for nonpayment of rent. Any move, whether forced or voluntary, is likely to require some savings for utilities and damage deposits, a month's rent in advance, and costs of relocating. Renters who have been highly cost-burdened in the past may then be unable to secure new housing. Sosin, Colson, and Grossman (1988) found this to be the case among a substantial proportion of the Chicago homeless they surveyed.

The very vulnerable would seem to be paying rent burdens that are simply unsustainable for the long term, while the severely vulnerable do not have a realistic residual income remaining after rent. The demographic characteristics of the three categories of increasing vulnerability are comparatively analyzed for changes over time within and between groups. The two populations at greatest risk are also compared with low-income renters who pay less than 45 percent of income to rent. The less vulnerable are studied to determine what factors may protect these households, as low-income renters, from paying as high a percentage of income to rent as the groups at greater risk.

Among the factors that could protect the less at risk from an excessive rent burden is receiving a housing subsidy or occupying a public housing unit. Either benefit should ideally limit the rent-to-income ratio to 30 percent, although some subsidized renters may find it necessary to spend more than 30 percent of income. An analysis of the proportion of income spent on rent by all low-income unsubsidized renters removes the effect on the ratio of those renters whose rent burden is limited through a subsidy.

Affordability

In order to determine whether housing that is affordable to the low-income population exists within each metropolitan area, a comparison of what renters can afford and what they pay is necessary. Gross rents are adjusted to 1986 dollars and divided into seven categories, ranging from less than $50 per month to $350 per month or more. The available housing stock is compared with a hypothetical housing stock that would consume no more than 30 percent of income for low-income unsubsidized renters. This comparison demonstrates the extent of a mismatch between the housing supply by rent level and demand for housing based on affordability.

To be consistent with other studies, the maximum "affordable" rent-to-income ratio of 30 percent is employed here. However, I concur with Stone (1989) that for low-income households, such a percentage may not leave a sufficient residual income (what remains after rent is paid) to meet the nonhousing necessities of life.

Measuring Housing Deprivation

In addition to cost burden, two other measures of housing distress are employed in this study. They are the extent of overcrowding and whether or not the housing unit is of standard quality or has substandard characteristics that would qualify it as inadequate or severely inadequate according to guidelines suggested by HUD. The latter two factors are hypothesized to increase the risk of homelessness but are not considered to be definitional of the population at risk.

More than one person per room is the standard measure of over-crowding, a form of housing distress that has been shown to have substantial psychic and physical costs (Gove and Hughes, 1983). Nationally the proportion of renters who are overcrowded is more than double that of owners.[11]

A second measure, suggested by HUD, is the number of bedrooms needed by the household in order to have no more than two persons per bedroom, to separate children from adults, and to separate opposite-sexed children beyond the age of six (Milgram and Bury, 1987). Although there is undoubtedly greater tolerance for lack of privacy and over-crowded conditions within a family than among unrelated individuals, it can be argued that the second measure provides a more realistic assessment of the need for space, particularly for households that contain children. The most frequent category of number of persons per room in the AHS is one. Thus three persons in a three-room apartment, which presumably has one bedroom, would not be considered overcrowded by the person-per-room standard. Significant differences in the extent of overcrowding are found by these two measures.

Multivariate Analysis of Vulnerability

Having identified a population of vulnerable renters, it is desirable to determine how the household and dwelling unit characteristics of these vulnerable renters may have changed over time, holding all else constant. In each metropolitan area, multivariate analysis of the factors predicting vulnerability is shown for the three time periods. Because the dependent variable, vulnerability, can only have two values (1=low-income renters who pay more than 45 percent of income to rent; 0 = all others), a logit rather than a linear model is the more appropriate functional form. The significance tests of logit models are more adversely affected than those of ordinary least-squares regression by the inclusion of nonsignificant variables (Aldrich and Nelson, 1984). Accordingly, an additive model was first derived, and variables that were not significant in any of the three years were dropped from the equation. The final model includes a housing inadequacy binary variable, number of children, education, age, race, and sex of the head. To preserve sample sizes, the metropolitan area rather than central-city sample is used, and a dummy variable identifies central-city versus non-central-city residence. The coefficients are compared to determine if there are differences in the likelihood of being vulnerable renter households across time and in different metropolitan areas. The factors predictive of vunerability are related to the characteristics of the homeless as identified in metropolitan area or national surveys and are used to suggest how the population of homeless persons may be expected to change in the future.

MEASURING THE COST OF HOUSING RELATIVE TO ITS QUALITY

Variability across metropolitan areas in the contribution of rising rents and falling incomes to vulnerability is anticipated. Also expected to vary across areas is the extent to which increases in rent are associated with improvements in the quality of housing. Homelessness resulting from demolition or condemnation of the dwelling unit is presumed to be more likely to occur when the unit is physically dilapidated. I hypothesize that, in the aggregate, rising rents cannot be explained on the basis of improved quality.

There is surprisingly little recent literature on the quality of housing (Yezer, 1989). Because the Annual Housing Survey is the most thorough attempt to date to measure the quality of housing on a national basis,[12] it is desirable to use this information to the fullest extent possible. This analysis will provide a more accurate picture of housing quality than one that determines only whether or not a housing unit has adequate kitchen and plumbing facilities.

In using the quality guidelines suggested by HUD, I assume that the standards establish a threshold beyond which a housing unit is not of adequate quality. I would argue that minimum standards of housing quality should be uniform for all dwellings and that this assessment must be independent of the characteristics of the occupant.[13] The history of our public housing efforts indicates that lower standards of housing for the poor have not only been acceptable to the general public, but have even been promoted as equitable (Gilderbloom, Rosentraub, and Bullard, 1987). This two-tiered approach to housing standards has contributed to the failure of public housing in many parts of this country. Humane living environments, autonomy, and high standards in construction and maintenance have indirect redistributive social benefits that typically bypass the poor. We know that the great majority of substandard housing is rental property (Milgram, & Bury 1987). Renters in general, and low-income renters in particular, do not have control over the condition and quality of the unit they occupy in the same sense that owners have, and they would presumably not select a substandard unit over a comparably priced unit of standard quality. Analysis of housing quality is one mechanism for examining this indirect redistribution.

Hedonic Regressions of Gross Rent

Full use of the quality indicators in the AHS allows a more thorough test of the hypothesis that housing costs have gone up because quality has increased. This assumption, that people are paying more for housing because they are getting more in terms of better quality or more spacious housing, can be directly tested with the AHS data through hedonic equations, regressions in which the dependent variable is gross rent, or the log of gross rent, and the independent variables are attributes of the housing unit.

Housing can be viewed as a "bundle" of attributes that collectively determines the cost of a unit. Gross rent is assumed here to be a function of the size and quality of the unit, of the number of units in and the age of the building in which it is located, and of neighborhood characteristics. The number of units in the building was used by Gilderbloom and Appelbaum (1987) as a proxy for "professionalization," or the extent to which ownership of rental units is concentrated among a few professional landlords. As was discussed in the theory chapter, this was hypothesized to be positively related to gross rent. For lack of a better operationalized variable, the number of units is used in this study as well.[14]

Gross rent = f (size + quality + # units + neighborhood)

Hedonic equations are used to account for the variation in gross rent in different housing markets. They have been called "potentially the most useful single measure of housing now available" (Merrill, 1980:A-1). The coefficients in a hedonic regression represent a set of weights that reflect the contribution of each attribute of a dwelling or neighborhood to the total value.

The AHS makes it possible to substantiate whether substandard quality is associated with lower rent, as one would predict. Use of three surveys allows one to determine whether and how the aggregate effect of quality on rent has changed over time. Indicators of poor quality, such as inadequate plumbing or heat, would be expected to have negative weights, and to subtract from total value. Similarly, indicators of high quality, such as air conditioning, additional bathrooms, and new construction, would predictively be positively associated with gross rent, although the premium paid for such amenities may also change over time. To my knowledge, hedonic equations have not been previously employed to specifically measure the effect that quality indicators have on rent over time.[15]

The seven categories of inadequacy or severe inadequacy defined in the appendixes are compiled from 28 indicators of substandard quality. The quality variables are

lacking or sharing a complete kitchen,
inadequate electrical system,
structural deficiencies,
public hallway inadequacies,
inadequate sewer,
inadequate heat, and
inadequate plumbing.

They are combined with

number of rooms,
age of the structure,
number of bathrooms,
number of air conditioners,
number of living quarters in the building,
whether or not the unit is in the central city and
whether there are boarded-up buildings on the street, as observed
    by the interviewer.

The regressions of gross rent on these variables over each of the three years of the survey indicate whether changes in gross rent are associated with changes in the effect of these variables.

Specification of the Regression

The specification of the functional form to be used for the hedonic equation is problematic. Kain and Quigley (1975), in arguing that "there is no clear cut criteria for deciding which of the various estimates is 'best,'" present three—an additive, a semilogarithmic, and a logarithmic. The authors find that none of the three could be singled out as superior, either on the basis of theory or goodness of fit, and that each of them had drawbacks as well.

The assumption of the additive form, that the price of each attribute is not dependent on the other attributes, is clearly not true. The cost of a room, for example, is not independent of its size or the quality of its construction. The semilog and log forms do not share this problem, in that the coefficients are interdependent. The cost of a quality attribute is dependent on size of the unit.

But, Kain and Quigley argue, the same interdependencies make little sense when applied to attributes that have an effect on rent but are outside of the dwelling unit, such as the quality of the neighborhood. There is no rationale for the interaction that occurs in a semilog or logarithmic equation between the cost of living on a bad street, for example, and the size of a room.

All three forms are easily interpretable and have been used in a number of studies. The semilog coefficient is the percentage change in the dependent variable that would result from a one-unit change in an independent variable. The nonlinearity of the semilog more accurately represents the diminishing returns that exist in the price of housing attributes.[16] Housing costs may rise indefinitely, but do so along a curve whose slope grows less steep.

The coefficients of the logarithmic form are interpretable as the percentage change in the dependent variable resulting from a 1 percent change in an explanatory variable. The coefficients are constant elasticities, and the logarithmic form would be most useful in a study of the elasticities of housing prices.

The coefficients of the additive model have the advantage of being directly interpretable as dollars. Various bundles of housing services can be compared in terms of price. Additive models have the drawback of assuming that rent increases linearly, which it clearly does not.

Merrill (1980) also assessed the advantages and disadvantages of the semilog and linear forms in her study of the effect of housing allowances on housing consumption. Like Kain and Quigley, she found no clear choice could be made between the two on the basis of plausibility, error structure, or percentage of variance explained. The decision to retain both was based on the different uses to which each form was suited in her study. The semilog equation was useful in deriving a log linear demand function, while the linear form was used to create an index in dollars for cost comparisons.

The interpretation of the additive model is especially well suited to the purpose of this portion of the study, which is to show changes in the cost of quality attributes over time. The change in the dollar cost of a housing attribute such as a room, an air conditioner, or lack of a kitchen can be seen over time.

Furthermore, one of the advantages of the semilog form is not as applicable to the present study as to those of Merrill or of Kain and Quigley. Because the AHS data (prior to 1985) lack information on size in terms of square footage, number of rooms must serve as a proxy for size. The advantage that a semilog or logarithmic equation would provide in allocating price dependent on size is not of as much value when square footage is missing, whereas the disadvantage of the semilog in proportioning the cost of nonhousing attributes, such as being inside the central city, to the cost of other attributes might arguably be greater. With this justification, and because this is not a study of housing quality per se, only the additive models are reported. A sample comparison of semilog and additive models of one equation are provided in the appendixes.

The AHS data contain subjective indicators of the neighborhood and house that are not included in the regression models. An individual's dissatisfaction with neighborhood or house may reflect that it is unsuitable to the occupant's needs rather than that it is inherently inadequate. On the other hand, expressed satisfaction may be the result of the individual's need to ratify his choice of housing, however objectively substandard (Merrill, 1980). A study by King and Mieszkowski (1973) did find fairly good correspondence between objective and subjective assessments of neighborhood and house. It was decided for the purposes of the hedonic regression to limit the neighborhood quality indicator to the single observation on the part of the interviewer whether or not boarded-up units existed on the same street.

Characteristics of the Occupant

Theoretically, rent can also be influenced by factors that are not related to the housing unit or neighborhood, such as the race and sex of the occupant. The interpretability of the hedonic equation is based on the assumption that the coefficients are "reasonable approximations of current market cost structure" (Merrill, 1980:A-22). To the extent that a unified market exists, estimates of housing bundles will accurately reflect real costs. If the market is highly segmented, with blacks and whites, for example, competing in different submarkets, the interpretation of the hedonic is not straightforward. It may then represent only a hypothetical unified market rather than a real market.

Discrimination can lead to minorities paying more than whites do for a given bundle of housing services. Numerous studies have used hedonic regressions to determine whether blacks pay more for housing, all else held constant (Schafer, 1979; Hanushek and Quigley, 1979). King and Mieszkowski (1973) used race and other household characteristics as explanatory variables in a study of black-white price differentials in New Haven, Connecticut, and found that rents were higher in the ghetto. Kain and Quigley (1975) used demographic and life-cycle variables to compare housing expenditures for black and white renters and owners. They determined that in St. Louis blacks paid as much as a 6 percent discrimination markup above what whites would pay for identical housing bundles and that the ghetto price may have been as much as 12 percent more.

To completely test the data for racial price differentials is beyond the scope of this study. Furthermore, the geographical information on the AHS is limited to a distinction between the central and noncentral city, prohibiting an analysis of predominantly white, black, or boundary areas. However, because discrimination is hypothesized to play a role in the disproportionate representation of minorities among the homeless, racial submarkets will be estimated by running separate hedonics for white, black, and Hispanic renters in the Houston SMSA, an area that has the advantage of having two minority renter populations that are large enough to analyze and that has both groups of renters highly concentrated in the central city.

In all four metropolitan areas, it is important to know if and how the association between household characteristics and gross rent may have changed over time. All else held constant, do single female heads, those over 65, and families with children, as well as minorities, pay more for housing in the latter period than in the former?

A second hedonic model adds the characteristics of occupants to those of the unit. The following are included in the final model:

   income, a continuous variable;
   age (under 25 or over 65);
   education (high school dropout or beyond high school);
   female head;
   number of children; and
   black and Hispanic heads

Total household members was collinear ($r=.8$) with number of children and was dropped from the specification.

The constant term in the regression can be thought of as being both the effect of the omitted categories of all dummy variables (white, married, male high school graduates between the ages of 25 and 65, living in a standard quality unit not less than three nor more than nine years old, on a suburban street that does not contain boarded-up housing units), as well as the very basic exterior structure of a dwelling, on land but without rooms, amenities, or defects—the shell that will contain a bundle of housing attributes.

Based on the hedonic regressions, the price of several bundles of housing services is estimated for each city or metropolitan area in each of three time periods. In Houston it is also compared by race. Changes across time and metropolitan areas are analyzed for similarities and differences, and hypotheses about the observed differences are offered.

The analysis begins with Baltimore. As each metropolitan area is added, it is compared with those that have been analyzed before. The final analysis chapter examines housing quality in the four SMSAs. The concluding chapter summarizes the findings, offers some further hypotheses about the relationship between the extent of vulnerability and homelessness, and briefly considers the policy implications of the findings and directions for future research.

NOTES

1. Comment of Barbara Boyle Torrey, U.S. Bureau of the Census, seminar given at the University of Michigan, March 1988.

2. K. Peroff (1987). In the same time period, however, there was a 21 percent increase in the proportion paying more than 50 percent of income to rent. The reduction in substandard housing and rent burden for the elderly may reflect the targeting of subsidized new construction to the elderly in the 1980s.

3. The 1985 sample was redrawn from the 1980 census, and the questionnaire was considerably revised.

4. The error factor, which is specific to each area in a given year, is approximately 1.96 times the square root of the average weight. This is multiplied by the square root of the weighted number of observations. For percentages, the sampling error is the error factor multiplied by the square root of P(100P) divided by the base of the percent.(See Hadden and Leger, 1988:1-16—1-18).

5. This is the case with the SPSS-X statistical package that was used in this study.

6. Underreporting of income among the poor is a fairly substantial problem. Estimates of total income derived from the CPS, and to a greater extent the AHS, are less than from such independent sources as the Bureau of Economic Analysis. In the CPS, underreporting was greatest for interest income (about 45 percent) and least for wage and salary income (about 1 percent). For AFDC, the CPS reports about 76 percent of the amount collected by the independent source. It would appear that for the poor, sources of income that are underreported might include money received from the underground economy, while for the more affluent, there may be many more sources of income, such as dividends, the imputed rental value of owned property, and gifts or trusts, which might be overlooked or deliberately concealed. For a discussion of underreporting and a comparison of CPS with independent estimates, see U.S. Bureau of the Census, 1989.

7. For a list of the most frequently allocated variables, see Hadden and Leger (1988).

8. U.S. Federal Housing Administration, FHA Homes, 1967: Data for States and Selected Areas on Characteristics of FHA Operations Under Section 203, Washington, D.C. FHA, Division of Research and Statistics, 1976, as cited in Kain and Quigley (1975:118).

9. U. S. Bureau of the Census, 1988b. Calculations from p. 81. Nineteen percent of poor renters were in public housing, and less than 11 percent of poor renters occupied subsidized housing.

10. This effect is similar to the offsetting of in-kind income that has occurred because of the fall of the poverty line relative to median income. A study done by the U.S. Bureau of the Census shows that the effect of raising the poverty line by 25 percent would be offset by the inclusion of in-kind income. Cited in Wilson (1987).

11. Of renters, 6.7 were overcrowded in 1977 (Meyers and Baillargeon, 1985) vs. 2.7 for all households in 1983 (Irby, 1986).

12. Quality has been more thoroughly measured within a few metropolitan areas as part of the National Bureau of Economic Research urban studies program in the 1970s. (See Kain and Quigley, 1975) and more recently in studies evaluating the housing allowance program (Merrill, 1980.)

13. Some would argue that homelessness has resulted in part from unrealistically high housing standards, zoning ordinances, and building codes that have prevented private investors from building low-quality, inexpensive housing for the poor, as well as having prevented the poor themselves from erecting shanties as they might in the Third World. In some housing markets, regressive concessions have been made by local governments to investors, allowing a higher density of housing in exchange for dedicating a percentage of new development to low-income households.

14. This is not a satisfactory indicator of private concentration of ownership, since low-cost public housing units tend also to be concentrated in large buildings.

15. Merrill's (1980) study of the Housing Allowance program used hedonic equations to examine whether subsidies allowed or encouraged consumers to obtain better-quality housing.

16. Kain and Quigley (1975:193). Another reason the semilog is chosen, according to the authors, is to escape the potential problem of heteroscedasticity, or increasing variance of the dependent variable along some dimension, such as size. The authors conclude that although "heteroscedasticity may be a minor problem in our samples . . . we do not find it a compelling basis for preferring one equation form over another" (ibid., 194).

5

Baltimore

SUMMARY

If we want to examine the factors that create a climate for home-lessness, it would be instructive to look at an area that has a high percentage of poor minority residents (the population that is dis-proportionately represented among the homeless) but an apparently low per capita rate of homelessness. Baltimore is, according to a number of accounts, such an area. (U.S. Department of Housing and Urban Development, 1984; Cowan, Breakey, and Fischer, 1986; Health and Welfare Council of Central Maryland, 1986). While the rate of homelessness implied by the HUD study was 28 per 10,000 for Chicago, it was 3 per 10,000 for Baltimore, the lowest found among the 18 metropolitan areas that were considered for this study. Bal-timore is also distinguished by an unusually high percentage of females among its homeless compared with national estimates (Cowan, Breakey, and Fischer, 1987; Cohen and Burt, 1989).

The results of the analysis of renters show that, to the extent that Baltimore's homeless problem is less severe than that of the other metropolitan areas studied, it is attributable to a more moderate increase in gross rents over the period of the study, as well as to stability in both the size of the large low-income renter population and the large stock of low-quality housing available to it. About one in five rental housing units were inadequate or severely inadequate in Bal-timore in both 1976 and 1983. Substandard housing, historically home to the poor, has not disappeared in Baltimore, and as a consequence, the poor of Baltimore have not been forced into homelessness to the extent that they have in other cities.

INTRODUCTION

Baltimore was identified as having in 1983 a per capita rate of homelessness that was much less than in other areas that share Baltimore's high spatial concentration of poor minorities. Among the 15 largest metropolitan areas in which HUD conducted a telephone survey of local experts in 1983, Baltimore had the lowest per capita rate of homelessness. While the figures on homelessness in Baltimore are not insignificant and do not diminish the seriousness of the problem of providing for the homeless of Baltimore, they do lead to the speculation that, based on the hypothesized relationship between a housing squeeze and homelessness, Baltimore should demonstrate moderate changes in the rental housing market and in incomes of the renter population over the eight-year period of analysis. This chapter will begin with a discussion of some of the structural and demographic changes that have occurred in Baltimore, followed by estimates of homelessness for the city and metropolitan area and concluding with the analysis of incomes and rents in Baltimore.

THE BALTIMORE ENVIRONMENT

Baltimore has been called a divided city (Shlay, 1987a). A visitor expecting to see an aging industrial area past its prime may be surprised to find the downtown and harbor area revitalized and glittering, but may be unaware that decaying neighborhoods remain not far away. Prosperity in the central city is not widespread. The development of the broader metropolitan area has been described as a "double doughnut of concentric rings" (Szanton, 1986). The prospering business, commercial, and entertainment center downtown and the predominantly white gentrified neighborhoods surrounding it are ringed by largely black working-class and ghetto neighborhoods, which in turn are circumscribed by the more affluent and largely white suburban ring. Such a configuration, not unlike that of Detroit, appears to have been facilitated by discrimination in residential mortgage-granting. Shlay (1987a) finds substantial evidence that this pattern is maintained by "credit flows so unequal that they suggest that three lending submarkets exist within the Baltimore SMSA." Although the Baltimore SMSA as a whole has a high percentage of homeowners, residents of predominantly black areas in Baltimore have had less access to home mortgages, all else held constant.

The Baltimore SMSA consists of the city of Baltimore and the five counties surrounding it. The city has lost nearly a fifth of its population over the last 25 years, while the surrounding area has increased in population but at a rate below the national average. Baltimore lost a greater proportion of its white population between 1960 and 1980 than did nearby major cities, including Philadelphia and Washington, D.C. The massive outmigration of 44 percent of the white population in this time period left behind a predominantly black population that had a poverty rate that was four times that of whites (Szanton, 1986). The city of Baltimore now contains 34 percent of the population of the SMSA, but by 1990 will have 71 percent of its single mothers, 63 percent of its teen pregnancies, and 68 percent of all families in poverty (United Way of Central Maryland, 1987).

Although it has the major share of metropolitan social service needs within its boundaries, the city is unable to access the tax base of the larger, more affluent suburbs. Baltimore City was formerly highly dependent on federal aid, which made up 39 percent of the city's capital and operating budget in 1980 but which fell to 12.5 percent in 1985 and has continued to fall (Szanton, 1986). To compensate, the city has raised taxes and now has the second highest per capita property tax yield in the region from the lowest per capita tax base. Its assessed valuations are about double those in the county of Baltimore or in Washington, D.C. Such high taxes are a virtual Catch-22, in that they are a deterrent to the investment that might reestablish a viable tax base in the city (Szanton, 1986:6). Neither the central city nor the suburban ring of Baltimore is as highly segregated as Chicago,[1] but because the poor, renters, and minorities are all still heavily concentrated in the central city, most of the discussion and analysis of Baltimore will concern the central city.

STRUCTURAL ECONOMIC CHANGES

Like Chicago, Baltimore is one of the large older cities that was hard hit by structural changes in the national economy. Total employment in the central city fell from 367,000 in 1970 to 323,000 in 1985. Blue-collar and manufacturing jobs as a percentage of total employment were half in 1985 what they had been in 1953. The jobs gained in white-collar service industries and information processing did not compensate for jobs lost in the traditional industrial sector.[2]

The change in the structure of employment demanded a more highly educated labor force, but this need was not well served by the public educational system in Baltimore. A task force investigating the future of Baltimore recently identified "better schools" and a "sounder economy" as the two most critical needs for the city. The present school system is believed by some to be unsalvageable (Szanton, 1986). Although it had the highest local tax rate and the highest proportion of disadvantaged students, Baltimore City ranked near the bottom of the state's school districts in expenditures per pupil. Baltimore ranked 14th of the 15 largest cities nationally in the percentage of 20-to-24 year olds who were high-school graduates. Those who can afford to send their children to private schools. Although enrollment in both public and private schools dropped with the decline in the school-aged population, public enrollments fell more than twice as fast as private (Szanton, 1986).

The increasing concentration of poorly educated minorities in the central city contributed to a growing mismatch between job prospects and the labor force. Kasarda (1988) estimates that jobs that required less than a high-school education fell by 75,000 between 1970 and 1985 in Baltimore (whereas they increased by 219,000 in Houston). Educational levels increased moderately between 1976 and 1983. As a consequence, in 1980 only 52 percent of jobs in the city of Baltimore were held by residents of the city, a decline from 75 percent in 1960 (Szanton, 1986). Unemployment among blacks was four times that among whites.[3] In Kasarda's view Baltimore is one of the distressed cities that are "characterized by excess of structurally displaced labor as their blue-collar job bases wither. Large concentrations of the unemployed who are increasingly dependent on welfare or the underground economy, or both, pose negative externalities (crime, alcoholism, drug abuse, loitering, vandalism) that further dissuade new businesses from locating nearby. Eventually, neighborhood deterioration and residential abandonment will probably thin out the population."[4] (Note that these externalities are the social costs of negative redistribution described by Harvey). Kasarda speculates that racial discrimination, lack of low-income housing outside the central city, and "anchoring" of households to subsidized housing within the central city contribute to the continuing concentration of minorities in the central city as employment opportunities there continue to erode.

He also notes with Harvey the dependence of low-income minorities on public transportation, which is geared toward bringing suburbanites into the central city to work rather than to transport central city residents to suburban jobs. Kasarda refers to those who are "caught in a downward socioeconomic spiral that is unprecedented for urban dwellers in this country" as the "new immobiles." One might speculate that some of these have joined the "new homeless."

In Wilson's (1987) theory of the "truly disadvantaged," the lack of employment opportunities for black males prevents them from marrying and ultimately leads to the breakdown of the two-parent black family. In 1982 Baltimore had the highest rate of any U.S. city in the percentage of all black births (76 percent) to unmarried women (Szanton, 1986). It also had the second highest rate of teen pregnancy in the country (Melvin interview). These statistics are associated with very high rates of poverty for women, factors that undoubtedly contribute to the high percentage of females among the homeless of Baltimore.

Thirty-one percent of central city Baltimore renter households were below the poverty line, as compared with 23 percent of all central-city households. Given the bleak picture of Baltimore's structural transformation and its effect on blacks, who make up 62 percent of central city renters, what might explain the relatively low extent of homelessness, if we accept the reasonableness of the estimates previously discussed? [5]

HOMELESSNESS IN BALTIMORE

The range of homeless persons in the Baltimore metropolitan area was estimated by HUD in 1983 to be between 450 and 750 on any given night, with a "most reliable range" of between 630 and 750 persons.[6] As part of its report on the extent of homelessness in America, HUD also reported figures taken from other published sources on the number of homeless in individual metropolitan areas. Of the 15 large metropolitan areas for which HUD provided both published figures and surveys of local experts, the Baltimore estimates from local sources were the most discrepant with those from published sources. The *Baltimore Sun* and the *Atlantic* magazine, for example, had cited figures of between 8,000 and 15,000 homeless for Baltimore in 1982 and 1983.[7] In all of the 14 other metropolitan areas included in the report, there was at least an overlap, and frequently a good correspondence, between the figures from other published sources and those reported by local experts, while for Baltimore, the published figures were ten times the size of the local estimates.[8]

The per capita rate of homelessness was intended to be an estimate of the homeless population of the entire metropolitan area.[9] In Baltimore in 1983, 96 percent of shelters in the SMSA were located within the city of Baltimore (U.S. Department of Housing and Urban Development, 1984). If nearly all the homeless in the Baltimore SMSA were concentrated in the city, where services were located, the projection of the per capita figure over the entire metropolitan area would underrepresent the extent of homelessness in the city. The use of the RMA population rather than that of the central city inflates the denominator in the ratio of homeless to total population and hence gives a per capita estimate of homelessness that is too small. Since the homeless tend to be found in urban settings, this problem exists in other metropolitan areas as well, but perhaps to a lesser extent than in Baltimore.[10]

Given the extreme range of the Baltimore estimates, it is fortunate that more recent and more sophisticated studies have been done in

Baltimore. These surveys have largely substantiated the HUD estimate, if one takes into account growth in the homeless population between 1983 and 1986 and assumes that the homeless are indeed concentrated in the city.[11]

The most reliable of these local estimates utilized a "capture-recapture" methodology, matching individuals at four points in time through a combination of name, social security number, birth date, sex, and race (Cowan, Breakey, and Fischer, 1987). Four pairs of dates were selected to examine the seasonal use of shelters in Baltimore. Each pair constituted a capture-recapture count, with individuals matched by computer across counts. This allowed researchers to determine not only the shelter population on any given night, but also the total number of different people who had used shelters over the ten-month period.

Cowan, Breakey, and Fischer found that shelter use did not vary much across seasons, with a range of 874 to 1,022 persons per night. Overall, 2,102 different people, of whom 66 percent were male and 34 percent were female, used the shelters during this period.

The shelter count was supplemented with a street count taken in December 1986. Taking into consideration those found on the street who said they had utilized shelters, the authors' point estimate of homelessness was quite compatible with that made by the Health and Welfare Council of Central Maryland in 1986. The council had found that on any given night, approximately 1,160 persons, 64 percent male and 36 percent female, were homeless (Institute of Medicine, 1988). It is important to note that the estimates of female homeless in Baltimore are much higher than the 19 percent found nationally by Cohen and Burt (1989). I speculate that this is indicative of the high percentage of female-headed vulnerable renter households in Baltimore.

THE HOUSING AND INCOMES OF BALTIMORE RENTERS

In the following section, the analysis of the Annual Housing Survey data for 1976, 1979, and 1983 in Baltimore will be presented. To have a base with which to compare the vulnerable population, demographic characteristics on the entire renter population are disaggregated by central city versus non–central city. The quality of housing in both areas is discussed. I then focus more specifically on the central-city low-income renter who receives no housing subsidies and finally on the three categories of the vulnerable population. All incomes and rents are adjusted to 1986 constant dollars using the CPI-XI. "Low income" refers to those at or below 125 percent of the poverty line as define by the CPI-XI, whereas the "poor" are those below the poverty line. Income cutoffs for these two groups are given in the appendixes, as are full definitions for all abbreviations. All figures in the tables, except numbers of households, incomes, and rents, are percentages.

Changes in the Demographic Characteristics of Renters

The demographic characteristics of all renters within and outside of the central city are given in Table 5.1. Baltimore demonstrated, over the eight-year period, clear trends consistent with the transformations in the Baltimore population discussed earlier.[12] This table indicates the increasing propensity of central-city renter households to be headed by a black and/or a female, relative to households outside the central city. It also shows that while the proportion of renters who are married declined in both inner and outer metro areas, married households still tended to live outside the city and single heads within the central city.

As will become more apparent when Baltimore is compared with Chicago, Houston, and Seattle, an important finding to note is the relative stability in the percentage of renter households who fall below 125 percent of the poverty line. While this figure is very high, and in fact is the highest among the four cities included in the study, it changed very little between 1976 and 1983 and far less than in the other areas.[13]

Renter heads of households were older in 1983 than in 1976, reflective of both the aging population and the inability of renters to move into ownership in a period of rapidly inflating housing prices, stagnating wages, and discriminatory lending practices. The mean age of Baltimore central-city renters in 1983 was the highest among the four cities and two full years higher than the mean age of Chicago renters. It is also interesting to note the increasing percentage of renter heads both within and outside of the central city who are over the age of 65. Given that the great majority of the elderly are homeowners and that Baltimore is an area of high homeownership, these percentages are surprisingly high.

Baltimore has more public housing as a percent of total housing units than does Chicago, 2.75 percent versus 1.8 percent (Massey and Denton, 1988). If recently constructed units have been dedicated to the elderly in Baltimore as they have nationally, the increasing percentage of renters over the age of 65 may be attributable in part to the movement of the aging from owned homes into subsidized rental housing.

Income and Rent

The median renter household in the central city of Baltimore had considerably less income in 1983 than in 1976. Income measured in

Table 5.1
Demographic Characteristics of Baltimore Renters, 1976, 1979, 1983

Variables	Outside Central City			Inside Central City		
	1976	1979	1983	1976	1979	1983
Total Renter Households						
Number	129,300	137,400	154,100	146,700	149,400	143,100
Percent <125% Poverty	14.0	12.9	14.0	38.8	35.5	40.0
Race (in percents)						
White	87.4	86.0	84.1	41.9	39.9	37.4
Black	11.7	12.9	14.4	56.4	59.0	61.7
Marital Status (in percents)						
Married	55.6	47.2	43.6	33.5	28.6	27.3
Widowed	10.6	11.3	11.3	16.6	16.9	16.0
Divorced	9.5	13.6	14.9	10.4	13.1	11.9
Separated	6.6	7.0	7.0	16.4	17.1	17.0
Never Married	17.7	20.8	23.4	23.1	24.2	27.8
Sex and Age of Head (in percents)						
Male	71.3	64.1	61.3	48.6	48.2	44.4
Female	28.7	35.9	38.7	51.4	51.8	55.5
17–24	21.1	17.3	11.1	10.8	10.9	8.2
25–39	42.7	44.3	48.0	34.8	32.0	36.0
40–64	24.1	25.6	26.6	37.6	38.8	36.7
65+	12.1	12.8	14.3	16.8	18.3	19.0
Mean Age	39.0	40.0	41.4	44.7	45.6	46.0
Education and Employment of Head (in percents)						
Dropout	28.9	25.8	23.7	51.6	49.7	48.5
High Ed.	38.7	38.0	40.9	19.8	18.5	20.9
Employed	79.1	75.7	76.5	55.1	54.1	55.4
Household size and Composition						
Mean H.H. Member	2.5	2.4	2.4	2.6	2.5	2.4
% Large Family	3.0	2.1	2.6	7.9	6.7	6.9
% Subfamily	1.2	1.0	.7	1.4	1.2	3.2
% With Children	40.2	39.7	40.6	41.6	40.1	42.6
Mean No. Children	.72	.70	.70	.95	.90	.92
Gross Rent, Income and Poverty in 1986 Dollars						
Med. Gross Rent	$380	$377	$407	$291	$290	$308
Mean Income	$25,768	$23,586	$24,943	$16,740	$16,466	$14,836
Med. Income	$22,289	$22,434	$22,271	$13,653	$13,155	$11,494
Med. Per Capita	$10,054	$10,861	$10,350	$5,837	$6,205	$5,610
Percent Poor	5.7	7.4	8.8	24.9	26.7	31.0
Med. Pov. Gap	$1,367	$2,095	$1,815	$2,403	$2,511	$2,995
% Poor w. Pov. Gap >$5000	4.5	11.2	12.2	18.1	18.9	23.1
Med. Residual	$658	$756	$676	$340	$365	$311

1983 probably reflected to some extent the recession year of 1982. The decline in median income of central-city renter households to only $11,500 in 1983 is indicative of the concentration of renters at very low-levels of income. In 1976, 64 percent of low income renters were below the poverty line, but by 1983, 78 percent were poor.

The mean poverty gap, or that amount of income that would be required to bring a poor household up to the poverty line, rose by $500 in the central city. The percentage of the poor with a deficit of more than $5,000 in central-city Baltimore, those who might be considered profoundly poor, increased from 18 percent of poor renters in 1976 to 23 percent in 1983.

Rents in Baltimore had increased beyond the rate of inflation between 1976 and 1983. Outside the central city, median rents rose from $380 to $407 over this period, while inside the central city median rents were substantially less, but rose from $291 to $308. The central-city low-income renter was most severely disadvantaged by the growing mismatch between income and the cost of available housing. I refer to a mismatch between the actual cost to renters of the units they occupy and what would be affordable to these renters if they were able to spend no more than 30 percent of income on rent, as federal guidelines suggest. Keep in mind that 30 percent of the income for a low-income household often exceeds what that household can realistically afford to spend on rent and still retain adequate income for food, clothing, medical care, transportation, and any other nonhousing necessities. The mismatch in income of renters relative to the cost of rental housing in Baltimore is shown in Figure 5.1 for the low-income population.[14] The solid bars are the rent distributions of the housing currently occupied by this population, while the hatched bars might be thought of as the rent distribution of the hypothetical housing stock that would match the (30 percent of) incomes of these renters. This figure does not tell us whether incomes or rents drive the mismatch. It does illustrate, however, that to assure that households whose income is below 125 percent of the poverty line (about $12,800 for a family of four in 1986 dollars adjusted by the CPI-XI) need not exceed a 30 percent rent-to-income ratio would require a doubling in the number of units with rents below $200 per month. The percentage of central-city residents who needed such units increased from 30 percent to 35 percent between 1976 and 1983, while those occupying such units declined from 20 to 19 percent (not shown).

Housing this inexpensive cannot be profitably built or maintained by the private sector.[15] With the 1986 tax reforms working to the disadvantage of private investment in such housing[17] and with the expiration of many commitments for subsidized housing (Clay, 1987), this gap between affordability and availability is all too likely to

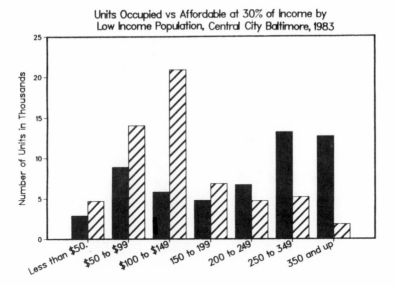

Figure 5.1

widen. Since larger units are generally more expensive, the shortfall becomes more pronounced for large units at lower rents.

Rent-to-Income Ratios

Half of all renters nationally now exceed the maximum "affordable" percentage of income that should be spent on rent, according to government standards.[17] This ceiling was revised upward from 25 percent for occupants of public and subsidized housing in 1981 (Bratt, 1986). When Section 8 subsidized rental housing was first available, the rent-to-income ratio was a sliding scale that varied from 15 to 25 percent (Struyk, Mayer, and Tuccillo, 1983). It should be kept in mind that as recently as 1968, the median proportion of income going toward housing costs for all Americans was only 15 percent.[18] The evidence suggests that even among the poor, the percentage of income spent on rent in recent decades was generally below 30 percent.[19] But what of the poor and nearly poor renters today? Figure 5.2 illustrates that more than 80 percent of low-income Baltimore renters who receive no housing subsidies paid more than 30 percent of income to rent, even in 1976. By 1983, the majority of low-income unsubsidized renters spent more than half their income on rent. Among Baltimore central-city renters, the percentage of low-income households paying

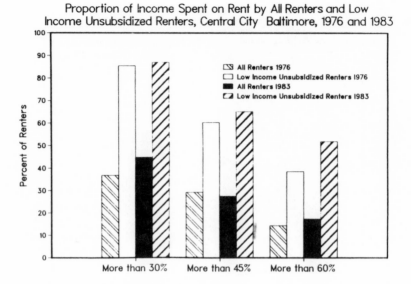

Proportion of Income Spent on Rent by All Renters and Low
Income Unsubsidized Renters, Central City Baltimore, 1976 and 1983

Figure 5.2

more than 60 percent of income to rent increased from 40 percent in
1976 to 52 percent in 1983.

Translating these high rent-to-income ratios into residual incomes,
or what remains after rent, Figure 5.3 plots monthly income, gross
rent, and residual income for those unsubsidized renter households
below 125 percent of poverty in the Baltimore central city over three
survey periods. In constant 1986 dollars, the median monthly income
of these Baltimore households fell from $457 to $452 and median gross
rent increased from $260 to $303.

Note that rents for these renters increased more sharply than for
renters overall. Whereas median gross rent of all renters had increased
a moderate 6 percent (Table 5.1), the median rent of the low-income
unsubsidized population had increased by nearly 17 percent. Decom-
position of the change in the rent-to-income ratio for renters in the
central city as a whole showed that the change was about equally
attributable to an increase in rent and to a decrease in income. For
unsubsidized low-income renter households in Baltimore, the rise of
the median rent-to-income ratio from 53 to 63 percent over the 1976
to 1983 period was nearly exclusively due to an increase in gross rent.

The significance of a very high rent-to-income ratio may be made
more clear by examining its inpact on residual income, or what remains after rent is paid, as shown in Figure 5.3. Median residual
income for these households declined from $212 to $149 between 1976

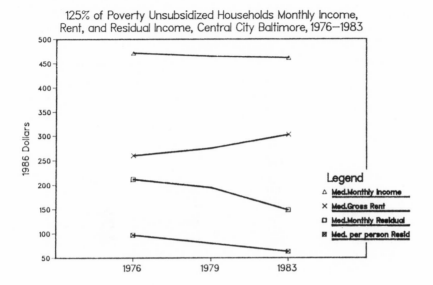

125% of Poverty Unsubsidized Households Monthly Income, Rent, and Residual Income, Central City Baltimore, 1976–1983

Figure 5.3

and 1983. To adjust for family size, the per person monthly residual is shown; it declined from $97 to just $63 per month. Because the AHS income data does not include noncash transfers such as food stamps and because total money income reported in the AHS is about 94 percent of that captured by the Current Population Survey, and even less of an independently derived source (Hadden and Leger, 1988), these residuals will somewhat underestimate actual household resources. Nevertheless, steep declines in residual income over time allude to the hardship such households must increasingly encounter in maintaining a current residence or seeking a new one. In addition to rent itself, renting frequently entails paying additional initial costs such as a damage deposit to the landlord and a security deposit to utility companies. Low-income renters who are forced to move thus may be faced with financial demands that are simply unmeetable.

The finding that changes in the median rent-to-income ratio for the low-income unsubsidized renter is attributable to rising rent does not exclude the possibility that erosion of income was a significant factor for some renters, particularly public assistance recipients. Maryland was not among the three states that have fully indexed public assistance benefits to inflation, and thus, over time, the income of these recipients has fallen further from meeting basic needs. The 1983 Maryland monthly general assistance allowance for a household of one (in 1986 dollars as inflated by the CPI-XI) was $139 while an AFDC allotment for a family of four was $391. Although Maryland has the 6th highest per capita income in the nation, it ranked 27th in income maintenance allowances (U.S. House of Representatives, 1986). Based on the availability of rental units below $100 and below $200 dollars per month, it is not difficult to see that welfare recipients might easily have been faced with homelessness.

A 1983 survey of those who contacted the six departments of social services in the Baltimore SMSA for help in averting homelessness found that 31 percent of families seeking assistance had been receiving AFDC for nine months or more, and overall, 20 percent were recipients of either AFDC or general assistance (Health and Welfare Council of Central Maryland, 1983). These figures indicate two things. First, the proportion of those verging on homelessness who receive welfare is low, and second, those who receive public benefits do not have income adequate to afford the housing that is available. The futility of providing social service benefits at levels below subsistence has been most notably documented for New York City and surrounding communities, where daily payments to provide emergency shelter to AFDC recipients in welfare hotels and motels may outstrip what recipients are allowed in monthly shelter allowances.[20]

The Quality of the Housing Stock

The quality of the housing stock is relevant to a study of housing vulnerability and homelessness for at least two reasons. First, in attempting to account for the increase in gross rent that we have seen in Baltimore, it is important to know whether rents have been driven up by an increase in the quality of the housing stock. Second, because studies of the homeless have shown that a substantial proportion of the homeless have lost their housing units due to demolition or condemnation (Sosin, Colson, and Grossman, 1988; Health and Welfare Council of Central Maryland, 1983), the amount of substandard housing and the percentage of vulnerable renters that occupy such housing are indicators of potential housing loss. As indicated in the methodology chapter, this study takes advantage of the superior data on housing quality gathered in the Annual Housing Survey to provide a more accurate assessment of the quality of rental housing than is available in any other known study. The relationship between housing quality and rent is further explored in Chapter 9.

Substandard housing is highly concentrated in the central city of Baltimore, and the city has a high proportion of substandard rental housing relative to other large cities. An examination of the housing stock revealed that little change had taken place over the eight-year time period in the percentage of all rental housing units that were of low quality, either in the central city or outside of it. Table 5.2 shows the percentages of substandard units by types of inadequacies that are identified in the AHS.

Two indicators of substandard quality suggested by HUD identify units that have one or more inadequacies or severe inadequacies (see Appendixes A & B). About 12 percent of the central-city Baltimore rental housing stock was inadequate and 8 percent was severely inadequate, both in 1976 and in 1983. Although the total rental housing stock in the central city had declined, the proportion of remaining stock that was substandard did not decline. As might be expected, the poor occupied a disproportionate share of this substandard housing. Calculation from AHS data tapes (not shown) indicate that approximately 30 percent of the central-city poor lived in inadequate or severely inadequate housing in 1983.

Housing Deprivation

Housing deprivation is typically divided into three forms: living in substandard housing (as defined in the appendixes), having more

Table 5.2
Percent Rental Housing Stock with Inadequacies or Severe Inadequacies: Baltimore

Type Inadequacy	Outside Central City			Inside Central City		
	1976	1979	1983	1976	1979	1983
Inad. plumb.	1.3	1.3	1.0	1.2	1.5	.5
Inad. struct.	1.7	3.5	2.4	12.1	13.6	13.6
Severe inad. struct.	.2	.3	.4	2.4	4.1	3.5
Inad. hall	0	.1	0	.3	.3	.4
Inad. heat	.5	.3	0	1.9	.3	.8
Severe inad. heat	1.5	2.2	1.0	3.4	2.4	2.8
Severe inad. elec	0	0	0	.2	.1	0
Inad. sewer	.5	.1	.3	.7	.3	.3
Severe inad. sewer	3.1	2.7	2.8	2.2	2.2	2.3
Inad. kitch.	1.0	1.3	1.0	2.3	2.1	.6
1 or more inad.	2.3	3.7	1.9	12.2	12.6	12.7
1 or more severe	5.0	5.8	5.5	8.6	9.9	8.3
No. inadequate	3070	5100	2915	17,850	18,877	18,150
No. severe inad.	6630	8043	8604	12,604	14,742	11,210

As defined by HUD in Appendices A and B.

than one person per room, and paying more than 30 percent of income to rent (Milgram, and Bury, 1987). Only 38 percent of central-city Baltimore renters were not experiencing one or more forms of housing deprivation in 1983. Figure 5.4 shows that increased cost burden is the primary cause of the decrease between 1976 and 1983 in the percentage of all households who had no form of housing distress. The categories of housing deprivation shown are mutually exclusive, and they sum to 100 percent. About one-third of all renters had two or more types of housing problems. Even though paying a high proportion of income to rent, about 17 percent of all renters were still living in overcrowded or substandard housing. While housing problems are nearly universal among low-income renters, nearly two-thirds of all renters have one or more forms of housing distress.

The Vulnerable Population

As previously indicated, the percentage of renter households in Baltimore who had incomes below 125 percent of poverty and paid more than 45 percent of income to rent (the vulnerable) remained quite stable over the period. Two more stringent measures of vulnerability were assessed. The very vulnerable are low-income renters who pay more than 60 percent of income to rent, while the severely vulnerable

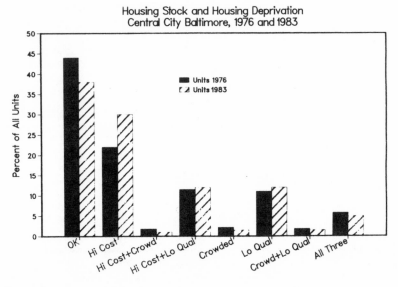

Figure 5.4

are those households with less than $50 per person per month remaining in residual income after paying rent.

In Figure 5.5, the three measures of vulnerability are plotted over time. Low-income households that pay more than 45 percent of income in rent continue to make up about 20 percent of central-city Baltimore renters. The more stringent definitions of vulnerability must be applied before an increase in the number of households rises, from 21,700 to 22,300 for the very vulnerable and from 15,200 to 18,500 for the severely vulnerable. Thus the fastest-growing population at risk is composed of severely vulnerable households, which increased from 10 percent of all renter households in 1976 to 13 percent in 1983. This is again reflective of concentrations of the poor at extremely low levels of income. Inflation in the housing market and stagnating incomes are likely to have exacerbated the problems since 1983.

The vulnerable are overwhelmingly female and, like the homeless, are made up increasingly of blacks. Figure 5.6 compares the very vulnerable with all renters. These contrasts would be more pronounced if the comparison included owners, but even within the central-city renter population, those at high risk have become increasingly distinct over time. Females in Baltimore, which has an unusually high percentage of homeless who are women, form 78 percent of those at risk of homelessness. The proportion of all renter heads who were female had increased

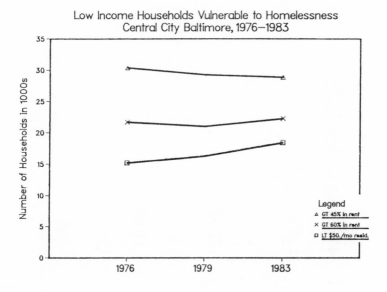

Figure 5.5

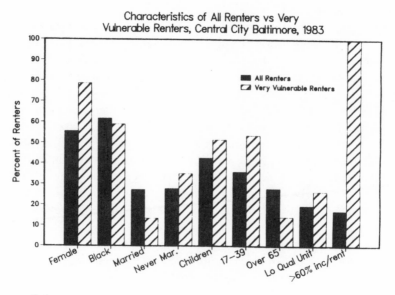

Figure 5.6

from 51 to 55 percent in Baltimore between 1976 and 1983. Thus, female renters are disproportionately at risk. Sixty percent of the vulnerable are black, about equal to the representation of blacks among all central-city Baltimore renters. This figure is consistent with the percentage of blacks among the homeless reported by Clark (1985) and more recently by the Maryland Department of Human Resources (1988).

The percentage of families with children increased significantly among the vulnerable. A higher percentage of vulnerable households have children than do all renter households. Family size and mean number of children have also increased among the very vulnerable.

Multivariate Analysis of Vulnerability

To test the relationships between these characteristics and vulnerability holding all else constant, a logit regression of vulnerability was run in which vulnerability was a dichotomous variable (1 = low-income household paying more than 45 percent of income to rent; 0 = all others). Table 5.3 displays the results for the Baltimore SMSA. It shows, perhaps surprisingly, that living in the central city was no longer positively associated with vulnerability by 1983, whereas it had been in the earlier two years. This may indicate that even though

Table 5.3
Logit Models of Homeless Vulnerability for Baltimore SMSA

Variable	Baltimore					
	1976		1979		1983	
	coef.	t	coef.	t	coef.	t
Inadequate	.32	3.09***	.15	1.54	.16	1.40
Female Head	.62	7.23***	.61	7.40***	.56	5.49***
Black Head	.15	1.51	-.04	-.43	.03	.24
Children	-.03	-.83	-.01	-.43	.11	3.24***
Central City	.23	2.53**	.36	3.81***	.12	1.04
Head Age	.002	.60	-.004	-1.70*	-.005	-1.63
Head Educ.	-.11	-3.38***	-.23	-6.70***	-.30	-6.74***
Intercept	3.73	15.81***	4.48	20.62***	4.61	16.36***
Degrees of Freedom	1676		1733		1587	

Log (p/(1-p)/2+5)=Intercept +BX

*=p < .10 ** p= <.05 *** p= <.01

incomes of suburban renters have not fallen to the same extent as those within the central city, higher housing costs outside the central city have put these renters at similar risk.

The number of children in the household, while negatively associated with vulnerability in 1976, was positively and significantly related to vulnerability by 1983. The finding helps to explain why children are now, and may continue to be, among the homeless. These children face extreme deprivation, since the incomes of their families have little remaining, after rent is paid, for food, clothing, and all other expenses.

Living in inadequate housing was positively but no longer significantly related to vulnerability in 1983 as it had been in 1976. This finding will be shown (in Table 5.4) to be related to the fact that among the low income who are "less vulnerable," by virtue of paying less than 45 percent of income to rent, a high percentage also live in substandard housing. Female headship was positively and significantly related in all three years, but black headship was not. As with the relationship between vulnerability and substandard housing, this is related to the fact that blacks are even more prevalent among the low-income who are less at risk than among the vulnerable. There is an indication that the heads of vulnerable households have become younger over time. The negative association between age and vulnerability is significant in 1979 and very nearly so (t = 1.63) in 1983. Education is a very strong predictor of vulnerability. The logit suggests that those who are vulnerable to homelessness share characteristics, including a high proportion of women and the presence of children, with the new homeless in Baltimore.

Comparison of Very Vulnerable and Less Vulnerable Renters

A comparison of very vulnerable renters with those whose incomes are below 125 percent of poverty income but who pay less than 45 percent of income to rent indicates that it is possible to identify significant differences between the vulnerable and those less at risk (see Table 5.4). Among these differences are the higher percentage of never-marrieds and younger heads among those at high risk. The percentage of very vulnerable heads who are 17 to 39 years of age increased 8 percentage points in Baltimore over the eight-year period. There was a 12-percentage-point increase in the less vulnerable who were elderly. Sixty-six percent of the less vulnerable in Baltimore were living in public or subsidized housing as compared with 12 percent of the vulnerable.[21] This appears to be a strong endorsement of housing subsidies as an entitlement for all who qualify on the basis of income,

Table 5.4
Comparison of Very Vulnerable with the Low Income Less at Risk Population, Central City Baltimore, 1976 and 1983

Variables	Low Inc >60% in Rent		Have <$50.00 Residual Income		Low Inc <45% in Rent	
	1976	1983	1976	1983	1976	1983
Number of Households	21,687	22,268	15,226	18,422	25,620	28,597
% of all Households	14.9	15.5	10.4	12.9	17.3	20.0
Characteristics of Household Head						
Married	11.6	13.3	13.5	16.1	24.0	14.6
Widowed	16.4	14.5	10.4	11.9	21.9	25.9
Divorced	16.6	17.2	15.8	15.7	7.5	13.9
Separated	28.0	19.8	30.7	22.5	23.7	20.0
Never Married	27.4	35.1	29.6	33.7	22.9	26.0
Head < 25	15.5	19.6	16.6	18.9	12.1	8.8
Age head 17–39	45.5	53.5	51.8	54.7	40.5	33.0
Age head 40–65	36.9	32.5	39.0	33.3	42.9	38.5
Age head > 65	15.5	14.0	9.2	12.0	16.7	28.5
Female Head	72.8	78.6	73.9	75.0	66.1	76.5
Black Head	58.9	59.	62.4	63.1	72.3	78.1
H.S.Dropout	63.3	62.3	64.0	62.4	75.7	75.2
Beyond H.S.	14.2	12.5	11.7	10.6	3.1	4.2
Employed	21.0	14.6	19.5	10.6	24.9	21.5
Characteristics of Family						
Mean HH Mem	2.5	2.7	3.2	3.2	2.5	2.7
Large Family	7.7	11.8	15.0	15.8	22.5	12.3
Welfare	44.0	57.7	53.0	64.2	46.0	51.3
Mean No. Children	1.1	1.3	1.7	1.8	1.8	1.4
Subfamily	0	3.6	0	4.9	1.2	4.6
Characteristics of Housing						
>1 Person/Room	10.5	6.0	16.0	8.7	18.1	8.8
Too Few Beds	21.2	17.7	28.3	21.3	28.6	26.1
Inadequate Unit	19.7	14.0	23.0	16.2	12.3	17.0
Severely Inad	10.2	12.4	13.0	11.6	16.3	8.0
Public Housing	13.4	2.9	17.0	8.4	39.7	39.5
Subsidized	0	5.6	1.2	5.4	0	26.8

rather than only for the fortunate few. There is a 15 year waiting list for public/subsidized housing in Baltimore (Health and Welfare Council of Central Maryland, 1986). The higher percentage of elderly among the less vulnerable is indicative of the inability of younger households to obtain subsidized units due both to federal cutbacks and to the concentration of remaining federal housing funds on units for the elderly and disabled (Clay, 1987:15). The incomes of the elderly have also been protected from decline by the cost-of-living increases in social security.

Those at high risk were less likely to be employed than the less vulnerable in spite of having higher levels of education. While the percentage of blacks has increased over time within all the categories of vulnerability, the percentage of blacks is highest among the less vulnerable. Low-income blacks spend a lower percentage of income on housing than do whites in Baltimore central city as a whole, a finding that may be related to the majority proportion of public housing that is occupied by blacks (Massey and Bickford, 1988). As will be discussed in Chapter 9, it cannot be assumed from this finding that within submarkets to which they may be restricted, blacks may not pay higher housing costs.

Women and Vulnerability

Even though women represent a high proportion of the homeless in Baltimore, a much higher percentage of female vulnerable than female homeless emerges. The physical vulnerability of women compels them to make extraordinary efforts to avoid becoming homeless, and because of this or in addition to it, women may have more sources of social support for doubling up that help them prevent becoming homeless. But the financial vulnerability of women may also portend that the proportion of women among the homeless is likely to continue to increase unless steps are taken to reduce their risk. Single female heads and elderly women are more than twice as likely as all households to have a housing problem and more than three times as likely to be cost-burdened. More than half of female heads with children under the age of 18 have a housing problem, a higher rate than that experienced by blacks or Hispanics (Birch, 1989).

Women, particularly women with children, have been found to suffer discrimination in obtaining both rental and owned housing. A task force investigating such discrimination for HUD collected the following testimony:

The woman alone with a child or children really has the worst time of all because of the entanglement of all kinds of discrimination, the layers of discrimination. And if the woman is of a minority group it adds another layer . . . and if she's on welfare, it adds another layer, and if she's got a large family, it adds another; it becomes impossible (National Council of Negro Women, 1975).

Coupled with this is the fact that female heads, despite their low level of income in comparison with two-parent families, pay nearly as much in rent as these families do. In Baltimore, black female-headed households had incomes that were 54 percent of black two-parent families but paid 89 percent of the median rent paid by these families. These differences are even more pronounced among all renters. All Baltimore female heads, for example, had incomes that were 42 percent of two-parent renter households but paid 91 percent of the median rent paid by these households. The very high rent burdens for women suggested by these figures have led to a very high proportion of women among the homeless in Baltimore.

NOTES

1. Twenty-one percent of Baltimore area blacks lived in the suburbs in 1980 as compared with 16 percent of Chicago blacks. Baltimore blacks were also less segregated from whites within the suburbs than were Chicago blacks. Index of dissimilarity in 1980 (representing the proportion of blacks who would have to move in order to achieve racial balance) was .545 for suburban Baltimore blacks and .754 for suburban Chicago blacks. (See D. Massey and N. Denton, 1988.)

2. Kasarda (1988). Numbers employed in manufacturing fell from 130,000 in 1953 to 105,000 in 1970 and 55,000 in 1985. Service industries, excluding government, retail, and wholesale trade, employed 108,000 in 1970 and 139,000 in 1985, while blue-collar services declined from 44,000 to 40,000.

3. Black unemployment was 12.5 percent versus 3.1 percent for whites in 1985 (United Way, 1987).

4. Kasarda (1988:191). The population of central Baltimore did decline during this period by 142,000 or nearly 16 percent (See P. Dearborn, 1988).

5. It must be kept in mind that the period referred to by both the HUD estimates and the AHS data is 1983. Substantial growth in the Baltimore homeless population is evident in figures reported by the Maryland State Department of Human Resources in 1988 as compared with those reported by the Health and Welfare Council of Central Maryland in 1983. Of the six counties making up the Baltimore SMSA, the total number of homeless served in emergency services (excluding mission beds) increased from

11,227 in 1982 to 40,541 in 1988 (yearly prevalence figures). Respective figures for Baltimore city were 5,055 and 18,445.

6. Estimates were based on telephone interviews conducted with 8 to 12 local experts in the Baltimore area, both within and outside of the central city. What HUD termed the "most reliable estimate" was based on its own assessment of the reliability of each estimate received. For example, estimates based on street counts and statistics of shelter users were given more weight than estimates dependent on impressions. The expertise of the interviewee was also taken into consideration.

7. As reported by HUD (1984). One of the four sources on which HUD based its estimates was the highest reported figure from a published source. A straight-line extrapolation of the sum of these estimates produced a national estimate of 586,000, the high range of HUD's four national estimates. The national extrapolation from the estimate based on interviews with local experts produced the lowest of the four estimates, 254,000.

8. It is important to distinguish between point estimates, or the number of persons estimated to be homeless on any given day, and yearly estimates, or the numbers of different people estimated to be homeless over the course of a year. The HUD report states that the number referred to in the published sources is the number of homeless at any given point in time. However, the published estimates for Baltimore reported by the *Atlantic* magazine and the *Baltimore Sun* are much more similar to the total number of homeless served in 1983 (11,227), according to the Health and Welfare Council of Central Maryland (1983). The failure to fully distinguish between point estimates and ever homeless may be a common source of the extreme discrepancy in local as well as national estimates.

9. One criticism of the HUD study was that it employed not widely used Rand McNally Metropolitan Areas (RMAs) rather than SMSAs to define the population. According to HUD, the 300 RMAs in the United States capture 92 percent of the population of 286 SMSAs, but contain only 28 percent of the area of the SMSAs. Applebaum (1988) cites this as the most significant problem with the report. RMAs can contain more than one city, each of which may have its own homeless problem.

10. Currently only 76 percent of emergency beds and 88 percent of transitional beds for the homeless are located within Central Baltimore, indicating an expansion of services outside of the central city. In the SMSA as a whole, emergency beds tripled between 1982 and 1988. (Health and Welfare Council of Central Maryland, 1930 and Maryland Department of Human Resources, 1989).

11. The State of Maryland Department of Human Resources summary of homeless services in 1988 shows that the total served in the city of Baltimore over the course of one year was 18,445, while the figures for the five additional counties that make up the Baltimore SMSA were 1,485 in Baltimore County, 2,569 in Anne Arundel County, 586 in Carroll County, 792 in Hartford County, and 520 in Howard County. Baltimore city thus served 76 percent of the homeless in the SMSA.

12. The sample of Baltimore renters included a total of 2,362 records for the SMSA, of which approximately 1,850 were renters in 1976 and 1979 and 1,700 were renters in 1983, when the sample size was reduced.

13. The low-income population was increasingly composed of those below the poverty line, however, as evidenced by a 6-percentage-point increase in the central city and a 3-percentage-point increase outside of the central city in the proportion of this population below the poverty line.

14. Removing subsidized renters and public housing residents from this comparison would intensify the mismatch. Baltimore has a higher percentage of its renter population in such housing than most other cities have.

15. Even the nonprofit sector finds it necessary to set rents beyond what many of the unsubsidized poor could afford. The Coalition on Temporary Shelter (COTS) in Detroit, for example, rents single-room occupancy units (SROs) with baths for $175 per month. The Transitional Housing program in Baltimore shelters homeless women with children in one-bedroom self-contained units for $200 per month (Peggy Posa and Steve Cleghorn interviews).

16. For an analysis of pre-1986 federal tax policies encouraging speculation in and conversion of rental housing and a study of how the 1986 tax reforms will affect investment in rental housing, see J. Gilderbloom and R. Appelbaum (1987).

17. The concept of "affordability," while somewhat arbitrary, is now considerably higher in the United States than in most of the Western industrialized world. Sweden, for example, has largely met a national goal of limiting housing costs to 20 percent of income (Gilderbloom and Appelbaum, 1987:164).

18. The median percentage of renter income spent on housing exceeds that of owner income and has increased more rapidly. Bureau of Census data cited in Farley (1983) shows that the median rent-to-income ratio for nonfarm housing was 17 percent in 1950, 18 percent in 1960, and 21 percent in 1970. When the Annual Housing Surveys were begun in 1973, the median was still .21, but it increased nearly 10 percentage points by 1983. The median percentage of income being spent on housing by home owners with a mortgage advanced slowly from 18 percent in 1976 to 20 percent in 1983.

19. A historical footnote on the rent burdens of the very poor is provided in *Tally's Corner*, by Elliot Liebow (1967). This classic ethnographic study of black "street corner" men in the early 1960s reports that in the Washington, D.C., slums, the proportion of income going to rent for a one-room SRO was about 20 to 33 percent of income. He contrasts this with the median income West Ender of Boston, who, according to Herbert Gans (1962), paid only 12 percent of income for an apartment of several rooms. Although the residents of the Washington slums were paying more and getting less than their West End counterparts, the comparison of rent burdens with those faced by the poor today suggests why those who once occupied marginal housing could now have become homeless.

20. The *New York Times* (July 11, 1989) reports that Westchester County in New York pays $143 per family per day to house families in motel rooms, and one-fifth of the county emergency housing budget of $54 million is spent to house 4,380 people in 50 such motel rooms. Cases in New York City are also discussed in Kozol (1988).

21. Ostensibly there should be no vulnerable households living in public or subsidized units since occupants of these units are supposedly limited to 30 percent of gross income to be spent on rent. However, considerable numbers of occupants exceed this rent to income ratio (Newman and Schnare, 1988). Further, the questions on public and subsidized units in the AHS prior to 1985 did not distinguish between these units and those that have been publicly owned by a college or church (estimated to be a very small proportion of the housing stock).

6

Chicago

SUMMARY

Nowhere is the controversy over the numbers of homeless more acute than in Chicago. What is not in doubt is the deterioration of the economic position of renters that occurred between 1975 and 1983. Compared with Baltimore, Chicago had a steep increase over the eight years in both the numbers and percentage of renters who were vulnerable to homelessness. Both falling incomes and rising rents were factors in the increased rent-to-income ratios. By 1983, 28 percent of all renters in the central city had incomes below 125 percent of the poverty line and paid in excess of 45 percent of income to rent. Rent burdens on average were substantially higher than in Baltimore. As in Baltimore, there was no change in the percentage of all rental housing that was inadequate or severely inadequate, and only 38 percent of all renters were neither cost-burdened, overcrowded, nor living in substandard housing. Among vulnerable renters, the percentage who were overcrowded doubled over the eight-year period of the surveys, while the percentage of those in substandard housing remained stable. Blacks, females, and households with children were increasingly at risk over time.

THE HOMELESS IN CHICAGO

Chicago is one of the four urban areas where a profoundly poor urban underclass appears to be growing most rapidly (Bane and Jargowsky, 1987). Although not generally discussed in the context of the underclass, the homeless might be considered its most impoverished members. The factors contributing to the formation and growth of the underclass in Chicago have been most notably discussed by Wilson (1987). Yet Wilson admits to having given little attention to the role that rising rents may have played in maintaining and exacerbating poverty.[1]

Like Baltimore, Chicago has experienced structural economic changes that have led to a dislocation between jobs and workers. Both cities have also sustained an overall population loss in the central city, while the numbers and percentages of minority households have increased. Unlike Baltimore, however, Chicago has a low rate of home ownership, particularly in the central city. Sixty percent of central-city residents were renters in Chicago, as compared with 51 percent in central Baltimore (*Annual Housing Survey*, 1983). An increasing percentage of these renter households have black, Hispanic, or female heads.

The number of homeless in Chicago continues to be controversial. Whereas HUD's 1984 estimates of homelessness in metropolitan areas have generally been criticized for being too low (Hartman, 1988), a study by Rossi, Fisher, and Willis (1986) indicated that for Chicago they were too high. The 1984 HUD estimate of 17,000 to 26,000 homeless persons for the SMSA (approximately 28 per 10,000 persons) is more in accord with that reported by the Illinois Coalition for the Homeless, which estimated 25,000 homeless in the city in 1983 (Kivisto, 1989).

Rossi's study included a census of all sheltered homeless in the city and a sample of the unsheltered street population from blocks where the homeless, according to informants, were said to congregate. Interviewers, accompanied by police officers, surveyed the selected blocks at two time points, six months apart. They estimated that an average of 2,700 persons were homeless on any given night, and 7,000 were estimated to be homeless over the course of a year (Rossi, 1988:90).

Although the study was scientifically rigorous compared with previous studies of the homeless, it was widely criticized by homeless advocates, who claimed that the estimate diminished the size of the homeless problem in Chicago. A more valid criticism concerned the use of police officers to accompany the interviewers. Critics speculated that fear of the police may have led to fewer than 10 percent of those found on the street admitting to being homeless.[2] Some doubt was also cast on the results by the fact that no homeless children were identified on the street. In contrast, the U.S. Conference of Mayors 1986 report on homelessness estimated that homeless families with children made up 40 percent of the homeless population of Chicago (Institute of Medicine, 1988). A more recent study has put the proportion of homeless families with children in Chicago at 30 percent (Sosin, Colson, and Grossman, 1988). Although it might be extremely rare to find young children on the street rather than in shelters in a city such as Chicago, the Chicago

Coalition for the Homeless estimated that there were 4,000 unaccompanied homeless youth under the age of 18 in the city, and only 30 emergency shelter beds were designated for youth (Chicago Coalition for the Homeless, 1985).

Rossi (1988) believes that the huge discrepancy between estimates is largely the result of differences in the definition of homelessness, as well as in the greater amount of error inherent in "guesstimates." His own figures are of the "literal homeless," and do not include the marginally housed, families in welfare hotels, and others who, according to the New York State definition of homelessness cited earlier, do not have a legal right to remain for a definite period of time.

The present study cannot solve the dilemma of the number of homeless in Chicago. As Rossi has stated, the absolute numbers are not so important as the fact that a significant number of people in Chicago are without homes (Rossi, 1987). It is possible, however, to shed some light on the roles that housing and income may have played in the development of the recent homeless population of Chicago.

HISTORY OF THE HOMELESS IN CHICAGO

The poor and homeless of Chicago have been more widely studied than those of most other cities, and an examination of the historical evidence is informative when compared with recent studies. In a classic survey of skid row in the late 1950s, Donald Bogue (1963) conducted a census of the dilapidated hotels, rooming houses, and single room occupancy (SRO) units in the several skid row districts of Chicago, as well as of the Cook County hospital and jail. It is important to take note of Bogue's broader definition of the homeless. He estimated that there were 12,000 to 13,000 homeless, of which about 3 percent lived on the street or were in jail or hospitalized, while about 8 percent lived in missions. The remainder were what we would probably today classify as renters rather than homeless. Though the conditions in which they lived were often deplorable, the occupants of the SROs were neither in barracks shelters nor on the street, and their residences were relatively permanent. Sixty-eight percent had been living in the same dwelling for a year or more.

The population was 96 percent male, although a recent drop in the sex ratio had occurred as the skid row district had become home to inmigrating black families, some female-headed. The skid row population as of 1950 was still 96 percent white. This was at least in part attributable to racial segregation in the hotels and rooming houses in the districts surveyed by Bogue, which were typically all white or all black. Hoch and Slayton (1989) state that 9 percent of skid row residents throughout the city were black. Thirty-five percent of the population had less than six years of education. The size of the skid row population had been quite stable over the 1940 to 1950 decade, with some evidence that the numbers were shrinking after 1950 (Bogue, 1963).

The homeless of Chicago in 1958 were disproportionately foreign-born, marginally employed, middle-aged or older men, with a median age of 49. Twenty percent were 65 or older. About twice the number of pensioners lived in the skid row district as in the rest of the city. Bogue found that more than 1,200 old-age pensioners lived in the district primarily because it offered the cheapest rent in the city. Thirty to 35 percent of the skid row population were problem drinkers. Another 10 percent were too disabled to work. In all, about 70 percent had at least a partial disability that would prevent them from being fully employed.

Bogue examined both social psychological and sociological explanations of why individuals ended up on skid row. He concluded that from the former perspective, the residents of skid row were victims of economic hardship, poor mental health, maladaptive social adjustment (the so-called marginal man), and/or poor physical health, disability, or low intellectual ability. From the sociological perspective, Bogue argued that "skid row exists to provide continued survival for familyless victims of society's unsolved social problems while these persons are in the terminal phase of their affliction and after society at large has abandoned all hope for them and has ceased to try to rehabilitate them....Skid row exists because the working processes in our contemporary civilization create certain types of circumstances for which society at large accepts minimal responsibility" (1963:405-6).

Bogue's study of the conditions of Chicago's "homeless" concludes with the conviction that the great majority of the population could and should be rehabilitated and all skid row residents should be rehoused, in institutional settings if necessary. Others who have studied the skid row district argue that skid row existed primarily because of the economic need, rather than the physical or mental disabilities, of its inhabitants (Hoch and Slayton, 1989).

Whether or not Bogue was correct in his assessment of the skid row environment, his policy recommendations were clearly humanitarian in intent. It is ironic, in reading Bogue's plea of 30 years ago to eliminate skid row, that we now attribute the growing phenomenon of homelessness, at least in part, to the loss of this generally substandard housing. This is the most concrete indication we have that societal expectations of what the poor deserve have seriously diminished in the last decade.

The elimination of skid row districts did take place in Chicago, as Bogue advocated, but it was accompanied by displacement rather than replacement. Half of the 22,000 SROs that existed in 1970 had been demolished by 1980 (Sosin, Grossman and Colson, 1988:45). A further 22 percent decline in SROs renting for less than $50 per week, small apartments for less than $75 a week, or dormitory or hotel rooms for less than $30 per week occurred between 1980 and 1983 (Rossi, 1988:111). Of the 24,000 rental housing units that were destroyed in central-city Chicago between 1979 and 1983, 21 percent were single rooms. Thirty-six percent of the rental units lost had been occupied by tenants with incomes below $5,000 in that year. Nearly five times as many units were lost as were built in that period (*Annual Housing Survey* published tabulations, 1983).

THE NEW HOMELESS

As Rossi (1989) notes, being homeless today connotes a much more severe state of shelter deprivation than was true for the population studied by Bogue. The new homeless in Chicago are quite different in some ways from their counterparts of 30 years ago, but in others may be more like the former inhabitants of skid row than the new homeless of other cities. Because better quality data exists on the Chicago homeless than those of the other cities examined here, more attention will be given to comparing and contrasting these populations for Chicago than elsewhere.

According to the study by Sosin, Colson, and Grossman (1988), those who have been recently homeless in Chicago are much younger, far less likely to be retired, and much more likely to be black and to be female than the historic homeless population. The sample of those who had ever been or were currently homeless studied by Sosin was a stratified random sample of program users (shelters, meal sites, and treatment programs). Those surveyed were 67 percent black, 9 percent Hispanic, and were, on average, less than 38 years old. Whereas Rossi, Fisher, and Willis had found nearly 20 percent of their sample to be over 55,[3] Sosin, Colson, and Grossman found only 12 percent of those ever homeless were above this age. Compared with the population as a whole, the sample of ever homeless in the latter survey was over-representative of the 26-to-40-year age group and underrepresenta-tive of the elderly.[4] Rossi's sample differed significantly in racial composition—57 percent black and 4 percent Hispanic. Both surveys, however, were disproportionately black and underrepresentative of Hispanics for the Chicago population at large.[5] Rossi reports that the ethnic group most disproportionately represented was the American Indian, who made up 0.1 percent of the census population but 5 percent of the homeless sample (1988:93).

In the Sosin study, among the currently homeless, 37 percent were female, while among the ever homeless the figure was 30 percent.

Nearly one-fourth of homeless households or individuals were single parents with children, while another 6 percent were intact families. Among homeless women in the sample, 87 percent had had children, and 61 percent currently had custody. The authors speculate that the small percentage of currently married (9 percent) is more reflective of extreme poverty than of homelessness in particular. "In some ways," they conclude, "our entire sample seems to consist of many individuals who others have called members of [the] underclass."

Rossi (1988) describes his sample of homeless as a population composed primarily of alienated men with a high rate of disability, past history of institutionalization and substance abuse, and lack of familial ties or social support—in short, much like the population Bogue described, only now predominantly minority. Drawing conclusions similar to Bogue's, Rossi (1988:114) states that "homelessness in our society is the result of the failure of institutions to provide for the familyless poor, especially unaffiliated males."

Whether the characterization of the homeless population of Chicago emphasizes the "new homeless" women, children, and minorities or the continuum with the past of a population of marginally functioning adults may be largely the bias of those reporting the results. An increase in the proportion of women from 4 percent to 25 to 30 percent seems noteworthy, as does the emergence of children among the homeless. But recognizing that 42 percent of young black males are unemployed in Chicago (Wilson, 1987:43), it is quite likely that the homeless of Chicago will have more of the characteristics associated with long-term joblessness—disaffiliation, depression, and substance abuse—than will the homeless elsewhere.

THE ROLE PLAYED BY HOUSING PROBLEMS AMONG THE CURRENTLY HOMELESS

Sosin and his associates wanted to determine what distinguishes the homeless from the domiciled poor. Although the number of respondents to their survey is small (137), housing problems figure prominently among the stated reasons for homelessness among those currently homeless. Fifty percent had been evicted for nonpayment of rent. Twenty-one percent had had an argument with the landlord or roommate or were abused. Nearly 17 percent had occupied buildings that were torn down or condemned. Only 13 percent had been paying no rent in their last dwelling, and the average rent paid by the homeless had been statistically significantly higher than that paid by those who did not become homeless. The majority had most recently been living with others rather than alone.

These factors are all relevant to the present study because of the proposed relationship between homelessness and overcrowding, substandard housing, and high rent burdens. Inadequate dwellings are more likely to be demolished. Overcrowding or doubling up causes social pressures related to an overload of demands and insufficient privacy,[6] which can lead to arguments and eviction.[7] Higher than average rents may indicate a shortage of affordable housing.

Of the ever homeless respondents who lost their homes (N = 302), Sosin and his colleagues found that 32 percent did not look for another place to rent. Of these, 73 percent did not search because they had no money. Twenty-two percent of those who searched found no openings, and of those who found one, 70 percent could not afford to rent it. Twenty percent turned down a unit for being too dilapidated. Nearly 20 percent were themselves turned down by the landlord. The authors conclude that, given the similarities in the demographic characteristics of the very poor and the homeless, and as poverty has increased in cities over the last decade, the very poor have "a finite possibility of becoming homeless, and more such individuals were in this state, over time" (Sosin, Colson, and Grossman, 1988:93). Although it is difficult to separate out the effects of income and housing as they may create conditions for homelessness, we now turn to an exploration of these factors for the Chicago area. First the demographic characteristics of Chicago renters as a whole are examined. Then, as in Baltimore, we focus on the low-income population of the central city.

DEMOGRAPHIC CHARACTERISTICS OF CHICAGO RENTERS

Table 6.1 shows the demographic makeup of Chicago renters within and outside of the central city over the three years of the Annual Housing Survey. It indicates that renter households in both areas were increasingly minority, never married, and female-headed, reflecting demographic trends in the population at large. Compared with Baltimore, Chicago has a considerably smaller proportion of black and female-headed households in the central city. The proportion of renters who were married decreased in both metropolitan areas, both within and outside the central cities. Both mean household size and mean age of Chicago households have remained fairly constant, whereas the mean age of Baltimore renters has increased significantly.

Median family income or household income[8] and per capita income of renters has fallen in both central and suburban regions. By 1983, 10 percent of Chicago central-city renters had an income deficit of more than $5,000 below the poverty line. The percentage of the poor with a deficit of this magnitude increased from 13 to 30 percent over the 1975-83 period.

Table 6.1
Demographic Characteristics of Chicago Renters, 1975, 1979, 1983

Variables	Outside Central City			Inside Central City		
	1975	1979	1983	1975	1979	1983
Total Renter Households						
Number	348,985	367,493	413,100	664,135	644,950	634,200
Percent <125% Poverty	13.4	9.6	14.0	32.7	29.0	37.7
Race (in percents)						
White	92.6	90.3	89.4	61.0	57.6	50.9
Black	6.3	7.9	8.6	36.8	39.7	41.8
Hispanic[a]	4.4	4.3	5.1	9.7	12.2	14.2
Marital Status (in percents)						
Married	53.1	42.0	39.6	37.9	33.1	31.6
Widowed	12.5	13.4	15.8	16.1	15.0	12.8
Divorced	12.8	15.3	17.6	12.0	13.0	13.8
Separated	3.3	3.1	4.3	10.5	11.1	10.8
Never Married	18.3	26.3	22.7	23.4	27.0	31.0
Sex of Head (in percents)						
Male	69.9	63.8	59.5	57.8	53.9	50.7
Female	30.4	36.2	40.5	42.2	46.1	49.3
Age, Education, Employment of Head						
% 17–39	53.7	54.6	53.6	43.8	44.7	47.4
% 40–64	25.4	23.5	22.2	32.6	31.6	28.3
% 65+	20.9	21.8	24.3	23.6	23.8	24.4
Mean Age	41.4	41.1	41.8	44.5	45.3	44.0
% Head H.S. Grad	78.2	74.7	76.1	55.9	57.3	60.1
% Head Employed	74.6	75.0	b	56.0	59.3	b
Household size						
Tot. H.H. Mem.	2.4	2.2	2.3	2.5	2.4	2.5
% with Children	36.9	33.6	33.6	38.2	38.6	41.2
Mean No. Children	.72	.61	.61	.93	.87	.89
Income and Rent						
Mean Income	$26,364	$26,110	$24,075	$19,840	$19,562	$17,087
Med. Income	$21,938	$23,607	$22,002	$14,762	$16,129	$13,201
Med. Per Capita	$11,259	$12,097	$11,117	$7,164	$7,812	$6,286
Med. Rent	$388	$411	$424	$293	$305	$325

[a] Hispanic ethnics may be black or white. Totals do not equal 100%   [b] Head employed not asked in 1983

MISMATCH OF AVAILABLE AND AFFORDABLE UNITS

Figure 6.1 shows the mismatch in income of renters relative to the availability of rental housing in the central city of Chicago for the low-income population. The solid bars represent the gross rent in constant 1986 dollars of the housing units occupied by low-income renters who receive no housing subsidies. The hatched bars represent the hypothetical housing units that would be affordable to these renters if they were able to spend no more than 30 percent of their incomes on rent. This figure then is a graphic description of the mismatch between affordable rents and available rents.

The mismatch is much more severe in Chicago than in Baltimore (see Figure 5.1). Provision of housing that would cost no more than 30 percent of income would require nearly 80,000 units renting below $100 per month in 1983, whereas about 22,000 such units existed, a ratio of about four to one. In Baltimore, the comparable mismatch was two to one. For Chicago, this is a 69 percent increase since 1975 in the shortfall of units, including vacancies, at this level of affordability.

A similar mismatch between size of the housing unit and what renters require in order to avoid being overcrowded (not more than two persons per bedroom) exists in both cities (figure not shown). The shortfall in terms of size alone emerges at four or more bedrooms, units that the rental vacancy market virtually does not provide. In Chicago, in 1983,

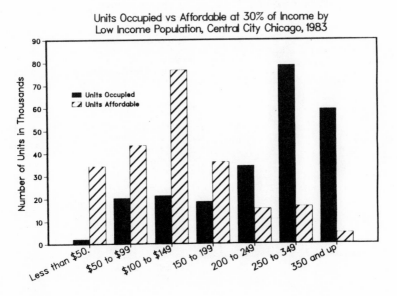

Figure 6.1

for example, 22,500 more units with four or more bedrooms were needed to avoid overcrowding. Since larger units are generally more expensive, the shortfall becomes more pronounced at lower levels of affordability.

RENT-TO-INCOME RATIOS

Figure 6.2 shows the proportion of income that central-city households with incomes below 125 percent of the poverty line and no housing subsidy spend on rent. It illustrates that within the central cities, the low-income renters of Chicago were more highly cost-burdened than those of Baltimore. Among Baltimore central-city renters, the percentage of low-income unsubsidized households paying more than 60 percent of income to rent increased from 40 to 52 percent between 1976 and 1983. The increase for comparable central-city Chicago renters was from 46 to 61 percent in approximately the same time period.

Residual income, or what remains after rent, is plotted in Figure 6.3, along with monthly income and gross rent for unsubsidized renter households below 125 percent of poverty in the Chicago central city over three survey periods. In constant 1986 dollars, the median monthly income of Chicago low-income unsubsidized renters fell from $442 in 1975 to $404 in 1983 while median rent rose over this period from $275 to $303. The resulting residuals have also declined more sharply over time

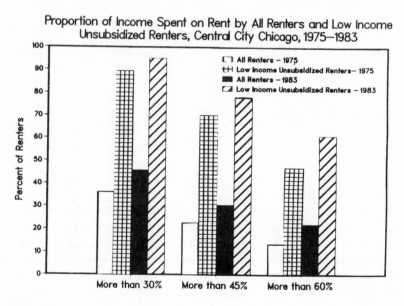

Proportion of Income Spent on Rent by All Renters and Low Income Unsubsidized Renters, Central City Chicago, 1975–1983

Figure 6.2

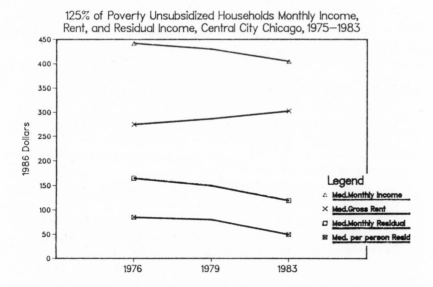

125% of Poverty Unsubsidized Households Monthly Income, Rent, and Residual Income, Central City Chicago, 1975–1983

Figure 6.3

in Chicago than in Baltimore, and the median per person residual fell for these unsubsidized low income renters to just $50 per month.

For unsubsidized low-income renters in Baltimore, increased rent was the more significant factor in the rise of the ratio of median rent to income from 53 to 63 percent over the 1976 to 1983 period. For Chicago, falling incomes contributed slightly more than increasing rent to the rise in the median ratio from 59 percent in 1975 to 73 percent in 1983.

THE QUALITY OF THE HOUSING STOCK

Table 6.2 shows the percentage of housing units that had inadequacies or severe inadequacies over the three time periods. As was found in Baltimore (see Table 5.2), there has been little improvement in these figures over time. In Chicago as in Baltimore, the major share of inadequacies are structural, defects not detected in the decennial census. Table 6.2 more accurately portrays the quality of the housing stock and helps explain why a much greater percentage of housing appears to the objective observer to be visibly dilapidated than census figures would indicate. About 16 percent of the central-city stock and about 7 percent of the suburban stock were substandard (either inadequate or severely inadequate) in both 1975 and 1983. Because the suburban rental stock was growing and the central-city stock was shrinking, the number of inade-

Table 6.2

Percent Rental Housing Stock with Inadequacies or Severe Inadequacies: Chicago

Type Inadequacy	Outside Central City			Inside Central City		
	1975	1979	1983	1975	1979	1983
Inad. plumb.	.7	.5	.6	3.4	2.4	1.8
Inad. struct.	2.8	3.3	3.3	6.2	7.8	6.8
Severe inad. struct.	.2	.3	.2	.8	1.6	1.6
Inad. hall	0	.1	.1	2.3	1.2	1.3
Inad. heat	.0	.2	.1	.1	.6	1.2
Severe inad. heat	1.2	1.5	.5	2.1	3.0	2.3
Severe inad. elec	.1	0	0	0	.1	.1
Inad. sewer	.1	.3	.1	.4	.8	.2
Severe inad. sewer	1.3	2.5	1.3	2.1	2.2	2.4
Inad. kitch.	1.0	1.0	1.1	2.8	2.5	2.4
1 or more inad.	3.2	3.8	4.0	7.8	9.0	8.5
1 or more severe	3.3	4.1	2.5	7.9	8.2	7.5
No. inadequate	10,340	14,600	21,770	52,760	57,840	53,560
No. severe inad.	11,425	15,360	10,250	52,540	53,150	46,900

As defined by HUD in Appendices A and B.

quate units outside of the central city increased, while there was a slight decrease in the number of substandard units within the central city.

HOUSING DEPRIVATION

The three forms of housing deprivation—more than one person per room (Crowd), substandard housing (Lo Qual), and cost-burden (Hi-Cost)—are illustrated in Figure 6.4. The great majority of Chicago renters were experiencing one or more forms of housing deprivations in 1983. The pattern in Figure 6.4 is strikingly similar to that of Figure 5.4 for Baltimore. Of the occupied central-city rental housing stock, only 38 percent in either Baltimore or Chicago housed renters who were neither overcrowded, cost-burdened, nor living in substandard

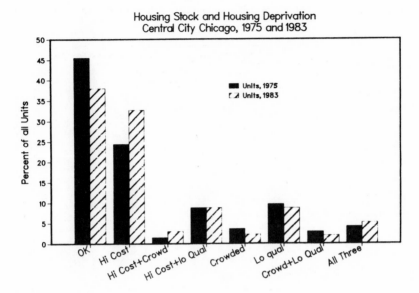

Figure 6.4

housing. These figures show that increased cost burden is the primary cause of the decrease between 1975-76 and 1983 in the percentage of all households who had no form of housing distress. The extent of crowding, as measured by persons per room, is higher in Chicago than in Baltimore. About 20 percent of Chicago central-city renters had two or more forms of housing deprivation. It should be noted that renters are much more likely than home owners to be overcrowded and to live in substandard housing, as well as to be more highly cost-burdened (U.S. Bureau of the Census, 1983). Therefore, renters experience much higher levels of housing distress vis-à-vis owners than a comparison of incomes and housing costs alone would indicate.

THE VULNERABLE CENTRAL-CITY RENTER POPULATION

How has the size of the vulnerable population changed over time? While the number of renter households in Baltimore who had incomes below 125 percent of the poverty line and paid more than 45 percent of income to rent remained quite stable over the period, the numbers of those at risk of homelessness in Chicago by this criterion had risen quite dramatically. By 1983, it included 175,000 central-city households. In Figure 6.5, the three measures of vulnerability are plotted. Even by the most strict of the three criteria, the number

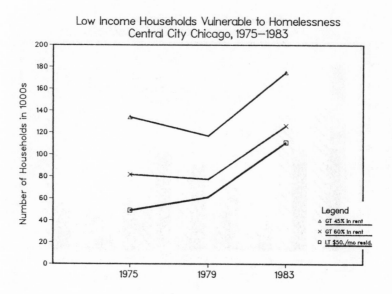

Figure 6.5

of households at risk in Chicago was 111,000 in 1983, or nearly 18 percent of the renter population, up from 49,000, or 7 percent, in 1975. Low-income households spending more than 45 percent of income on rent were now 28 percent of central-city Chicago renters, as compared with 20 percent of central-city Baltimore renters. These differences in the size of vulnerable populations in 1983 should have a bearing on the extent of homelessness in the two cities.

Of course, not all of the most vulnerable have become homeless or are likely to become so. Many will find a way to get by. But these figures do tell a story of a greatly increased population at very high risk in Chicago and a substantial but more slowly growing high-risk population in Baltimore.

Figure 6.6 compares the characteristics of the very vulnerable and all central-city renters. Again, these contrasts are less pronounced than a comparison of vulnerable renters with owners would be, but the figure shows the disproportionate representation of female and black heads among the very vulnerable. Females make up 68 percent of those vulnerable in Chicago. The proportion of all renter heads who were female had increased from 42 to 49 percent in Chicago between 1975 and 1983. Thus female renters are disproportionately at risk in Chicago, as they are in Baltimore.

In both Baltimore and Chicago, about 60 percent of the vulnerable are black. This is not disproportionate to the representation of blacks among

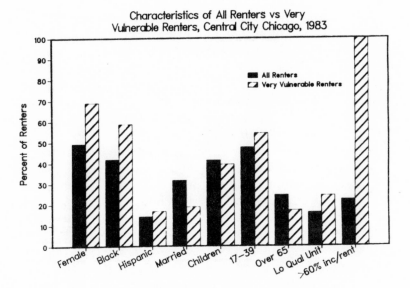

Figure 6.6

all central-city Baltimore renters, but in Chicago, blacks are much more likely to be at risk than renters overall. This figure is about midway between the estimates of blacks among the homeless as found by Rossi, Fisher, and Willis (1986) and by Sosin, Colson, and Grossman (1988). Seventeen percent of the very vulnerable in Chicago are Hispanic, slightly more than the percentage of Hispanics among the entire renter population and higher than the percentage of Hispanics among the samples of homeless in either of the above studies. That Hispanics are more prominent among the vulnerable than among the homeless may be due to the greater tolerance of Hispanics for overcrowded conditions as found by Gove and Hughes (1983).

Minorities in Chicago may be especially prone to both housing distress and homelessness because of racial discrimination in housing, which affects their ability to freely participate in the housing market (Kain and Quigley, 1975). Farley and Allen (1987:141) show that Chicago has the highest index of racial residential segregation among the 25 central cities with the largest black populations. The index of dissimilarity, which has a value of 100 when there is complete segregation, was 92 for Chicago in 1980, nearly 20 points higher than that of Detroit. It had dropped by only one point since 1970. The index of segregation was much higher for blacks in the Chicago SMSA (88) than for Hispanics (64), but Hispanics as well as blacks were more highly residentially segregated in Chicago than in nearly all other large metropolitan areas (Farley and Allen, 1987:144).

A logit regression of vulnerability (see Table 6.3) on a number of these characteristics for the Chicago SMSA shows that central-city residents are much more likely to be at risk than those outside of the central city. In Chicago, as in Baltimore, it shows that, whereas in 1975 presence of a child in the household was negatively associated with high risk, by 1983 it was positively and significantly related to vulnerability. The heads of vulnerable households are also significantly younger than in 1975. While the coefficient of vulnerability for female heads has declined somewhat over time, females remain significantly more vulnerable than males in all three time periods. In Chicago, as was not true in Baltimore, black heads of households are significantly more vulnerable. The logit suggests parallels between those who are vulnerable to homelessness and those who are literally homeless. It particularly shows that the circumstances of children in rental housing have changed unfavorably.

A comparison of very vulnerable and severely vulnerable renters with those whose income is below 125 percent of poverty income but who pay less than 45 percent of income to rent (the less vulnerable) is shown in Table 6.4. This shows that in Chicago, the vulnerable as well as the less vulnerable were more likely to be either married or to be never married in 1983 as compared with 1975. The vulnerable are much less likely to be widowed, or to be over 65, a further indication that this aged population has been moved out of vulnerability either through income or rent transfers or through both. A much higher percentage of the less vulnerable were living in public or subsidized housing in either year, but this percentage grew substantially between 1975 and 1983. Rossi (1989) notes that the majority of subsidized units that were built in Chicago in recent years were specified for the elderly.

Younger heads were increasingly among those at high risk. The percentage of very vulnerable heads 17 to 39 years of age increased 13 percentage points in Chicago over the seven-to-eight-year period. Those at high risk were less likely to be employed than the less vulnerable in spite of having higher levels of education. This too is reflective of the younger ages of the vulnerable, as the general level of education has been increasing. Whereas only 19 percent of Bogue's (1963) skid row population had a high school diploma, 55 percent of Rossi's (1986) sample were graduates, a figure nearly identical to the percentage of high-school graduates—56 percent—for the Chicago population at large (Institute of Medicine, 1988). This may indicate that the returns to education or the quality of education, for the poor and minorities, have declined.

Table 6.3
Logit Models of Homeless Vulnerability for Chicago SMSA

Variable	1975		1979		1983	
	coef.	t	coef.	t	coef.	t
Inadequate	.16	3.09***	.25	4.51***	.16	2.41***
Female head	.62	15.54***	.66	14.17***	.49	9.82***
Black head	.28	6.51***	.19	3.86***	.23	4.35***
Children	-.05	-3.25***	.02	1.16	.09	5.05***
Central city	.18	3.72***	.33	5.79***	.36	6.26***
Head age	.001	.59	-.002	-1.51	-.004	-2.59***
Head educ.	-.14	-9.21***	-.18	-10.76***	-.17	-9.44***
Intercept	4.10	38.92***	4.08	34.87***	4.40	34.23***
Degrees of Freedom	5687		5347		3372	

$(\text{Log}(p/(1-p)/2+5)=\text{Intercept} +BX$

$*=p < .10; ** p= <.05 *** p= <.01$

Table 6.4
Comparison of the Very Vunerable with the Low Income Population Less at Risk, Central City Chicago, 1975 and 1983

Variables	Low Inc. >60% in Rent		<$50 Residual Inc.		Low Inc. < 45% in Rent	
	1975	1983	1975	1983	1975	1983
Number of Households	81,767	126,017	49,101	110,896	87,779	68,878
% of all Households	12.3	20.0	7.4	17.6	13.2	10.9
Characteristics of Household Head (in percents)						
Married	15.3	18.8	18.4	20.3	26.0	30.0
Widowed	27.9	14.0	21.5	8.7	23.5	19.4
Divorced	14.2	16.3	13.4	17.4	11.0	10.5
Separated	19.7	20.0	24.5	21.1	20.5	15.4
Never Married	22.9	31.0	22.2	32.5	19.1	24.8
Age <25	14.7	14.6	19.2	17.0	12.1	8.8
Age Head 17–39	41.1	54.2	47.9	59.4	45.9	46.3
Age Head 40–65	34.3	28.8	32.2	30.3	28.9	33.9
Age Head > 65	24.6	17.1	19.9	10.4	25.2	19.8
Female Head	68.4	69.6	67.7	70.9	62.1	67.9
Black	51.2	58.7	55.0	60.9	62.2	66.0
Hispanic	9.6	16.7	10.9	17.9	11.2	18.4
H.S.Dropout	59.6	54.2	55.4	55.3	73.1	65.3
Beyond H.S.	17.3	19.7	18.9	18.0	7.3	12.7
Employed[a]	15.6	16.0	20.3	16.1	21.6	34.9
Characteristics of Family						
Mean H.H. Mem.	2.0	2.8	2.6	3.2	3.8	3.8
% Large Family	3.7	8.0	9.1	12.5	25.2	20.6
% Welfare	40.8	60.3	39.4	67.4	52.1	50.0
Mean No. Children	.69	1.4	1.1	1.7	2.2	2.1
% Subfamily	.6	.7	.7	.8	1.2	1.2
Characteristics of Housing (in percents)						
>1 Person/Room	4.6	10.7	7.6	16.5	26.8	26.9
Too Few Beds	24.4	38.8	30.1	44.5	47.4	43.6
Inadequate Unit	10.9	11.4	11.0	11.2	12.5	14.6
Severely Inad.	10.8	10.1	11.4	11.2	14.1	9.5
Public Housing	2.1	4.1	4.9	5.7	32.0	41.1
Subsidized	1.1	3.5	1.5	3.8	3.7	12.4

[a] "Head employed last week" in 1975; any wage and salary earnings in 1983.

While the percentage of blacks has increased over time within all the categories of vulnerability, the percentage of blacks among the less vulnerable is, as in Baltimore, even higher. But those who are less at risk financially are seen to pay a price in terms of overcrowding and living in inadequate housing. Twenty-seven percent of less vulnerable families are overcrowded, and 24 percent live in substandard housing. Thus a substantial proportion of those identified as "less vulnerable" in terms of the rent-to-income ratio may be more at risk of losing their homes due to demolition or interpersonal conflict. There were few low-income renter households in the central city of Chicago that were not experiencing housing distress.

The analysis of vulnerable renters in Chicago suggests that Rossi's estimate of the homeless, however accurately it may have captured the literally homeless, is just the tip of a huge iceberg. For every person who has become literally homeless by this estimate, there are perhaps ten or more households very precariously housed—crowded, living in dilapidated housing, and paying a very high proportion of an already marginal income to rent. The fact that this population, by all three criteria, increased so rapidly between 1979 and 1983 in Chicago should concern us. It is an indication that redistributive policies have harmed these already marginal households and that the growth of the urban underclass in Chicago, some of whom are homeless, may be an inevitable consequence of such policies.

NOTES

1. William Julius Wilson, personal conversation, seminar at the University of Michigan, April, 1989.

2. A criticism raised by Gilderbloom as cited in Institute of Medicine, 1988.

3. The percentage of older adults found by Rossi et al. was by far the highest among 13 studies reported in Institute of Medicine (1988:16). Another Chicago study had found only 8 percent above this age in 1983 (see Chicago Coalition for the Homeless, 1983).

4. Sosin, Colson, and Grossman, (1988) report that 29 percent of the Chicago population in the 1980 census were over the age of 55 and 28 percent were between the ages of 26 and 44, while 49 percent of the sample were in this younger age group.

5. The 1980 census figures for Chicago were 50.3 percent white, 39.8 percent black, and 14.1 percent Hispanic (Sosin, Colson, and Grossman, 1988).

6. Gove and Hughes (1983) found in their study of Chicago residents that those most likely to be negatively affected by overcrowding were households

of single parents with children, with or without other adults, and couples with both children and other adults present.

7. Interestingly, currently homeless blacks in the Sosin et al. study were significantly more likely to have been evicted because of an argument. This is consistent with the Gove and Hughes study, which found blacks, among the three racial/ethnic groups compared, to be the most reactive to the social pressures of overcrowding.

8. Total family income rather than total household income is reported in 1975 for Chicago. Subsequent years include income for nonrelatives who may live in the household. Though the income of nonrelatives does not greatly affect total household income, the effect of including nonrelatives' income in 1975 would have been to increase the income reported and thus to exaggerate even further the income decline that occurred after 1975.

7

Houston

SUMMARY

Houston has a poverty rate that, overall, is much lower than that of Baltimore or Chicago,[1] a vast surplus of housing, and yet a per capita rate of homelessness that is reportedly several times that of Baltimore's, according to both the 1984 HUD estimate and estimates by advocates. This chapter seeks to identify factors that might explain the extent of homelessness in Houston. The primary findings follow:

Despite a vacancy rate that was more than twice as high as that found in Baltimore and Chicago, Houston median gross rents increased both at a faster rate and to a higher level than in these metropolitan areas. Rent increases were most severe for low-income blacks. Because the median income of all Houston renters did not decline in the 1976 to 1983 period, the increase in the Houston median rent-to-income ratio was the result of rising rent rather than a combination of falling incomes and rising rents, as was the case in Chicago. The proportion of income spent on rent by low-income unsubsidized renters in Houston in 1983 was equivalent to that found in Baltimore. This group of Houston renters was less cost-burdened than similar Chicago renters. The mismatch between what is affordable to the low-income household at 30 percent of income and what is available, however, is more severe at the lowest levels of rent in Houston than in either Baltimore or Chicago. Thus, although the average low-income renter in Houston spends a smaller proportion of income on rent than would be spent in Chicago, the shortage of inexpensive units may increase the vulnerability of the Houston renter to homelessness.

INTRODUCTION

Although Houston has had an "extraordinary excess supply of housing" (Smith, 1986) of both rental and owned properties,[2] it has not escaped a growing problem of homelessness. The HUD 1984 estimates of homelessness for Houston ranged from 5,200 to 7,500, with an implied per capita rate (from the midpoint) of 22 per 10,000, the highest among the cities previously classified as "high minority, high rate of homeownership."[3] Not as much is known about the homeless of Houston prior to 1983 as in the other cities in this study, but the establishment of homelessness as a significant social problem in the early 1980s can be inferred from the convening in 1982 of a Task Force on Homelessness, followed in 1983 by the establishment of the Coalition for the Homeless of Houston/Harris County (McKinsey, 1989). All indications are that homelessness and hunger have increased considerably since the time of the HUD study.

A 1989 scientifically based study estimates that there are 10,000 literally homeless persons in Houston on any given night (McKinsey, 1989), a 33 percent increase from the high point of the 1983 HUD estimate. This study and one reported by Andrade (1988) indicate that, as in other parts of the country, there is a substantial representation of women and children among the homeless. Blacks were disproportionately represented while Hispanics were not. The majority of those interviewed had first used a shelter within the previous 12 months. Although a mild climate might be speculated to favor a transient homeless population, the great majority of shelter residents were long-time Texas residents.[4] The recent study corroborates estimates that have been made by the Houston Coalition for the Homeless, which has also used the figure of 10,000 literally homeless (Collier interview, 1989). The study further estimated that there were 150,000 persons who were "marginally homeless," both doubled up and precariously housed (McKinsey, 1989).

In trying to determine why Houston may have a relatively high rate of homelessness for a metropolitan area with a high rate of homeownership and much surplus housing, several factors are worthy of examination. Economically, Houston has waxed and waned, first as a boom town riding the crest of oil development and international trade, then as a bust town in the recession years of declining oil prices, and most recently as a city staging a comeback (Waldrop, 1987).

Among the factors that might be associated with increasing homelessness in Houston are high unemployment, growth in the proportion of the population that has historically had low incomes, discrimination, increased housing costs, and housing and social policies that do not help the poor.

UNEMPLOYMENT

The recession triggered by the crash in oil prices hit Houston in the 1982-83 period (Feagin, 1988:97), bringing about the loss of 150,000 jobs (Smith, 1986).[5] The rate of unemployment increased from 3.6 percent in 1980 to nearly 10 percent in 1983. As recently as 1987, unemployment remained at this level (U.S. Bureau of the Census, 1983 and 1987) and the work force had failed to regain about 102,000 jobs held in 1982 (Feagin, 1988:99).

Blacks were much harder hit by the recession than were whites. Whereas black unemployment was less than twice that of whites in 1982, in 1983 it was three times as high (Shelton et al., 1989). By 1987, unemployment among black adult males in Houston was nearly four times that for whites (Farley, 1989). It was not until the fourth quarter of 1987 that positive growth in nonagricultural and energy dependent employment resumed, and analysts concluded that the recession had bottomed out (Smith, 1988).

GROWTH OF THE LOW-INCOME POPULATION

In a multivariate analysis by Redburn and Buss (1987), a positive relationship was found between the rate of population growth in a metropolitan area and the per capita rate of homelessness. From 1975 to 1980, the Houston metropolitan area grew at a rate that was the fastest in the nation. By 1983, Houston had become the fourth largest metropolitan area in the United States. In contrast to the old industrial central cities of Baltimore and Chicago, the city of Houston did not experience sustained population loss, even as unemployment soared in 1982-83. Following a loss of 11,000 households in 1983 and a comparable recovery in 1984, Houston's population remained quite stable until resuming positive growth in 1987 (Smith, 1988). The 1980 SMSA population of 3 million is currently projected to reach 4 million by 1990, with a decade growth rate of 35.7 percent. The central city has been growing at a slower rate, projected to be 18.4 percent over the decade, which would lead to an estimated population of 1.9 million by 1990 (U.S. Bureau of the Census, cited in Feagin, 1988).

Blacks still outnumber Hispanics in Houston, but Hispanics are rapidly narrowing the gap. While the population of blacks increased by 41 percent between 1970 and 1980, the Hispanic population of Houston grew by 130 percent (James, 1984). Hispanics are now conservatively estimated to number at least 400,000 in the metropolitan area and 700,000 in the Houston "market" area. This would place Houston just behind San Francisco and Chicago as the seventh largest Hispanic community in the country (Feagin, 1988:254). Forty percent of the increase in Hispanics within the greater Houston metropolitan area has come from Mexican and Central American immigration (Word, 1989). While these immigrants typically have high rates of employment, the problem of homelessness in Houston is thought to have been aggravated by the national immigrant amnesty program that has resulted in some Mexican and Central American immigrants remaining in Houston but being unable to work.[6]

Houston is notable for a vast discrepancy in the incomes of blacks and whites. Farley (1989) found that the income of Houston blacks as a ratio of white income had fallen from 61 percent in 1980 to only 41 percent in 1988. Among the 17 large metropolitan areas he studied, only New Orleans and Memphis had a lower ratio of black income to white. There was a 22-percentage-point difference in the poverty rates of blacks and whites in 1988, an increase of 6 percentage points from 1979 (ibid.).

INCOME AND HOUSING ASSISTANCE

Analysts of social welfare in the state as a whole have found "the safety net for poor people in Texas is among the weakest in the nation" (Shapiro and Greenstein, 1988:1).

Houston ranks among the lowest of large metropolitan areas in the country in the percentage of households (2.6 percent) receiving income assistance. Of those who do receive welfare 55 percent pay more than 30 percent of income to rent. Overall, 41 percent of all Houston households were either overcrowded, cost-burdened, or lived in substandard housing (Newman and Schnare, 1988). As will be seen, the percentage of renter households who experience one or more housing problems is even higher. Meeting the need for shelter assistance has not been a top priority of local government. Some critics charge that this inattention to the needs of the poor is deliberate. "Historically, Houston has not been aggressive in pursuing its claim for a fair share of the federal housing assistance pie" (Gilderbloom, Rosentraub, and Bullard, 1987).

Houston has, by any account, a very low number of public housing units. Conventional public housing caused such a controversy in Houston that in 1950 a referendum was passed that severely

restrained the program (James, McCummings, and Tynan, 1984:133).
A comparison of the numbers of public housing units in 16 large cities
showed that Houston, the fourth largest city, ranked fifteenth, with
only 4,268 units. Within Texas, Houston had fewer public units than
the smaller cities of Dallas and San Antonio. Houston not only has far
fewer units than comparably sized cities,[7] but one-fourth of its units
have been scheduled for demolition since 1984, and of these only 80
remain occupied. As in a number of other cities, the condemnation of
these public housing units has been highly controversial.[8]

In terms of providing housing subsidies to low-income renters, Houston
ranks near the bottom (13th of 16 cities) in providing subsidies through
the Section 8 housing voucher programs, with only 11,754 units subsidized. Whereas nationally about 20 percent of those who qualify receive
housing assistance, only 6 percent of those qualifying for Section 8 assistance in Houston receive it, including 9 percent of those who are disabled
and 5 percent of those who are elderly (Gilderbloom, Rosentraub, and
Bullard, 1987). Waiting lists for public and subsidized units tripled between 1980 and 1987 (Feagin, 1988:263; Shelton et al., 1989). To the disadvantage of families, subsidized housing has also focused primarily on the
elderly (James, McCummings, and Tynan, 1984). Housing for the elderly
is less controversial among local residents than is housing for minorities
and families, especially since three-fourths of the elderly served are non-
Hispanic whites (James, McCummings, and Tynan, 1984).

For those fortunate few who do receive housing assistance, the
payment is among the lowest in the country. Texas ranks 45th in the
amount of shelter payment per recipient, and Houston provides only
29 percent of the Fair Market Rent (FMR) to recipients. Of the largest
metropolitan areas, Baltimore also provides 29 percent of FMR, while
only Miami, at 26 percent, is lower than Houston (Newman and
Schnare, 1988).

What accounts for Houston's apparent lack of commitment to better
conditions for the poor? A spirit of self-reliance and abhorrence of
regulation prevails. Houston in particular is a "widely cited model of
the positive consequences of a free enterprise, laissez-faire approach
to urban development" (Feagin, 1988:1), and is a city that has ostensibly solved the housing crisis through reduced housing regulations,
lack of zoning restrictions, and an emphasis on supply-side economics
(Johnson, 1982). That viewpoint is challenged by Feagin (1988:264),
who claims that the poor and minorities of Houston have paid a
disproportionate share of the social costs of development. The "modest taxes and moderate services provide a context in which the less
affluent residents face serious everyday problems even in times of
prosperity, when their main benefit is a low wage job. These everyday
problems are aggravated not only by periods of economic recession

and depression but also by Houston's long history of racial discrimination and oppression" (Feagin, 1988:264).

DISCRIMINATION IN HOUSING

While it has been estimated that an effort by local government to obtain Houston's fair allocation of federal housing subsidies could double or triple the amount currently available (Gilderbloom, Rosentraub, and Bullard, 1987:40), the effort by whites to restrict provision of subsidized housing continues to hamper such an effort. Two recent projects were canceled by the Housing Authority following protests by whites.[9]

Evidence of discrimination in rental housing was reported in a 1973 study by the League of Women Voters that found that half of all rental developments in Houston discriminated against minorities. Blacks were more often subjected to discrimination than Hispanics (James, McCummings, and Tynan, 1984:131). Nearly 60 percent of Hispanics and 53 percent of blacks were renters in 1980 and as such were constrained in their housing choices by discrimination as well as by their incomes. Little effort has apparently been made in Houston to use housing programs to further neighborhood integration (ibid.). Although the city of Houston has stronger enforcement of open housing laws than do the surrounding suburbs, the power of the Fair Housing Division has been weakened by lack of support from the city council and reduction of its staff of compliance officers from four to one between 1977 and 1984. Three-quarters of nearly 1,800 complaints to the Houston Fair Housing Division between 1975 and 1983 were filed by blacks and Hispanics. Of these, two-thirds were dismissed and only six went to litigation (Shelton et al., 1989).

Failure to aggressively enforce fair housing statutes contributes to the continued isolation of blacks in central-city black neighborhoods.

INCREASED HOUSING COSTS IN A SURPLUS MARKET

It can be concluded that a number of factors could be contributing to the growing problem of homelessness in Houston. But an examination of the rental housing stock shows that rising rents may be a most critical factor. In a 1988 study that assessed the opinions of service providers, health and human service administrators, and community leaders on the most important unmet need contributing to homelessness in Texas, affordable housing was by far the most frequent response (Andrade, 1988).

Perhaps because of the rapid expansion of the population in the previous decade, the economic collapse of 1982-83 was not perceived quickly enough or otherwise did not deter builders from adding 63,000 housing units to the stock in 1983. Vacancies increased by 67 percent in one year, and aggregate vacancies did not begin to decline until 1986 (Smith, 1986,1988). The "laws" of supply and demand would argue against an increase in constant gross rents in a surplus housing market. Instead, we would expect that housing prices would fall in response to a rapidly increasing rental vacancy rate. To the contrary, while the Houston central city had a rental vacancy rate of 18.8 percent in 1983, up from 8.3 percent in 1976, median rents in constant 1986 dollars (CPI-XI) had climbed from $347 to $411. In the metropolitan area as a whole, mean rent had increased from $360 to $443 over this period. Some of the increase was undoubtedly due to the high proportion of the housing stock that was newly constructed. Forty-seven percent of Houston's 1980 housing stock had been built since 1970 (James, McCummings, and Tynan, 1984:25). In spite of the vast amount of new construction, only 6 percent of Hispanic and 2 percent of black renters in 1983 lived in housing that had been constructed since 1979 (Annual Housing Survey machine readable data, 1983).

While rents did decline precipitously after the most recent Annual Housing Survey was conducted in 1983, they did not return to pre-1981 levels. As Figure 7.1, the Rental Price Index for Harris county,(the Houston SMSA), indicates, average monthly rent, excluding electricity (essentially contract versus gross rent)[10] increased in constant dollars from $263 in 1979 to a high of $389 in 1982. It fell to a low of $306 in 1987 and has since increased, despite the continued high vacancy rate of 16 percent, to $313, or 19 percent higher than in 1979.[11] Rents were projected to have returned to their 1983 level by 1989 and then to increase sharply to nearly twice the 1979 level by 1991. Contract rent would then exceed $500 dollars per month as vacancies fall and competition is restored to the market (Smith, 1986). Currently, the amount of housing being retired from the stock exceeds the number of units being added by new construction, leading to a decline in the surplus (Smith, 1988).

Low-income renters, however, occupy an older, less expensive submarket of rental units that is not inflated to the extent that new construction is, nor does it enjoy the surplus that high vacancy rates would indicate. The median gross rent of low-income renters, while showing a more dramatic increase between 1976 and 1983 than that of renters overall, remained well below the median gross rent for renters as a whole and was unlikely to have declined substantially after 1983.

The vacancy rate is a poor indicator of the amount of housing that is affordable to the low-income population, particularly when size of

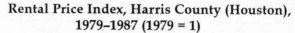

**Rental Price Index, Harris County (Houston),
1979–1987 (1979 = 1)**

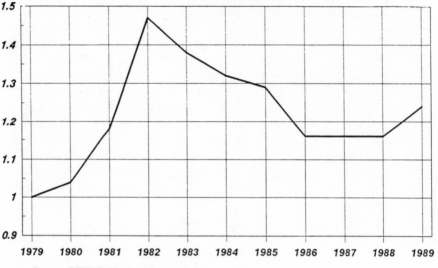

Source: REVAC. Used with permission.

Figure 7.1

the unit is taken into account. Of 67,450 vacancies in Houston in 1983, there were no rentals available for under $50, only 4 percent were available for between $50 and $200, and the 275 units that had as many as four bedrooms were renting for $900 or more dollars per month. The number of rental vacancies increased monotonically with increasing rent, up to $450 per month. Low-income renters must compete with higher-income renters who may seek low-cost units. A decline in median gross rent after 1983 may have allowed low-income renters to increase their bundle of housing services but not to have decreased their rent expenditure. Because of these factors, I will assume that the estimates of those vulnerable to homelessness in 1983 will not have declined significantly in subsequent years because of the temporary drop in rental housing costs.

THE DEMOGRAPHIC CHARACTERISTICS OF HOUSTON RENTERS

Table 7.1 provides a picture of the changing characteristics of all Houston renters within and outside of the central city over the 1976 to

Table 7.1
Demographic Characteristics of Houston Renters, 1976, 1979, 1983

Variables	Outside Central City			Inside Central City		
	1976	1979	1983	1976	1979	1983
Total Renter Households						
Number	81,900	128,200	163,900	253,500	283,900	292,000
Percent <125% Poverty	18.8	20.8	26.5	16.3	17.9	22.4
Race and Marital Status of Household Head (in percents)						
Non-Hispanic White	47.1	51.4	47.8	60.6	50.9	50.4
Black	46.6	41.2	36.5	24.8	26.2	26.8
Hispanic	6.0	8.4	7.9	12.9	16.2	17.1
Married	52.7	49.3	47.0	43.8	37.1	37.6
Widowed	7.4	7.3	5.7	8.1	7.9	7.1
Divorced	13.5	14.9	17.3	16.4	17.3	16.3
Separated	10.3	9.0	8.7	8.1	8.1	7.9
Never Married	16.0	19.5	21.3	23.7	29.5	31.0
Sex and Age of Head						
% Male	71.3	70.4	67.8	68.1	65.3	60.4
% Female	28.7	29.6	32.2	31.9	34.7	39.6
% 17–24	22.5	21.8	17.5	21.2	21.4	15.3
% 25–39	43.7	46.6	53.1	46.2	48.1	52.2
% 40–64	26.5	24.5	25.7	24.6	21.7	25.1
% 65+	7.3	7.1	3.8	8.0	8.9	7.4
Mean Age	36.9	36.5	35.5	36.9	36.7	37.4
Household Size and Composition						
%Med. H.H. Members.	2.9	2.9	2.8	2.4	2.3	2.4
%Large Family[a]	7.2	6.6	4.4	4.7	4.3	5.1
%Children	50.3	48.2	51.4	36.0	33.3	34.4
%One Person	24.3	24.5	26.1	34.3	37.2	36.5
%Subfamily	1.6	1.9	1.4	1.0	1.2	1.5
Education and Employment of Head (in percents)						
Beyond H.S.	27.7	30.1	34.0	41.1	41.1	44.9
Dropout	38.7	34.0	30.4	29.9	29.2	27.9
Employed	78.6	80.4	82.1	80.4	82.3	80.0
Housing and Rent in Constant 1986 Dollars						
Med. Gross Rent	$314	$359	$396	$347	$374	$411
Med. Rent/Inc Ratio	20	22	25	21	23	24
%Public Housing	5.0	6.5	4.5	3.1	4.9	3.2
%Subsidized	1.0	1.4	2.4	.9	1.1	2.4
%> 1 Person /Room	10.5	10.1	7.6	7.4	7.6	9.7
%> 1.5 Persons /Room	2.5	2.6	2.1	2.4	3.5	4.0
%Inadequate[a]	6.7	8.0	9.5	6.1	6.1	7.3
%Severely Inadequate	8.2	7.2	6.6	6.2	5.7	5.5
Income and Poverty in Constant 1986 Dollars						
Med. Income	$18,281	$20,528	$18,746	$20,007	$20,528	$20,957
Med. per capita	$8227	$8248	$7158	$9733	$10999	$11001
Percent Poor	13.0	15.4	21.2	13.9	12.6	17.8
Med. Pov Gap	$2878	$2821	$3245	$2664	$2642	$3590
% Poor w Povgap >$5000	6.0	4.3	5.3	4.3	3.5	5.8

[a] excludes units without adequate heat.

1983 period. Poverty was not concentrated in the central city of Houston as it was in Baltimore and Chicago. There was a more significant increase in the percentage of renters who were below the poverty line outside of the central city than within it, although there was a small increase in the median income of all renters in the 1976 to 1983 period. Median household income in constant 1986 dollars was $20,000 in the central city in 1976 and $20,950 in 1983. For those outside the central city, the figures were $18,281 and $18,746.

The percentage of all renter households with children remained quite stable, with 51 percent of suburban and 34 percent of central-city households containing children.

Female-headed renter households had increased but had not reached the proportions seen in Baltimore or Chicago. The percentage of female-headed households increased from 32 to 40 percent in the central city and from 29 to 32 percent in the suburban area. Never-married heads increased from 16 to 21 percent of suburban renters and from 23 to 31 percent of central-city renters.

The high-school dropout rate for Texas as a whole is one of the highest in the country (Andrade, 1988:28), but among Houston renters the percentage who have not completed high school fell. Employment levels overall remained very high both within and outside of the central city, relative to Baltimore and Chicago.[12]

While national trends indicate an increase in the median age of renters, this is true only in the central city of Houston. In both areas, the Houston renter population is considerably younger than in Baltimore and Chicago. However, there is a substantial drop in the proportion of renters who are between 17 and 25, indicative of a delay in household formation among the young, as has been found nationally (McGough and Casey, 1986). Elderly renters made up only about 6 percent of all Houston renters in 1983.

LOW INCOME BLACK AND HISPANIC RENTER HOUSEHOLDS

The population of interest in this study is low-income renters, and the percentage of all renters who had incomes below 125 percent of the poverty line in the Houston SMSA increased from 18 to 24 percent between 1976 and 1983. Because the majority of these low-income renters are either black or Hispanic and because the two groups are quite distinct demographically, a separate analysis of these renters is shown (see Table 7.2). Black and Hispanic renters with incomes below 125 percent of poverty are heavily concentrated within the central city, although this has become less true over time for Hispanics than for blacks. Eighty-three percent of black and 71

Table 7.2
Low Income Black and Hispanic Houston Central City Renters, 1976, 1979, 1983

Variables	Low Income Black Renters			Low Income Hispanic Renters		
	1976	1979	1983	1976	1979	1983
Total Renter Households						
Number	18,598	22,650	30,904	7,935	11,245	14,999
Percent of all Renters	7.4	8.0	10.5	3.1	4.0	5.1
Percent Central City[a]	87.5	81.4	83.4	84.2	72.3	71.4
Marital Status of Household Head (in percents)						
Married	20.2	14.8	28.5	62.8	65.5	73.1
Widowed	20.4	20.6	17.9	13.0	4.7	2.0
Divorced	12.0	17.3	12.4	6.4	9.5	11.6
Separated	25.1	24.0	16.4	11.2	7.7	9.6
Never married	22.3	23.3	24.8	6.5	12.5	3.7
Sex and Age of Head						
% Female	67.7	75.7	66.8	33.5	23.5	28.9
% 17–24	14.5	12.9	11.7	16.6	24.4	11.7
% 25–39	40.1	37.7	37.3	38.2	43.2	62.8
% 40–64	32.0	32.8	39.7	35.8	24.5	21.9
% 65+	13.4	16.6	11.0	9.4	7.9	3.6
Mean Age	38.0	39.0	40.0	38.0	32.0	33.0
Household size and Composition						
Mean H.H. Members	3.1	3.1	3.4	4.4	4.2	5.0
% Large Family	19.5	12.8	14.2	32.8	26.2	29.7
% with Children	52.1	59.8	60.5	69.8	71.6	88.7
Mean No. Children	1.6	1.6	1.6	2.4	2.2	2.8
% Subfamily	1.9	1.0	3.2	3.6	2.0	7.6
Education and Employment of Head						
% Dropout	62.1	60.7	50.3	83.3	87.3	80.3
% High Educaton	7.8	9.2	12.5	8.2	2.7	2.3
% Employed	41.9	41.0	56.1	65.7	77.3	79.4
Housing and Rent in Constant 1986 Dollars						
Median Gross Rent	$201	$223	$284	$237	$271	$300
% >30% Income to Rent	67.3	70.2	78.0	69.3	70.7	82.3
% >45% Income to Rent	49.5	55.4	66.1	46.1	48.5	49.0
% >60% Income to Rent	36.5	38.1	54.6	35.9	34.0	35.3
% Public Housing	14.5	18.5	13.4	6.6	12.2	6.3
% Subsidized	3.7	7.7	9.9	0	3.2	4.3
% > 1 Person per Room	22.8	18.7	17.3	41.9	45.4	53.0
% Inadequate	17.0	16.3	17.5	14.5	10.1	17.8
%Severely Inad.	10.3	10.2	6.8	5.8	7.6	5.7
Income and Poverty						
Median Income	$4,497	$4,523	$4,528	$6,581	$7,918	$8,800
Median Per Capita	$2,106	$2,111	$1,678	$1,950	$2,199	$1,914
Median Per Person Residual	$88	$91	$41	$92	$108	$86
% Below Poverty	80.2	78.9	80.3	78.0	65.0	86.1
Med. Poverty Gap	$2,169	$1,903	$3,129	$2,037	$1,393	$2,446
% Pov. Gap >$5000	25.4	24.7	29.6	27.4	21.7	31.3
% Receive Welfare	30.3	36.3	33.8	15.6	11.9	17.0

[a]Percent of all low income black or Hispanic renters in central city.

percent of Hispanic low-income renters lived in the Houston central city. The numbers of minority low-income renters nearly doubled in the period in which the numbers of all renter households in the central city increased by only 15 percent. By 1983, about 70 percent of all low-income central-city renters were either black or Hispanic, although, as will be shown, a somewhat smaller percentage of the vulnerable, those who are both low-income and pay at least 45 percent of income to rent, are minorities.

The cross-tabulations reveal striking differences between blacks and Hispanics in nearly all the variables considered, with the exception of the percentage of each group who live in substandard housing. About 24 percent of either group lives in housing that is either inadequate or severely inadequate. In many cases the differences between blacks and Hispanics have become more pronounced over time. Low-income Hispanic renters are much more likely to be married, to have children, to have larger families and subfamilies, to be overcrowded, and to be employed, despite having lower levels of education. In 1976, the median age of household heads for both renter groups was 38, but it increased for black low-income renters over the eight-year period to 40, while for Hispanics, it decreased to 33. Hispanic renters are nearly twice as likely to be between the ages of 25 and 39 as are blacks, perhaps a reflection of the fact that a high proportion of Hispanics are immigrants, who tend to be younger. Hispanics are much more likely to be married and thus may establish separate households at earlier ages.

Low-income blacks and Hispanics had much greater increases in median gross rent than did renters overall. The median gross rent of low-income Hispanic renters still exceeded that of blacks in 1983, but it had grown 27 percent beyond the rate of inflation since 1976, while that of low-income blacks had increased by an astonishing 41 percent. Because blacks had lower incomes, a much higher proportion of blacks than Hispanics were devoting more than 45 percent or more than 60 percent of income to rent by 1983, whereas the two groups had been very similar in 1976. Blacks were also twice as likely to receive welfare or to occupy public or subsidized housing as Hispanics. The differences observed between these black and Hispanic subgroups will later help to explain why blacks are disproportionately represented among those at risk of becoming homeless, while Hispanics are not.

THE MISMATCH BETWEEN SUPPLY AND AFFORDABILITY

The mismatch between what low-income unsubsidized renters could afford at 30 percent of income and what they actually paid is shown in Figure 7.2. This chart indicates that 10,000 households had incomes so

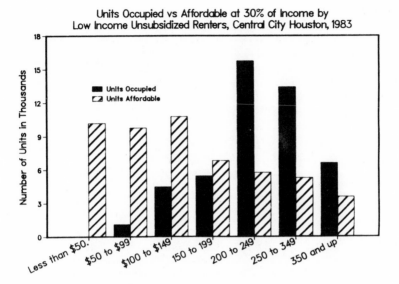

Figure 7.2

low that they could only afford to pay less than $50 per month, but no households were actually occupying units in this price range. The mismatch between what could be afforded at this percent of income and what was available was about 3 to 1 for units under $200, whereas it had been about 1.6 to 1 in 1976. Thus, the high vacancy rate of 1983 did not lead to an increase in housing available at low rent levels. As Gilderbloom and Appelbaum (1987:107) have argued, rental markets do not operate competitively at all levels of vacancy. While low vacancy rates are invariably associated with higher rents, the reverse is not necessarily true.

The proportion of income spent on rent by all renters and low-income unsubsidized renters in the central city is shown in Figure 7.3. Since only 6 percent of all renters occupied public housing or received housing subsidies, most renters are included in these figures. Of those who were not subsidized, 82 percent paid more than 30 percent of income to rent, and 53 percent paid more than 60 percent, an increase from 46 percent in 1976. The proportions of income going to rent for the low-income population are similar to those for Baltimore and less than those for Chicago central cities. Although Chicago had lower median rents, incomes were also considerably lower than in Houston.

Among low-income unsubsidized Houston renters, median income was not significantly different at $5,060 in 1983 than it had been in

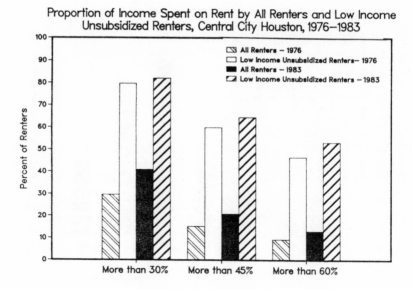

Figure 7.3

1976, although it had temporarily been higher in 1979. Incomes, rents, and residuals are plotted in Figure 7.4. Since median rents had increased over the period from $247 to $320, median residual incomes had declined substantially to about $50 per person, on a par with Chicago and considerably less than in Baltimore. The numbers of low-income unsubsidized renter households had increased by half over the period.

The position of low-income black renters relative to Hispanics declined significantly over the eight-year period. Per person residual income of blacks fell by half, while that of Hispanics declined only slightly. But as was shown in Table 7.2, more than half of all Hispanic low-income renters were overcrowded by 1983, whereas among black households, 17 percent had more than one person per room.

HOUSING STOCK AND HOUSING QUALITY

As in Baltimore and Chicago, there has been little change in Houston in the percentage of substandard units in the central city, over the 1976 to 1983 period. Table 7.3 shows, however, that substandard units outside the central city have declined as a percentage of all units.

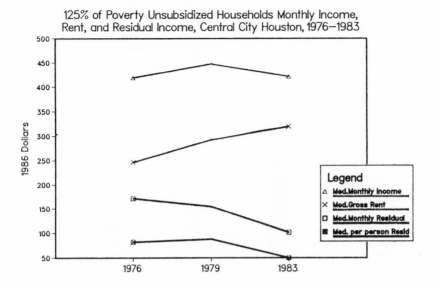

Figure 7.4

Because the size of the housing stock has increased, the number of substandard units has continued to rise. As will be more thoroughly discussed in Chapter 9, a large number of units in Houston lack adequate heating facilities. If these units are excluded from consideration, estimates of poor quality housing fall from 31 percent in the central city to about 16 percent, about on a par with Chicago. Outside of the central city, inadequate heat is even more common and excluding it lowers inadequate units from 33 percent to 11 percent. Heat is not totally unnecessary in Houston, but such large percentages of substandard units might be considered to inflate the extent of housing deprivation. Therefore in Figure 7.5, in which the three forms of housing deprivation are graphed, inadequate heat has not been included in the assessment of low quality. By this measure, 55 percent of all renters were experiencing housing problems in 1983, an increase of 12 percentage points since 1976. While most of this increase in housing deprivation is again due to households that are cost-burdened, there was an increase in the percentage of households with both high housing costs and overcrowding or substandard housing. Even though devoting a large share of income to rent, these renters still faced overcrowded and poor-quality living environments.

Table 7.3
Percent Rental Housing with Inadequacies and Severe Inadequacies: Houston

Type Inadequacy	Outside Central City			Inside Central City		
	1976	1979	1983	1976	1979	1983
Inad. plumb.	1.9	1.6	.5	1.4	1.5	.6
Inad. struct.	6.0	6.1	6.7	4.7	4.9	5.9
Severe inad. struct.	.5	.7	.6	.3	.5	1.0
Inad. hall	.2	.3	.5	.1	.2	.9
Inad. heat	26.8	23.5	20.3	18.4	18.9	18.1
Severe inad. heat	1.7	1.8	1.5	2.0	2.0	3.2
Severe inad. elec	0	0	0	0	0	.1
Inad. sewer	.7	.5	.4	.5	.4	.4
Severe inad. sewer	6.4	5.2	5.5	5.4	4.7	4.6
Inad. kitch.	2.5	1.8	1.4	1.7	1.5	.9
1 or more inad.	31.2	28.2	25.3	22.1	22.6	22.7
1 or more severe	9.3	8.2	7.2	8.5	7.8	8.5
No. inadequate	46,864	59,186	61,316	57,865	67,331	68,619
No. severe inad.	14,009	17,184	18,573	16,890	22,240	24,560
No. inad. minus heat	5,483	7,900	9,940	15,515	17,242	21,430
No. severe minus heat	6,703	8,704	10,993	15,840	16,050	16,150

As defined by HUD in Appendices A and B.

THE VULNERABLE POPULATION

Figure 7.6 charts the growth in numbers of households who have low incomes and pay more than 45 or 60 percent of income in rent or who have less than $50 per person remaining in residual income after rent is paid. The numbers of these households by all three standards were on the increase prior to the onset of Houston's economic misfortunes, but the rate of increase accelerated after 1979. Comparing this figure with those for Baltimore and Chicago, it can be seen that Baltimore and Chicago displayed a slight decrease in the percentage of renters who were vulnerable between 1976 and 1979, while in Houston all three categories of vulnerability increased between 1976 and 1979. The percentage of vulnerable households in Chicago in 1983 was twice that of Houston.

How do those who are vulnerable to homelessness differ from those who also have low incomes but do not have such high rent burdens?

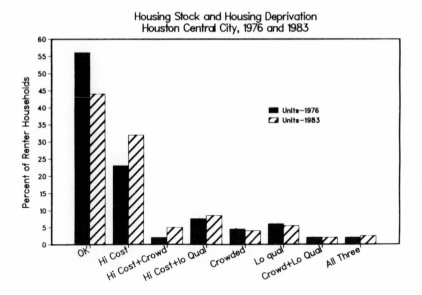

Figure 7.5

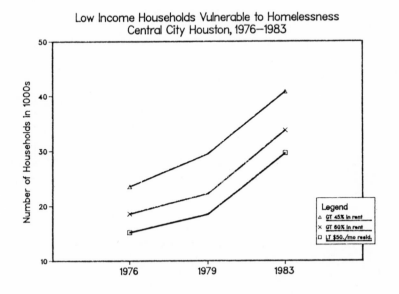

Figure 7.6

Table 7.4
Comparison of the Very Vulnerable with the Low Income Population Less at Risk, Central City Houston

Variables	Low Inc. >60% in Rent		<$50 Residual Inc.		Low Inc. < 45% in Rent	
	1975	1983	1975	1983	1975	1983
Number of Households	18,633	33,202	15,247	29,610	17,831	24,715
% of All Households	9.3	11.4	6.0	9.9	7.0	8.3
Characteristics of Household Head (in percents)						
Married	23.7	33.2	23.6	29.5	40.1	47.8
Widowed	18.2	16.0	10.7	12.4	19.3	18.6
Divorced	16.1	12.3	15.4	14.1	10.1	11.9
Separated	17.1	13.9	22.1	15.0	13.9	7.3
Never Married	24.8	24.6	24.8	29.0	16.5	14.4
Age <25	24.3	12.4	24.9	14.0	13.6	7.3
Age Head 25–39	30.0	42.6	38.1	48.5	36.6	49.9
Age Head 40–64	29.5	32.6	30.0	30.4	30.6	24.6
Age Head > 65	16.1	12.5	7.0	7.2	19.3	18.3
Female Head	65.2	62.4	64.8	61.5	46.7	42.6
White	47.0	28.1	40.5	26.9	23.0	26.9
Black	36.4	50.1	43.8	49.4	52.7	42.3
Hispanic	15.3	15.7	14.6	17.8	23.9	31.0
H.S. Dropout	51.7	48.1	51.0	47.5	66.3	58.5
Beyond H.S.	22.1	19.5	21.8	19.1	11.1	12.2
Employed	49.0	44.2	48.0	60.3	50.5	51.7
Characteristics of Family						
Mean H.H. Mem.	2.3	3.1	2.4	3.2	3.5	3.6
% Large Family	7.8	13.8	15.9	15.0	25.3	18.2
% Welfare	16.9	22.7	24.5	27.9	21.7	18.9
% with Children	37.0	55.2	47.8	57.5	54.4	56.7
Mean No.Children	.9	1.5	1.0	1.6	1.5	1.8
% Subfamily	1.9	2.0	2.8	1.0	1.2	3.6
Med. H.H. Income	$3,656	$3,920	$3,290	$2,750	$6,254	$5,809
Med. Per Capita	$1,952	$1,540	$1,472	943	$2,500	$2,231
Characteristics of Housing						
Med. Gross Rent	$301	$355	$293	$352	$183	$264
% >1 Persons per Room	11.7	19.3	19.7	22.1	28.9	31.2
% >1.5 Persons per Room	6.6	7.7	10.0	8.8	17.1	20.6
% Inadequate Unit	10.6	13.1	12.9	14.0	16.0	15.6
% Severely Inad. Units	5.7	7.9	7.2	6.9	9.5	4.8
% Public Housing	3.5	4.7	6.7	7.9	18.5	15.6
% Subsidized	1.8	6.0	2.1	7.5	3.5	9.5

Table 7.4 compares the characteristics of the very vulnerable, those who pay more than 60 percent of income to rent, and the severely vulnerable, those with less than $50 per person residual, with those low-income households who are considered less at risk because they pay less than 45 percent of income in rent. Of the 40,000 households who are vulnerable, 33,000 pay more than 60 percent of income in rent.

Among the very vulnerable, Hispanics are not disproportionately represented compared with the renter population at large. However, very vulnerable households are 50 percent black, 62 percent female-headed, and 55 percent with children. Total household members, the percentage of families with children, and mean number of children have increased over time for all three subgroups of low-income renters.

The characteristics of very vulnerable renters are compared with those of all renters in Figure 7.7. By definition, 100 percent of these renters pay more than 60 percent of income to rent. Very vulnerable renters are more likely than renters overall to live in overcrowded and substandard housing and to be over 65. They are much more likely to have children.

Holding all else constant, logit regression (see Table 7.5) indicates that in Houston, as in Baltimore and Chicago, children were negatively associated with vulnerability in 1976 and positively and significantly associated in 1983. This pattern underscores the worsening economic plight for children in rental housing. Children are not only increasingly likely to be raised in rental units, but to live in high-risk households

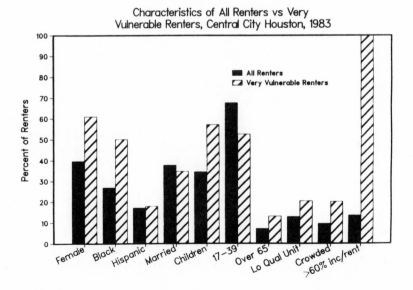

Figure 7.7

where income for nonhousing expenditures may be seriously insufficient. In an era of affluence for many people, these children also exist in an environment of increasing relative deprivation.

Unlike the findings in Baltimore and Chicago, however, age of the head is not negatively associated with vulnerability in 1983. In Houston, living in the central city did not significantly affect risk in any of the three periods. Hispanic renters were not significantly more vulnerable than whites in any year. Female heads and blacks were positively and significantly vulnerable in all three time periods, although the size of the coefficient for females diminished over time, while that for blacks increased by a substantial amount.

CONCLUSION

The relatively high rate of homelessness in Houston is proposed to be related to the cost of rental housing for low-income households, a cost that rose between 1979 and 1983 at a faster rate and to a higher level than in either Baltimore or Chicago. Continued high vacancy rates in Houston suggest that the problem is one of affordability rather than availability of housing. We have seen that among low-income blacks and Hispanics, rents increased dramatically over the eight-year period, with a larger percentage increase than that of renters overall. The median rent of low-income black households increased by 41 percent beyond the rate of inflation, a staggering increase in an eight-year period. Although there is not reliable data on the demographic characteristics of the homeless in Houston in 1983, two more recent surveys confirm that blacks are disproportionately represented among the homeless in Houston while Hispanics are not (Andrade, 1988; McKinsey, 1989). The evidence presented in this chapter indicates that the high proportion of the homeless who are black is paralleled by the fact that 50 percent of very vulnerable renters in Houston are black. While Houston blacks are highly segregated on only two of the five dimensions of segregation measured by Massey and Denton (1988), the disproportionate representation of blacks among the homeless may reflect the economic effects on low-income blacks that result when the size of this population is growing and the housing stock that is available to it is not and/or when more affluent blacks are limited by racial discrimination to black submarkets (Courant, 1978). In either case, the cost of housing rises under this internal competition, and the greatest economic consequences of confinement to these segregated housing markets fall to low-income blacks (Wilson, 1979).

Low-income Hispanics, while not becoming homeless to the extent that blacks have, are on the other hand much more likely than blacks

Table 7.5
Logit Models of Homeless Vulnerability for Houston SMSA

Variable	1976		1979		1983	
	coef.	t	coef.	t	coef.	t
Inadequate	.15	1.69**	.23	3.06***	00	02
Sev Inad	-.03	-.34	.14	1.66*	.10	.60
Female Head	.77	14.36***	.58	11.79***	.53	5.91***
Black Head	.16	2.47**	.27	4.66***	.40	3.84***
Hispanic Head	-.01	-.06	.11	1.47	-.18	-1.25
Central City	-.05	-.82	-.00	-.03	-.03	-.27
Children	-.03	-1.68*	.04	2.43**	.15	4.92***
Age Head	-.001	-.64	.004	2.42**	-.000	-.18
Head Educ.	-.18	-8.38***	-.14	-7.21***	-.16	-4.56***
Intercept	4.22	30.93***	3.86	30.28***	4.21	17.81***
Number of Cases	5,437		5,942		1,402	

(Log(p/(1-p)/2+5)=Intercept +BX

* p= <.10 ** p= <.05 $$ * p=<.01

to live in overcrowded conditions. As in the other cities studied, the proportion of female heads and households with children among the vulnerable would suggest that these groups will increasingly be represented among the homeless.

NOTES

1. The overall poverty rate for the central cities in 1983 was 22.9 percent for Baltimore, 20.3 percent for Chicago, and 12.7 percent for Houston (U.S. Bureau of the Census, 1983). As will be discussed, blacks and Hispanics had much higher poverty rates than whites.

2. The rental vacancy rate in 1983 was 18.8 percent (*Annual Housing Survey*) and was still above 16 percent in 1988 (Barton Smith, 1988). In 1986, 25,602 foreclosures, 90 percent of which were residential, occurred. This was a 65 percent increase over 1985 and a 178 percent increase over 1980. (Feagin, 1988:262). Of these units only two HUD financed units have been made available to the homeless (Collier interview, 1989).

3. The cutoff for "high rates" of home ownership was 60 percent, and Houston has 60.9 percent. The rate of home ownership for blacks is 47.2 percent and for Hispanics, 43.4 percent (James, McCummings, and Tynan, 1984:198-99).

4. Sally Andrade (1988). The survey found that the East Texas shelter population (primarily Houston) was 29 percent female and 71 percent male and that 18 percent of shelter residents were children. The shelter population was 44 percent black and 10 percent Hispanic, a higher percentage of blacks and lower percentage of Hispanics than among Houston renters as a whole. The characteristics of shelter users may not accurately reflect those of the total homeless population. Women and children have been shown to be more likely to use shelters than men, and the mild climate may enable more homeless to avoid shelters. Thirty-seven percent of those surveyed were natives of Texas, while the average length of residents for the remainder was 8.4 years.

5. The effect on the local economy was reflected in the number of pounds of food distributed by the nonprofit Houston Food Bank, which increased from 268,000 pounds in 1982 to 3 million pounds just two years later (Feagin, 1988:260).

6. Andrade (1988). Fifteen percent of homeless Hispanic men and 9 percent of homeless Hispanic women reported that they were unable to work because they lacked an ID or documentation.

7. Philadelphia, the fifth largest city, has five times the number of public housing units (Feagin, 1988:263).

8. Ellie Collier, interview, 1989. The 1,000 units of the now boarded-up Allen Parkway Village public housing project have been the object of a bitter struggle that has recently resulted in the resignation of the director of the Housing Authority who supported demolition. The units were constructed during the 1940s as low-to-moderate-income housing in the formerly white fourth ward. The

now predominantly black and Asian settlement has "long been a cohesive black community with friendly neighborhoods, numerous churches, and black-owned businesses" (Feagin, 1988:249), much like the picture of Chicago black neighborhoods painted by William Julius Wilson before the exodus of the black middle class. One resident, in a letter to the *Houston Chronicle*, described the fourth ward as "a beautiful place, where neighbors actually know each other, kids play outside in the streets, older folks sit on their porches and chat with neighbors... and there's a warm feeling of community that's found almost nowhere else in Houston." (Feagin, 1988:249). Because of the proximity of Allen Parkway to the booming downtown, developers tried to legitimize the desire to bulldoze the community by labeling the area as "blighted," beyond redemption. Predominantly white absentee landlords allowed rental housing to deteriorate in anticipation of the new development. Public housing residents organized and the ACLU filed a suit on their behalf, claiming that the assessment that Allen Parkway could not be renovated was deliberately "overly bleak" and that the city had withheld 10 million dollars in federal rehabilitation money (ibid.). A federal judge has recently ordered that no federal funds can be used for demolition, which may ultimately force the renovation (Collier interview).

9. James, McCummings, and Tynan (1984) report that a proposal for 105 units of low-income housing in the predominantly white Westbury section of Southwest Houston was met with the protests, marches, and threatened legal action of 1,500 citizens and a proposed 80-unit development in the Spring Branch area was the object of intense political pressure.

10. Contract rent is the specified rent owed to the landlord, whereas gross rent includes the cost or estimated cost of utilities.

11. Figures supplied by Al Ballinger of the University of Houston Center for Public Policy, which produced the chart. Prices are inflated by the standard CPI rather than the CPI-XI.

12. Because of changes in the AHS data, "employed" refers to those heads who worked "last week" in 1976 and 1979 and to those heads who had any wage or salary income in 1983.

13. About 75 percent of those over 65 in Houston own their own homes (Gilderbloom, Rosentraub, and Bullard, 1987:24).

8

Seattle

SUMMARY

Seattle is a prospering metropolitan area that has made a considerable investment in providing affordable housing to its poor residents. Yet, among the four metropolitan areas identified as having a high rate of homeownership and a low percentage of minorities (see Table 3.7 in chapter 3), Seattle was estimated to have by far the highest per capita rate of homelessness. The 1984 HUD study reported a midpoint of the "most reliable range" of homeless persons per night of approximately 3,200, or 20 homeless per 10,000 persons. Seattle ranked seventh, just beyond Houston, in per capita homelessness among the 15 major metropolitan areas studied. This chapter examines the factors that may explain why homelessness exists to such an extent in an area that has not been faced with many of the problems found in Chicago, Baltimore, and Houston.

Compared with these SMSAs, Seattle has a smaller population in poverty, a housing stock with a smaller percentage of substandard units, and fewer overcrowded renter households than those of the other SMSAs studied. Yet, the crisis of affordability may affect the Seattle low-income renter as much as, if not more so, than the low-income renters in Houston, Baltimore, and Chicago because the mismatch between availability and affordability of low cost rental units in Seattle is very pronounced for units renting below $200 per month.

As in the other metropolitan areas studied, median gross rents in the Seattle SMSA rose well beyond the rate of inflation between 1976 and 1983. Although median incomes of low-income unsubsidized renters also increased, the median per person residual declined by 35 percent, in part because of increased family size among this segment. All three categories of vulnerability increased, and by 1983, nearly 15 percent of central Seattle renters, or about 17,000 households, were vulnerable to homelessness based on low income and excessive rent burden. The vulnerable households of Seattle, like those of Baltimore, Chicago, and Houston, disproportionately contain children and are female and/or minority-headed.

INTRODUCTION

The Seattle metropolitan area represents an important contrast to the other three areas studied. It is the only SMSA among the four with a low percentage of minority population and a high rate of homeownership,[1] and thus is an area in which we would predict that homelessness would be less prevalent, according to the hypothesized relationship between these factors. Yet the homeless population of Seattle is estimated to be larger on any given night than that of Baltimore. Seattle is now economically thriving, the "center of Pacific rim trade," and a city that has undergone such rapid expansion that voters have recently overwhelmingly passed a referendum limiting further growth in the downtown area (*New York Times*, May 18, 1989). A city of only 233,600 households, Seattle has more high-rise buildings than cities several times its size (National Public Radio, May 16, 1989). It has been described as "one of the hottest urban housing markets in the country".[2] Unemployment, at 4.8 percent, is below the national average, and Boeing, the major employer, has recovered from the employment slump it experienced earlier in the decade.[3] More building permits for residential construction were issued in 1987 than in any year since 1959, yet the vacancy rate for multifamily and single-family dwellings combined was only 2.6 percent.

EFFECTS OF REVITALIZATION AND DEVELOPMENT

The rapid development of Seattle was accompanied by a substantial restructuring of the urban landscape and displacement of the inner-city population. Downtown Seattle was the home of the original "Skid Road," named for the structure on which logs were skidded down to the sawmill for processing. The road was bordered by the inexpensive taverns and rooming houses that were patronized by loggers. Eventually, the term became an abbreviated reference to the district itself, with the term *skid row* "implying the bottom of a path of downward social mobility" or being on the "skids" (Miller, 1982).

Seattle, because of its port location and access by rail, had a larger skid row population than many cities of its size. As the city entered the prosperous 1960s, the interests of businesses and skid row residents increasingly came into conflict. Although much of the Seattle skid row district was ultimately restored and preserved rather than demolished (Miller, 1982), the loss of housing units that had been occupied by the poor, the unskilled, pensioners, and the disabled was dramatic. Between 1960 and 1981, the number of SROs fell by 15,000 (Hoch and Slayton, 1989). In one two-year period from 1970 to 1972, 40 hotels and buildings in the skid row and surrounding area were demolished, eliminating 2,732 housing units (Miller, 1982). There was little evidence that the demolition of skid row was due to any decline in the size of the population who had lived there (Bahr and Caplow, 1974). Thus, the "revitalization" of the skid row area and other Seattle neighborhoods resulted in considerable displacement of the low-income population.

A study by the Seattle Office of Policy Planning (1979) found that 7 percent of all households in the city moved at least once because of displacement in the 1973 to 1978 period and nearly half of all elderly in the study had been displaced from their previous residences. Displacement can, of course, have its cause in other than the demolition of the housing unit. Rent increases beyond what is affordable to the tenant and sale of the housing unit to another owner are also frequent causes for a forced move by renters. Lee (1978) found that in a sample of skid row residents that excluded those whose housing units were closed, 24 percent of those he surveyed in 1975 were "unexpected movers" in the following year. While Lee did not determine what motivated these unanticipated moves, he attributed them to "pushes which skid row dwellers and other powerless people find difficult to resist" (ibid.:198). A study of displacement in two "revitalizing" Seattle neighborhoods, which were close to the downtown but did not include skid row, found that 23 percent of all renters who moved between 1979 and 1980 were displaced, about half because of unaffordable rent increases. Most of those displaced had low incomes and were forced to pay higher rents in their new location.[4]

HOMELESSNESS IN SEATTLE

It is impossible to determine in any of these studies whether homelessness resulted from displacement for some of these residents, but in Seattle, the growth of homelessness is concurrent with the "re-vitalization" of the city. One piece of evidence of the growing problem of homelessness and increasing need for emergency shelter is seen in the level and source of funding for services. Seattle, like most large cities, has long had a Salvation Army and Union Gospel mission serving primarily indigent men. The city of Seattle did not begin funding shelters until 1978 and quickly became the single largest source of revenue for the emergency shelters in King County. King County itself began funding emergency shelters in 1982 (Seattle–King County Emergency Shelter Study Update, 1986). Statistics com-piled by the Emergency Housing Coalition show a fourfold increase between 1982 and 1983 in the numbers of homeless served in a one-month period. Only 34 percent of total demand for shelter was met in 1983. In spite of a rapidly expanding network of shelters, primarily for women and families with children, the majority of those requesting shelter were turned away for lack of space, and households with children were twice as likely to be turned away as single adults (Seattle–King County Emergency Shelter Study Update, 1986).

THE SEATTLE HOUSING ENVIRONMENT

The population of Seattle has continued to experience rapid growth since the most recent data of the present study were collected. It is informative to examine what has occurred since 1983 and how these factors may have contributed to a continuing high rate of homelessness.

Data provided by the city of Seattle indicate that, since 1983, in-creases in rent have continued to outstrip both the growth in the consumer price index (CPI) and the rising cost of owned housing. Between 1983 and 1988, rents increased by 35 percent, while home prices and the median income both rose by 18 percent, and the CPI grew by only 10 percent (Seattle 1989 Housing Assistance Plan).

Unlike the city of Houston, which historically has not aggressively pursued federal funds for low-income housing nor initiated local referendums to provide housing for the disadvantaged, the city of Seattle has had a long-standing commitment to house the poor, has actively sought the federal housing monies to which it was entitled, and has increasingly taken responsibility locally for raising the money to meet the demand for affordable housing as federal funds have dim-inished (Seattle 1989-90 Overall Housing Development Plan, 1988). The active role that the city has taken may have prevented the problem of homelessness from growing substantially worse since the HUD estimate was made in 1983. The State Department of Community Development reports that King County has approximately 3,400 homeless on any given

night, about 45 percent of the state total (Washington State Department of Community Development, 1989). This represents an increase
of less than 200 from the midpoint of the HUD estimate made in 1983.

The city is reportedly one of the best in the country in terms of its
progressive housing policies (McIntire interview). A lack of affordable housing has been identified by the city as the primary reason
for the substantial numbers of homeless in Seattle.[5] Since 1982, voters
in the city of Seattle have approved $100 million in local housing
initiatives. Principal among these is a $50-million housing levy that
will produce 1,000 low-cost rental housing units by 1994. At least half
of these units are to be affordable to households at 30 percent or less
of the median income, and the remaining are for households earning
between 30 and 50 percent of median income.[6] In response to a housing needs assessment indicating that the longest wait for public or
subsidized housing is for the largest units, the present number of units
with three or more bedrooms will be increased by 15 percent.[7] The
levy initiative will join an existing program in preserving low-cost
downtown housing and in building new SROs to replace those that
have been lost to development.[8] The city housing authority has been
said to have very different concerns from those of the SMSA and the
state and to place a much higher priority upon providing housing for
the poor (McIntire interview). The state of Washington was, on the
other hand, the 48th in the nation to pass a law authorizing a state
housing finance agency.

HOUSING AND THE LOW-INCOME POPULATION

The central-city poverty rate for Seattle was 11.2 percent in 1982,
second only to Phoenix as the lowest poverty rate among the 18 cities
discussed in Chapter 3 (U.S. Bureau of the Census, 1983). The poverty
rate among female heads in Seattle, at 20.7 percent, was the lowest
among all of the cities included in the study and about half of the
percentage of female heads in poverty in Baltimore and Chicago. The
city estimated that in 1988 there were 32,000 households, or about 25
percent of all renters, below 80 percent of the median income who pay
more than 30 percent of their income to rent.[9] It should be noted that
the households with incomes below 125 percent of the poverty line,
as adjusted by the CPI-XI, who are considered low income in this
study would be considered very low income according to the city
housing needs assessment. A family of four by this criteria would have
an income below $12,700 1986 dollars, placing it at 33 percent of the
median income. The city assessment concluded that households that
have at least 50 percent of the median income should be able to afford

housing on the market. Those below 50 percent would not be able to stay within suggested income guidelines. The city of Seattle uses 35 percent of income as its affordability criterion, a percentage that seems unrealistically high for poor households.

Availability of affordable housing must be gauged in relation to the income of poor renters. Public assistance recipients represented only 3 percent of the 1.4 million people in King County, but public assistance payments in Seattle have been eroded relative to median income and now average only 18 to 24 percent of the median income, or 60 to 68 percent of the official poverty line. It has been estimated that an AFDC recipient would need to pay as much as 99 percent of income to rent the average one-bedroom apartment in Seattle. Similarly, 97 percent of an average General Assistance income would be required to rent the typical studio or SRO apartment.[10]

Seattle data provide a good example of the difficulty encountered in trying to estimate the supply of low-cost housing available to the low-income population. A study by the Office of Management and Budget found that there were about 18,000 families with children or with a disabled member who had incomes below 125 percent of poverty. Of these, only 3,000 were living in Seattle Housing Authority units, leaving 83 percent of these households to compete in the open market with higher-income renters and with each other for the very limited stock of low-cost housing. We know that the existing inexpensive housing is not exclusively occupied by the poor. A 1983 HUD study indicated that only 54 percent of identified low-cost units were occupied by low-income people (Seattle Human Services Strategic Planning Office, 1989:14). Although there is likely to be a floor of housing quality below which higher-income renters will not seek housing, a rise in rent may compel these households to try to maintain a stable ratio of income spent on rent by reducing their housing aspirations. Similarly, a growth in the size of the low-income population, in the absence of any increase in housing that is affordable to these renters, will increase competition and hence rent for these low-income renters.

Seattle does have a much higher per capita availability of housing subsidization than exists in Houston. In 1988 there were 18,680 public or assisted rental housing units in Seattle.[11] About 11 percent of all renters in central Seattle live in public or subsidized housing, as compared with 6 percent of central Houston renters. The city estimates, however, that over 4,000 privately owned subsidized units are at risk of being withdrawn from the subsidized stock within the next 20 years as their terms of commitment to low-rent expire (*Seattle's 1989 Housing Assistance Plan,* 1988:67). Even public and subsidized housing units are not exclusively occupied by the very poor (Salins, 1987).

DEMOGRAPHIC CHARACTERISTICS OF SEATTLE RENTERS

The minority population of Seattle is considerably smaller than that of Baltimore, Chicago, and Houston, but as with the other metropolitan areas, it is concentrated in the central city. The 1980 census showed that in the SMSA as a whole, 88 percent of households were white. In 1983, 77 percent of renters within the central city and 94 percent of those outside the central city were white. Blacks constitute the major minority group, and there is a substantial and growing Asian population, as well as smaller Hispanic and American Indian components. Fifty percent of the central-city school district's students are nonwhite (McIntire interview), indicating that the proportion of the city that is minority is likely to continue to increase rapidly in the coming years. Because of the concentration of minorities as well as the homeless in the central city, the present analysis will examine the central city of Seattle separately and in more depth.[12]

Demographic characteristics of renters within and outside of the central city are presented in Table 8.1. Statistically significant changes over time include increases in the proportion never married, increases in female and black heads of households, decreases in the proportion of heads under the age of 25, and increasing levels of employment.

Compared to the other SMSAs studied, Seattle renters have much higher levels of education. Fifty percent of renters both within and outside of the central city had education beyond high school. Seattle has the smallest mean household size among the four cities and one of the smallest in the nation. This remained stable, with half of all central-city renter households consisting of a single person. At 38 percent, Seattle ranked with Minneapolis and just below Washington, D.C., and San Francisco in the percentage of single-person central-city households (including homeowners) in 1983 (See Table 3.5).

RELATIONSHIP OF INCOME AND RENT

Median income of Seattle renters grew moderately between 1976 and 1983, but rents increased far more rapidly, with most of the growth during the period covered by this study occurring between 1976 and 1979. While median incomes grew by 5 to 8 percent beyond the rate of inflation, median rents rose by 17 to 25 percent, outside of and within the central city, respectively. Median income of city renters was about half of the median income of all central-city households and that of suburban renters was about two-thirds of all suburban households. In both areas incomes increased about $2,000 between 1976 and 1979 and then fell by more than $1,000 between 1979 and

Table 8.1
Demographic Characteristics of Seattle Renters, 1976, 1979, 1983

Variables	Outside Central City			Inside Central City		
	1976	1979	1983	1976	1979	1983
Total Renter Households						
Number	97,617	119,888	140,978	103,500	112,800	117,200
Percent <125% Poverty	16.6	14.1	17.5	21.3	19.8	23.9
Race (in percents)						
Non-Hispanic White	94.9	93.8	93.3	84.1	80.3	77.4
Black	1.3	1.5	1.6	8.9	9.7	11.4
Hispanic	1.2	1.8	1.1	1.9	2.1	2.4
Other	2.5	2.9	4.0	5.1	7.9	8.8
Marital Status (in percents)						
Married	44.0	41.2	39.5	27.7	23.8	26.2
Widowed	8.7	7.1	5.9	12.6	11.0	10.1
Divorced	19.1	20.1	23.0	20.1	19.4	19.1
Separated	4.7	4.1	4.7	4.0	4.3	4.5
Never married	23.6	27.6	27.0	35.6	41.6	40.0
Sex of Head (in percents)						
Male	67.1	69.1	63.3	56.7	56.6	53.2
Female	32.9	30.9	36.7	43.3	43.4	46.8
Age, Education, and Employment of Head						
% 17–24	24.0	24.5	18.3	21.1	21.8	15.5
% 25–39	42.8	46.2	53.1	37.5	41.9	48.7
% 40–64	22.7	19.8	21.6	22.7	20.2	19.6
% 65+	10.5	9.5	7.1	18.4	16.1	16.1
Mean Age	37.7	36.9	36.3	41.3	40.0	40.1
% Dropout	18.3	15.2	12.9	20.0	16.6	18.7
% Beyond H.S.	43.4	45.5	50.1	51.4	54.4	51.9
% Head Employed	71.5	79.3	80.3	57.3	66.6	67.1
Household Composition						
Tot. H.H. Mem.	2.3	2.3	2.3	1.8	1.8	1.9
% Large Family	3.1	2.1	3.7	1.3	1.2	2.3
% One Person	33.9	31.6	31.9	50.5	51.0	50.7
Mean No. children	.68	.62	.69	.36	.33	.39
% Subfamily	.6	.5	1.1	.3	.4	.6
Income and Rent in Constant 1986 Dollars						
Med. Income	$21,208	$23,490	$22,361	$15,166	$17,595	$16,326
Med. Per Capita	$10,481	$11,730	$11,001	$9,141	10,330	$10,176
$Welfare	9.8	7.1	7.2	12.4	9.8	10.6
Med. Rent	$356	$417	$418	$285	$333	$357
Med. Rent.Inc. Ratio	20	24	23	23	25	26
% Public Housing	4.1	3.6	2.9	7.6	7.3	6.2
% Subsidized	1.5	1.8	2.4	2.3	2.0	4.7

1983. The median rent-to-income ratio increased by 3 percentage points both within and outside the central city during this period, but to a higher level in the central city.

Contrasting the proportion of income spent on rent by all renters with that spent by low-income unsubsidized renters, Figure 8.1 shows that a higher percentage of Seattle renters overall paid more than 30 percent of income to rent than did renters in Chicago, Baltimore, and Houston. Among low-income renters, however, the pattern is very similar in all cities studied. More than 85 percent exceeded federal affordability guidelines, and well over half paid more than 60 percent of income to rent. The percentage of low-income Seattle renters who pay more than 45 percent of income to rent is equivalent to that of Chicago, but the percentage who pay in excess of 60 percent in Seattle is significantly less than in Chicago.

The mismatch between the cost of units occupied by the low-income population who do not receive a housing subsidy and the rent that would be affordable for these renters at 30 percent of income is shown in Figure 8.2. As was the case in Houston, in 1983 there were no low-income unsubsidized renters occupying units renting for less than $50, although in Seattle about 2,000 households had incomes for which this would have been an affordable rent. Similarly, there was no demand (based on income) among the low-income population for units renting above $350 per month, yet this was the

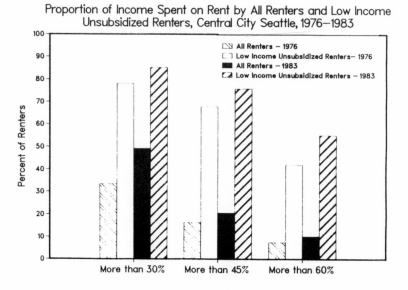

Proportion of Income Spent on Rent by All Renters and Low Income Unsubsidized Renters, Central City Seattle, 1976–1983

Figure 8.1

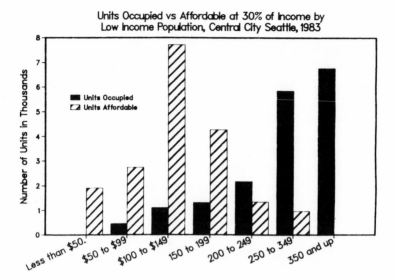

Figure 8.2

modal category for units occupied by these renters. The most striking discrepancy between affordable units and occupied units occurs for units with rents between $100 and $150 per month, where the ratio of affordability to availability is about eight to one.

The excess of demand, based on 30 percent of income, to supply for the period 1976 to 1983 is shown in Figure 8.3. Here it can be seen that the mismatch has worsened over time. About 14,000 low-income households who could afford only units renting for less than $200 per month were occupying more expensive units. This does not represent the entire population of those in need of housing subsidy, but is an indication of those most in need.

HOUSING STOCK AND HOUSING DEPRIVATION

Seattle's aggressive housing policies have been successful in reducing the total percentage of units that are inadequate or severely inadequate according to the guidelines suggested by HUD (see Appendixes A and B). As Table 8.2 shows, the percentage of all units that were in either category within the central city fell from 14 percent in 1976 to 11.5 percent in 1983. Outside the central city, the percentage of substandard units fell from 6 to 4 percent. These figures show that a smaller percentage of the total Seattle stock was inadequate or severe-

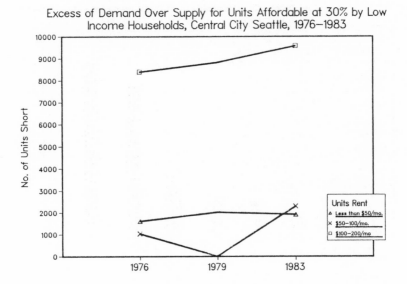

Figure 8.3

ly inadequate than was the case in Baltimore and Chicago. The Seattle
central city figures were only slightly lower than those of Houston (if
inadequate heat in Houston is excluded), but outside the central city
there was a considerably smaller percentage of substandard housing
than in suburban Houston. The percentage of units that were substandard in Baltimore and Chicago, 20 percent and 16 percent respectively,
remained constant, even as the number of central-city housing units
declined in those cities. In contrast, the percentage reduction of substandard units in the growing Seattle central city was sufficient to
result in slightly fewer units being of low quality. There has also been
a decline in the percentage of boarded-up units on the street, as
observed by the interviewer.

Figure 8.4 shows that the increase in the proportion of households that
experienced one or more forms of housing deprivation in the Seattle city
was almost entirely due to an increase in the proportion of renters who
were cost-burdened. As in Houston, about 45 percent of all renters were
free of any of the three forms of housing distress, in comparison with 38
percent of renters in both Chicago and Baltimore. In contrast to Houston,
however, crowding is rarely a problem in Seattle, which has one of the
lowest levels of housing density among all major metropolitan areas.
Only 2.7 percent of renters have an average of more than one person per
room. This may be predominantly related to the prevalence of single-
person households in Seattle, as noted above. Ten percent of Seattle

Table 8.2
Percent Rental Housing Stock with Inadequacies and Severe Inadequacies: Seattle

Type of Inadequacy	Outside Central City			Inside Central City		
	1976	1979	1983	1976	1979	1983
Severely inad. plumbing	.4	1.7	.4	4.1	4.4	2.7
Inad. structure	2.1	2.5	1.9	3.2	2.5	2.5
Severe inad. structure	.1	.4	.1	.3	.4	0
Inad. public hall	1	.1	.1	.3	.2	.4
Inad. heat	.4	.6	.2	.8	.7	.7
Severely inad. heat	1.1	1.8	.3	1.7	1.3	.7
Inad. electric	.1	0	0	.1	.1	0
Inad. sewer	.1	.4	.1	.3	.3	.1
Severe inad. sewer	1.9	1.7	1.0	1.3	1 6	2.6
Inad. kitchen	.5	.7	.2	2.8	2.6	1.9
1 or more inadequacies	3.1	4.0	2.3	7.2	6.1	5.4
1 or more severe inad.	3.3	4.1	1.6	6.9	7.3	6.1
Boarded up units on street	7.7	5.9	3.6	9.9	8.0	7.2
Number inad. units	2,753	4,072	2,950	7,407	7,179	6,303
Number severe inad.	2,719	4,094	1,994	7,124	8,581	7,190

renters had two or more housing problems, primarily a combination of high-cost and low-quality housing.

The residual income of low-income Seattle renter households declined over time (see Figure 8.5), but remained considerably above that of Baltimore, Houston, and Chicago renters. Although median monthly income grew by 13 percent between 1976 and 1983, rents increased by 24 percent over the same period. The household residual declined from $172 to $150 per month, while the per person residual declined from $135 to $87 per month, reflecting an increased household size among this low-income population.

THE VULNERABLE

By all three measures of vulnerability, the population at risk increased over time. Figure 8.6 shows a decline between 1976 and 1979 in the percentage of all renters who had low incomes and paid more

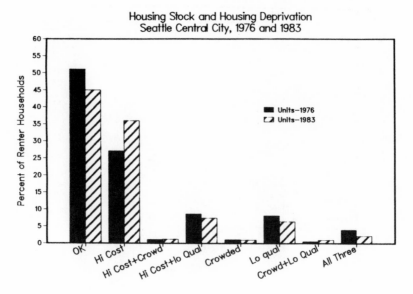

Figure 8.4

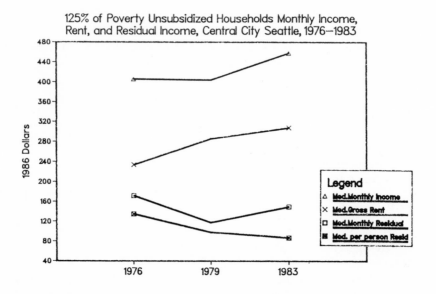

Figure 8.5

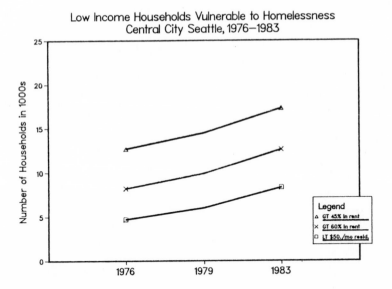

Low Income Households Vulnerable to Homelessness
Central City Seattle, 1976–1983

Figure 8.6

than 45 percent of income to rent, but by 1983, 17,300 renters inside the central city, as well as 12,700 outside the central city (not shown), could be considered at risk. For the entire SMSA, this represents an increase of 50 percent, or 10,000 renter households, over 1976. Of the 18,950 low-income unsubsidized renter households in the central city in 1983, 76 percent paid more than 45 percent of their incomes to rent, and 55 percent (the very vulnerable) paid more than 60 percent. The percentage of renters at risk in the latter category increased from 8 to 11 percent in the central city. Those who had less than 50 dollars per month per person remaining in residual income after rent was paid (the severely vulnerable) increased from 4.5 to 7 percent. Of all those at risk, 73 percent were very vulnerable and 48 percent were severely vulnerable. As a percentage of the total population, there were somewhat more households at risk in Seattle than in Houston or Baltimore. Increase in the population at risk parallels what has taken place in Houston, which also has had significant increases across all three categories, in contrast to Baltimore, where growth has occurred primarily among the severely vulnerable.

Median gross rents among all three categories of Seattle's vulnerable were higher than in Houston, even though central-city median rent in Seattle for all renters was substantially lower than in Houston ($54 less in 1983). This indicates that the low-income Seattle renter may have even less access to affordable housing than does the Houston renter. That this may be the case is supported by Figure 8.2. A very large affordability gap exists in Seattle, especially for units renting between $100 and $200 dollars per month. The modal rent of low-income unsubsidized renters in Houston fell between $200 to $250 dollars per month, whereas in Seattle, the modal category of these renters, as previously noted, was in excess of $350 per month.

LOGIT MODEL OF VULNERABILITY

Between 30 and 44 percent of the three categories of vulnerable households in Seattle contained children. Although this is a smaller percentage of vulnerable households with children than was found in the other three cities, a logit model of vulnerability (Table 8.3) for the Seattle SMSA residents shows a pattern similar to that found elsewhere. The association between children and vulnerability, which was negative in 1976, becomes positive and significant over time. This relationship has now been found in all four SMSAs and thus is evidence that the increasing representation of children among the homeless is being driven by the severe economic vulnerability among low-income renter households. It also may indicate that we will continue to see an increase in the proportion of homeless who are families with children.

Central-city Seattle residents are significantly more vulnerable, as are younger heads, females, and those living in substandard housing. Blacks were not significantly more vulnerable in 1983 than they were in 1976 and 1979, although the percentage of vulnerable who were black grew in all three categories.

In Figure 8.7, the characteristics of the very vulnerable, those paying more than 60 percent of income to rent, are compared with those of all renters. In all categories, the contrasts are not as pronounced between the two groups in Seattle as they are in Houston, but all are in the same direction. The very vulnerable in Seattle are less likely to be crowded or live in substandard housing than are their Houston counterparts. They are far less likely to be married or to have children.

Consistent with previous findings in the other three cities, females are seen to be disproportionately represented among the vulnerable in Seattle. While the percentage of all renter heads who were female increased in the central city from 43 to 47 percent between 1976 and 1983, the percentage of female heads among the three categories of vulnerability fell slightly over this period, but ranged from 55 to 60 percent.

Table 8.3
Logit Models of Homeless Vulnerability for Seattle SMSA

Variable	1976		1979		1983	
	coef.	t	coef.	t	coef.	t
Inadequate	.18	2.34**	.24	3.27***	.26	1.94*
Female Head	.64	12.03***	.46	9.04***	.36	4.42***
Black Head	.16	1.75*	.22	2.48**	.14	1.06
Children	.04	1.34	.10	3.76***	.15	4.13***
Central City	.22	3.94***	.18	3.39***	.26	3.11***
Head Age	-.004	-2.62***	-.00	-.15	-.005	-2.13**
Head Educ	-.14	-6.75***	-.16	-7.83***	-.19	-6.26***
Intercept	3.94	36.27***	4.05	37.66***	4.36	28.02***
Number of Cases	4,469		5,175		1,645	

(Log(p/(1-p)/2+5)=Intercept +BX

* p=<.10   ** p=<.05   *** p=<.01

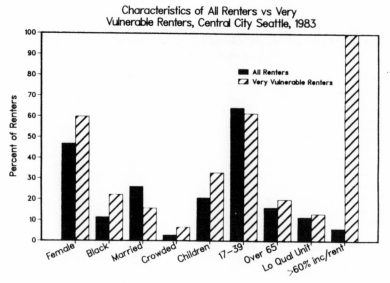

Figure 8.7

The age distribution of those at risk did not vary significantly from that of renters overall. Among very vulnerable renters, the percentage who were over 65 was considerably higher in Seattle than in Houston, but this was also true of renters in general. Per capita income was higher in Seattle among the very vulnerable than in Houston, and a significantly higher proportion of these very low-income households received welfare, probably indicative of more permissive welfare eligibility criteria in Seattle.

COMPARISON OF THE VERY VULNERABLE WITH LOW-INCOME LESS AT RISK

I have argued that vulnerability to homelessness does not simply identify poor or low-income households but distinguishes these renters from other low-income renters who do not share such high rent burdens. What sets very vulnerable renters apart in Seattle is shown in Table 8.4. Over time vulnerable households were less likely to contain a single person and more likely to contain children than less vulnerable households. Mean number of children in the very vulnerable households more than doubled. Although there were small increases in median income for all three groups, median per capita income fell for both the vulnerable and the less at risk. The percent

Table 8.4
Comparison of the Very Vulnerable with the Low Income Less at Risk Population, Central City Seattle

Variables	Low Inc. >60% in Rent		LT $50.00 Residual Income		Low Inc. <45% in Rent	
	1976	1983	1976	1983	1976	1983
Number of Households	8,172	12,667	4,675	8,302	9,458	11,213
% of Renter Households	7.9	10.6	4.5	7.0	9.1	9.4
Characteristics of Household Head (in percents)						
Married	14.3	15.8	16.6	23.9	18.6	13.8
Widowed	19.5	16.7	12.8	6.8	24.6	20.4
Divorced	20.6	18.3	19.3	25.6	26.2	29.4
Separated	10.0	7.6	9.1	8.3	6.3	10.5
Never Married	35.6	41.5	42.1	35.4	24.2	26.0
Age Head 17–24	25.7	15.8	28.1	17.6	11.4	8.6
Age Head 25–39	26.8	45.7	33.5	53.4	19.5	34.9
Age Head 40–64	21.1	18.5	23.2	22.2	30.5	20.0
Age Head >65	26.3	20.0	15.2	6.8	38.7	36.5
Female Head	64.5	59.8	58.3	54.7	49.0	61.4
White Head	76.5	63.3	72.2	58.7	70.3	63.1
Black Head	14.4	22.3	16.1	26.2	17.7	21.7
Hispanic	2.9	1.1	3.3	1.7	2.1	1.3
H.S. Dropout	35.5	35.4	30.9	32.5	42.9	43.9
Beyond H.S.	34.3	39.3	40.5	37.5	30.1	28.6
Employed	29.9	42.3	32.0	39.3	16.9	20.9
Characteristics of Family						
Mean H.H. Mem.	1.5	2.2	1.7	2.5	1.7	2.0
% Large Family	1.3	6.4	2.4	9.8	3.4	4.0
% One Person	65.0	50.4	59.2	40.9	66.8	55.9
Mean No.Children	.28	.74	.45	1.10	.51	.59
% w. Children	19.7	33.0	21.6	44.3	22.4	29.8
% Subfamily	0	0	.8	0	.4	1.3
Income (in constant 1986 dollars)						
Med. Income	$4204	$4928	$3042	$44125	$5219	$5245
Med. Per Capita	$2909	$2875	$1828	$1752	$4260	$3643
% Pov. Gap > $5000	3.7	9.8	9.2	20.1	2.9	3.9
% Welfare	25.1	30.5	26.0	30.3	31.4	37.6
Characteristics of Housing						
% >1 Persons per Room	1.4	4.3	3.3	6.6	2.9	8.9
% Inadequate Unit	12.0	6.5	14.4	1.8	13.5	5.4
% Severe Inad.	7.8	6.6	11.2	4.6	19.7	11.4
% Public Housing	2.4	9.8	3.4	8.5	34.2	41.0
% Subsidized	1.9	12.0	1.8	9.8	10.0	16.6
Med Gross Rent	$282	$363	$313	$374	$119	$124

receiving welfare increased for all three groups, as did the percent with a poverty gap of more than $5,000. Twenty percent of severely vulnerable households were more than $5,000 below the poverty line.

In spite of the lack of association between age and vulnerability in the logit model, 61 to 71 percent of the very and severely vulnerable were under age 40, as compared with 43 percent of the less at risk. Thirty-seven percent of the low-income less at risk were over the age of 65. It can be seen that the majority of the low-income population of Seattle, including those at high risk and those less at risk, were females. In spite of much higher levels of education over time across all three categories, the percentages employed were significantly smaller in the later period.

The less at risk were seen to pay rents that were only about one-third as large as those of the at-risk groups, although they were about twice as likely to live in severely inadequate or overcrowded housing, as well. Forty-seven percent of the low-income less at risk lived in public or subsidized housing and were therefore protected from extreme rent burdens. This figure places Seattle about midway between Baltimore (66 percent) and Houston (25 percent) in the percentage of less vulnerable renters who receive a subsidy.

Note that 6 to 9 percent of the vulnerable and less vulnerable populations in 1976 and 13 to 14 percent of these populations in 1983 were the omitted category by race. Thus we can presume on the basis of the Seattle census data that the percentages of low-income vulnerable and less vulnerable who are Asians and American Indians has increased, although the exact representation of these two ethnic groups among the vulnerable cannot be determined. About 2 percent of the central-city population in 1980 was American Indian and 8 percent were Asian. The representation of these two groups among the low-income population (those with incomes under $10,000 in 1980) was proportional. Since 1981, the city of Seattle has become home to about 15,000 Asian refugees, most of whom have low incomes (*Seattle's 1989 Housing Assistance Plan*). There is also a substantial Japanese population, most of whom do not have low incomes.

COMPARING THE HOMELESS OF SEATTLE WITH VULNERABLE RENTERS

Reasonably good data exist on the sheltered homeless population of Seattle, based on statistics collected via a standardized reporting form and automated data base in use at 20 out of the 28 shelters that are funded by the city. The data will underrepresent, according to the city report, the substantial numbers, estimated to be as high as 2,000, of homeless youth in the city. Seattle has become a mecca of sorts for runaway youth, many from other parts of the country. The only youth included in the study are those 18-to-21-year-olds who receive shelter in the adult facilities (Seattle Human Services Strategic Planning Office, 1989). Furthermore, because the data do not include a random sample of street dwelling homeless, they will not accurately represent the demographic characteristics of all Seattle homeless. Nevertheless, it is useful to compare the makeup of the sheltered population with those who may be at risk of becoming homeless.

Ideally, one would like to compare the population at risk in 1983 with those who became homeless in 1983 or 1984. However, reliable data on the demographic characteristics of the homeless do not exist for the earlier years. Table 8.5 compares the demographic characteristics of those sheltered in 1988 with the characteristics of severely vulnerable Seattle renters, as identified in the 1983 AHS. In 1983, 8,300 central-city Seattle households were identified in this study as severely at risk on the basis of having less than $50 per person per month remaining in residual income after rent was paid.

Some of the similarities to be noted between this high-risk population and the sheltered homeless include the percentage of blacks among the two groups. Thirty percent of the Seattle sheltered homeless were black, and 26 percent of the severely vulnerable were black. As in Baltimore and Houston, blacks were disproportionately represented among both the homeless and the vulnerable, since the percentage of blacks among all central-city Seattle renters was only 11 percent. Hispanics were found to be overrepresented among the identified homeless, but not among the severely vulnerable. The percentage of all central-city renters who were Hispanic was 2.4 percent in 1983, compared with 12 percent of the sheltered homeless in 1988. Since 1983, not only has the proportion of the population that is Hispanic increased, but also, as in Houston, unemployment among Hispanic undocumented aliens has risen. The city of Seattle reports that, as a result of the change in immigration laws, employers are more wary of hiring such workers, and thus the percentage of Hispanics in poverty and at risk of homelessness can be expected to have increased.

The race or ethnic background of the "other" category was not determined from the AHS data, but the Seattle homeless were found to include a substantial (9 percent) American Indian population and a smaller percentage of Asian homeless (2 percent) than would be proportional to the representation of Asians among renters. As has been previously noted for New York City, Asians are rarely found to be homeless, a fact that has been attributed to the greater tolerance among Asians for high-density living and doubling up (Bardy interview, 1988).

Table 8.5
Composition of Severely Vulnerable Seattle Renters as Compared with Seattle Sheltered Homeless Population

Variable Percent	Severely Vulnerable Renters[a]	Sheltered Homeless[b]
% White	59	46
% Black	26	30
% Hispanic	2	12
% Other[c]	13	12
% Female heads	55	30
% With children	44	37
% One person	41	60
% Age 17–25	18	17
% Age 25–44	57	61
% Age 45–59	12	17
% Age 60+	13	4
% Welfare[d]	30	35

[a]Severely vulnerable renters are those with less than $50 per person per month in residual income remaining after rent in 1983 as identified in the AHS.

[b]Based on those sheltered at 20 of the 28 Seattle shelters in 1988.

[c]Others sheltered were 9 percent Native American, 2 percent Asian, and 1 percent unidentified.

[d]Welfare recipients among the 668 families sheltered. Half of all sheltered clients were thought to be eligible for public assistance.

The ages of Seattle's homeless population were strikingly similar to those at high risk below the age of 44. The shelter figures indicate that only 4 percent of Seattle homeless were over the age of 60, a figure consistent with national trends. As previously noted, the percentage of those who are vulnerable above the age of 60 may have declined in recent years as a result of Seattle's subsidized housing program for the elderly. In 1981, Seattle voters approved $48 million for elderly and handicapped housing. Currently, 1,200 units have been built under this program since the 1983 survey was completed.

The number of homeless who were single adults in Seattle was found to be stable in the 1986 to 1987 period. However, the proportion of those homeless who were in families increased by 8 percent in 1987, and the number of "bednights" in family shelters increased 16 percent, indicating that part of the increase was due to larger family size among the homeless. Increasing family size was also found among the vulnerable, but not among renters in general. Female-headed families with an average of 2.2 children constituted 20 percent of those sheltered. The percentage of sheltered children under the age of five increased by 13 percent from the year before (Seattle Human Services Strategic Planning Office, 1989). The total bed capacity of 1,500 in the city of Seattle was inadequate to meet demand, and many homeless were turned away for lack of space. This problem was especially severe for single women and family units (ibid.:28). Recall that among the vulnerable, the percentage of families with children doubled between 1976 and 1983.

The city of Seattle provides about 40 percent of the budget of 21 Seattle shelters, more than any other segment of the economy. Its financial commitment has increased by 265 percent over the last five years as demand for services, particularly from women and children, has continued to grow. New shelters continued to open, including a 28-bed facility for women and children during 1988. The population of single homeless has stabilized in Seattle, while the numbers of Seattle's homeless families have continued to grow. How does the current picture of homelessness in Seattle as a growing phenomenon demanding a greater share of resources fit with the finding that per capita homelessness in Seattle has increased little over the HUD estimate? There are at least two possible explanations. First, and most likely, is that the 1983 HUD report overestimated the extent of homelessness in Seattle and that homelessness has indeed increased. Secondly, the size of the homeless population may have grown moderately but its composition may have changed dramatically in favor of women and children. The community may be more responsive to the demands of this more vulnerable population than it has been to single males.

CONCLUSION

The city of Seattle has made a greater investment in low-income housing than the other cities examined here. In part, this may be a reflection of the prosperity of Seattle relative to the other metropolitan areas. In part, it also seems to reflect a progressive attitude on the part of the city government and voters.

Because of these efforts, the case of Seattle effectively illustrates the inability of even a prosperous and resourceful community to fully compensate for the withdrawal of federal funds from housing and income programs. For example, the recently passed levy in Seattle will provide $6.25 million per year in local funds for eight years, whereas the federal housing contribution had been $42 million in 1979 alone. By 1985 the federal input had declined to only $5 million (*Seattle 1989-1990 Overall Housing Development Plan*, 1988.)

Whereas Houston has only a few private nonprofit organizations involved in providing low-cost housing, Seattle has many such organizations. The state of Washington also is more involved in housing than is Texas. The detrimental effect that the withdrawal of federal housing funds has had on the area is discussed in both the housing development plan and the study of homelessness in Seattle. The combination of state, local, and private sources cannot meet the needs of low-income households in Seattle, a city in which the pressure of market demand for housing is much greater than in Houston.

The case of Seattle most clearly points out that provision of affordable housing is appropriately a federal responsibility, even in the age of "new federalism." Only the federal government has the redistributive power to tackle a problem as severe and intractable as the mismatch between what the low-income population can afford and what is available to it in the market.

NOTES

1. In the Seattle SMSA, 63 percent of households were home owners in 1980, while in the city of Seattle, 49 percent of all units were owner occupied, 47 percent were renter occupied, and 3 percent were vacant. It is estimated that renters are now in the majority in the central city (*Seattle's 1989 Housing Assistance Plan*, 1988).

2. This paragraph draws on a conversation with Jim McIntire, Institute for Public Policy and Management of the University of Washington at Seattle, and author of a housing needs assessment for downtown Seattle.

3. The U.S. Bureau of Labor Statistics reported an unemployment rate in 1982 of 8.2 percent for Seattle SMSA and 10.9 percent for the central city.

4. M. Schill and R. Nathan (1983) studied a total of nine neighborhoods in five cities, including Seattle. On average, 50 percent of those displaced had incomes of less than $10,000. Displaced renters had an average increase in rent of 19 percent following the move, a substantial one-year increase.

5. Seattle Human Services Strategic Planning Office, 1989. Although the low vacancy rate might suggest an actual shortage of housing units, this does not seem to be the case except for the relatively rare large family. Only about 3 percent of all renter households contained more than 5 members (see Table 8.1).

6. Median family income was $38,200 in 1988 (*Seattle's 1989 Housing Assistance Plan*). A one-person household with income of less than $8,200 is below 30 percent of median income, while an income of $13,370 would be below 50 percent of median income.

7. Waiting periods for public housing are considerably shorter in Seattle than in the other cities studied and vary from five months for a one-bedroom apartment to two years for a four-bedroom. Only 16.5 percent of all Seattle Housing Authority units currently have three or more bedrooms, and 57 percent are targeted for elderly and handicapped renters (*Seattle's 1989 Housing Assistance Plan*).

8. An estimated 500 additional SROs were demolished in the past several years. Attempts by the city Housing Preservation Office to require replacement by developers was recently overturned by the Supreme Court (Jim McIntire interview).

9. These estimates are based on the 1980 census and are reported in the 1989 Housing Assistance Plan. Eighty percent of median income would be $30,560 in 1988. The present study indicates that the city probably underestimates the rent burden and overestimates the income of renters. Forty percent of all renters, even in 1983, paid more than 30 percent of income to rent, and median central-city incomes were about half of the median income overall.

10. *Seattle's 1989 Housing Assistance Plan*, 1989:13. Based on the 1988 average AFDC allotment of $412 and average rent of a one-bedroom apartment of $410. For General Assistance, the average income is $234; the rent of a studio apartment or SRO ranges from $219 to $323. Current rental housing prices are from the Cain and Scott *Apartment Vacancy Report*, a private subscription service which publishes semiannual rental and vacancy rates for rental properties of at least 20 units. Cain and Scott's report will underestimate low-cost units in smaller buildings.

11. The Seattle Housing Authority manages 6,600 public housing units, owns 1,200 elderly units, and has vouchers and Section 8 certificates for 2,814 units. There are 4,810 privately owned, federally assisted units, 2,400 Department of Community Development units, and 819 state-funded units (*Seattle's 1989 Housing Assistance Plan*, 1988). In contrast, Houston has a total of 16,822 public and subsidized units for a renter population that is roughly twice as large as that of Seattle (Feagin, 1988:263).

12. The Seattle SMSA is composed of two counties, King, of which the city of Seattle is the county seat, and Snohomish, of which the largest city is Everett, about ten miles north of Seattle. Much of Snohomish county is rural. Most of the external data available concerns the city of Seattle and King County.

9

The Relationship Between Housing Quality and Price

SUMMARY

Previous chapters have explored the roles of income and rent in increasing the vulnerability of the low-income population to homelessness. We have seen that in all four metropolitan areas studied, rents rose well beyond the rate of inflation between 1975-76 and 1983. Rising rent, relative to stagnating or falling income, leads to an increase in the rent-to-income ratio. For the poorest renter households with the highest rent burdens, this ratio has been hypothesized to be unsustainable for the long term. Because this is the principle mechanism proposed to have led to an increase in homelessness, it is desirable to account for changes in gross rent and to directly test the assumption that rising rents are attributable to rising quality.

This chapter employs hedonic equations, in which gross rent is regressed on characteristics of the housing unit, to assess whether changes have occurred over time in the effect that both positive and negative quality indicators have on gross rent. A second model adds the characteristics of the tenant to the regression, to examine cross-sectional changes over time in the price that individuals and households pay for housing, controlling for the characteristics of the unit. To preserve sample sizes that were severely cut in the 1983 survey, these regressions are done for the SMSA with a dummy variable identifying the central city. To compare how well the equation for the SMSA as a whole represents the central city, a separate set of equations is examined for the central city of Chicago. The potential effects of racial discrimination on rent are explored through separate equations for blacks and Hispanics in the Houston housing market.

The findings of this analysis, although limited by the effect on significance tests of the reduction in sample size, are generally supportive of the hypothesis that substandard quality has less effect on reducing rent than it has had in the past. The influence of quality on rent and on changes in rent varies substantially across the four metropolitan areas. The Houston analysis shows that rents paid by blacks are not as discounted by substandard quality as are those of renters overall. Furthermore, minorities may pay more than whites for bundles of housing of a given quality, even though on average they pay less rent than renters overall. In all metropolitan areas, households with children pay a premium in rent, holding size, quality, income and other factors constant.

INTRODUCTION

There are several factors that could account for an increase in gross rent, assuming that the rise in energy costs that occurred during this period has been accounted for in the rising consumer price index. The fact that gross rents rose fastest in Houston, where heating costs are low, would be an indication that the cost of energy is not the principle force driving rent levels up beyond the rate of inflation.

Housing construction costs have also risen. To the extent that the housing stock in a given metropolitan area is new, higher average housing costs would be anticipated. A greater proportion of newly constructed units in Houston and Seattle relative to Baltimore and Chicago undoubtedly plays a role in the faster rise in rent in the former cities than in the latter.

The poor do not generally live in newly constructed units, but the construction of new housing units has long been theorized to lead to a process of "filtering." As the more well-to-do move into newly constructed units, the housing stock once occupied by these higher-income groups is assumed to become available at reduced cost to lower-income groups. The filtering theory presupposes that the poorest-quality stock will be eliminated as higher-quality housing becomes available at a lower price. The filtering process "is sometimes defended as the principal way in which we can hope to raise the housing standards of the poor—and often attacked for having failed to do just that" (Heilbrun, 1973:253).

The filtering theory fails to take into account changes in the distributions of income and family size that affect the demand for housing of a given price and size. Increasing concentration of the poor at very low levels of income is likely to raise demand for the least expensive housing and to drive up the price. Gentrification, in which the affluent choose to rehabilitate older buildings rather than move to new ones, can also reverse the flow of older units to lower-income households and can lead to displacement from neighborhoods that they had previously occupied. Increased homelessness is a good indication that the process of filtering as a naturally occurring route to improved housing conditions for the poor has not worked very well.

It was proposed in the theory chapter that rents might have increased because of a growing professionalization of rental property. If ownership of rental property becomes concentrated among a few owners, collusion in the setting of rents among professional landlords could drive rents above levels that might occur in an unrestrained market. Concentration of ownership is difficult to document without examining records of property ownership, but Gilderbloom and Appelbaum (1987) have used the number of living quarters in a structure as a proxy for the concentration of ownership in a regression of gross rent on housing attributes. They found that rent was positively associated with the number of units in the building.[1]

Another possibility is that housing costs are higher because the housing we occupy is more spacious, of higher quality, and has more amenities. This is the argument that former president Reagan made in the 1981 President's Commission on Housing report (1981:18-19). It is predicated on a change in the effect of tastes on consumption. People may choose to spend more because they wish to consume more. There are two elements to the argument: (1) that housing is actually of better quality and (2) that choice to consume better housing has been exercised. In previous chapters it has been demonstrated that the rent burdens of low-income families are so excessive that they could not reasonably have been driven by a desire for higher-quality housing. This chapter will examine the extent to which lower-quality housing, which has historically been discounted in the market, still exists, and to what extent it remains less expensive than standard-quality housing.

A shortage of low-income housing might have occurred because the stock of cheaper, substandard-quality housing has been destroyed and replaced by higher-quality, more expensive housing (which did not filter down in price). The decennial census has provided a gross estimation of housing quality based primarily on plumbing and kitchen facilities. We know from this source that during the postwar period, at least through the 1970 census, there was a marked improvement in the quality of housing as measured by the presence of complete plumbing.[2] The argument has been made that as the presence of indoor plumbing and electricity has become virtually ubiquitous, such indicators have become obsolete as measures of variation in quality and fail to account for the obvious physical deterioration of housing taking place in some of our central cities.[3]

As noted in the introduction, the Annual Housing Survey was developed as a tool to assess whether and how the United States was moving toward the goal of the 1949 Housing Act "to provide a decent home and a suitable living environment for all American families" (U.S. Bureau of the Census, 1983:7). The survey collects the most complete information available, on a national basis, on the quality of housing within metropolitan areas, and thus offers an opportunity to track with greater sensitivity, changes that may have occurred since the survey was initiated in 1974.[4]

Housing costs essentially represent the combined market value of location, size, and quality. "Location" may include the centrality of the unit; access to services, jobs, and transportation; and the quality of the neighborhood or surrounding housing. Demand for housing is shaped by a household's income and family size. In the classic economic explanation of housing demand, the response of changes in the expenditure on rent to changes in income is called the "income elasticity of demand." It is the percentage change in expenditure divided by the percentage change in income (Heilbrun, 1973:247). A change in income will be expected to produce a change in the demand for housing of a particular size, quality, and location.

It has been empirically demonstrated that the demand for increased space with rising income is limited and that it is primarily an increase in quality rather than quantity that accounts for an increase in housing consumption with income.[5] As we have seen, overcrowding and the presence of subfamilies within low-income households have increased over the course of the survey in most areas. Many households can afford neither adequate quality nor sufficient space. This would be especially true if the price of substandard housing were now higher than it had been in the past. For these households, there may be a need for more space that may override the desire for better quality should income rise. If income falls, at it has for many low-income renters, concessions may be made in both the quality and the size of housing. Both overcrowding and substandard quality have been shown to be precursors to homelessness.

It has also been noted that as household income rises, renter households are more likely to become owners than to continue renting increasingly expensive units. Through ownership many benefits unavailable to the renter, including stabilized housing costs, tax breaks, and personal autonomy, can be enjoyed. As a consequence, with the exclusion of an exceptional rental market such as New York City, rents fall within a rather circumscribed range. In this study, maximum rents may be 15 times minimum rents, while maximum incomes may reach 50 times the minimum. Although higher-income renters can afford to spend a higher percentage of income on rent because they have sufficient residual income to meet nonhousing needs, affluent renters typically spend a smaller proportion of income on rent and thus have a greater proportion of disposable income. This increases the relative advantage of affluent over low-income households, beyond what might be expected from examining income alone. As housing costs have risen and become increasingly variable across the country, income alone becomes increasingly inadequate as a measure of well-being or quality of life. For low-income and moderate-income households, housing costs and residual income are important factors to consider.

MEAN LEVELS OF HOUSING SERVICES

In examining the characteristics of rental housing, we first want to look at whether there have been changes in the mean levels of housing size and services. If, for example, the mean size of rental units has increased, an increase in rent would not be unanticipated. This would in essence be a confirmation, at least in part, of President Reagan's hypothesis. Because square footage is not calculated in the Annual Housing Survey, we are limited in the assessment of size to the number of bedrooms and bathrooms in a unit and to the total number of rooms. In the regression analysis, bedrooms and total rooms proved to be highly collinear, and only number of rooms and bathrooms are used in the final regressions as measures of size of the unit. As a test of the Gilderbloom-Appelbaum hypothesis that professionalization is positively associated with gross rent, the total number of units in the building is also included. These variables are coded to facilitate their use in additive models and the recodes are provided in the appendixes.

The HUD-suggested criteria for assessing housing inadequacy as provided in Appendixes A and B are used in the regressions with the exception of the plumbing variable, which was essentially equivalent to and collinear with zero bathrooms and was eliminated from the model. The six remaining indicators of inadequacy are coded as zero if absent, one if inadequate, and two if severely inadequate. Overall, inadequacy and severe inadequacy of units are mutually exclusive dummy variables.[6]

MEAN VALUES OF HOUSING QUALITY AND CHARACTERISTICS OF RENTERS

Tables 9.1 through 9.4 present the weighted means and standard deviations of all the variables used in the regressions for the SMSAs. All incomes and rents are in constant 1986 dollars. We want to know whether

Table 9.1
Weighted Means and Standard Deviations of Quality and Renter Variables for Occupied Units, Baltimore SMSA, 1976–1983

variable	1976 Mean	1976 S.D.	1979 Mean	1979 S.D.	1983 Mean	1983 S.D.
	\$337.48		\$338.32		\$364.15	
Characteristics of Unit						
Gross rent	\$337.48	141.7	\$338.32	147.62	\$364.15	156.39
Central city	.535	.499	.535	.499	.491	.500
Number rooms	4.427	1.622	4.445	1.680	4.595	1.518
Number baths	1.161	.397	1.172	.426	1.161	.405
Bad street	.135	.342	.139	.346	.093	.291
New construction	.063	.243	.027	.162	.040	.195
Boom construction	.301	.459	.294	.456	.295	.456
Old construction	.558	.497	.541	.498	.482	.500
Inad structure	.102	.345	.136	.405	.115	.369
Inad public hall	.002	.042	.002	.049	.002	.047
Inad heat	.065	.338	.052	.313	.040	.276
Inad electricity	.002	.068	.001	.053	.000	.000
Inad sewer	.052	.309	.047	.299	.062	.343
Inad kitchen	.015	.121	.017	.128	.005	.072
1 or more inad	.077	.252	.083	.267	.073	.247
1 or more severe	.068	.267	.077	.277	.067	.260
Number units	4.593	2.165	4.658	2.198	4.565	2.222
No. Airconditioners	1.786	1.916	1.812	1.975	2.096	2.104
Characteristics of Renters						
Head Black	.358	.479	.363	.481	.359	.480
Head Female	.400	.490	.449	.498	.474	.500
Number Children	.844	1.322	.807	1.262	.793	1.207
Head Under 25	.159	.366	.142	.349	.099	.298
Head Over 65	.124	.330	.145	.352	.151	.359
Hi School Dropout	.408	.492	.383	.486	.356	.479
Beyond Hi School	.281	.450	.271	.445	.307	.462
Subsidized	.133	.340	.132	.339	.138	.345
Income	\$21,668	16,190	\$20,611	14,912	\$19,775	13,837
N of Cases		1669		1651		1565

Table 9.2
Weighted Means and Standard Deviations of Quality and Renter Variables for Occupied Units, Chicago SMSA, 1975–1983

variable	1975		1979		1983	
	Mean	S.D.	Mean	S.D.	Mean	S.D.
Characteristics of Unit						
Gross rent	$338.30	149.72	$353.60	150.56	$384.09	182.17
Central city	.658	.474	.638	.481	.605	.489
Number rooms	4.076	1.512'	4.111	1.540	4.079	1.408
Number baths	1.118	.397	1.099	.348	1.102	.344
Bad street	.128	.335	.161	.367	.102	.302
New construction	.046	.210	.033	.178	.025	.155
Boom construction	.239	.426	.237	.426	.232	.422
Old construction	.658	.474	.625	.484	.588	.492
Inad. structure	.064	.270	.085	.317	.075	.300
Inad. public hall	.016	.124	.008	.090	.008	.093
Inad. heat	.037	.268	.054	.317	.039	.262
Inad. electricity	.001	.053	.001	.038	.001	.035
Inad. sewer	.040	.274	.051	.305	.042	.284
Inad. kitchen	.021	.143	.020	.140	.026	.159
1 or more inad.	.063	.233	.072	.247	.071	.232
1 or more severe	.064	.244	.068	.252	.055	.229
Number units	5.913	1.921	6.015	1.911	6.004	1.955
No. airconditioners	.802	1.132	.835	1.222	.946	1.341
Characteristics of Renters						
Head black	.263	.440	.286	.452	.287	.453
Head female	.387	.487	.428	.495	.463	.499
Number dhildren	.845	1.441	.776	1.310	.779	1.239
Head under 25	.150	.357	.140	.347	.119	.324
Head over 65	.158	.365	.163	.369	.167	.373
Hi school dropout	.389	.486	.363	.481	.335	.472
Beyond hi school	.317	.465	.345	.475	.373	.484
Subsidized	.063	.242	.080	.271	.087	.282
Income	$21,039	16,285	$22,056	15,676	$19,911	14,914
N of Cases		5446		5106		3261

184

Table 9.3
Weighted Means and Standard Deviations of Quality and Renter Variables for
Occupied Units, Houston SMSA, 1976–1983

variable	1976 Mean	1976 S.D.	1979 Mean	1979 S.D.	1983 Mean	1983 S.D.
Characteristics of Unit						
Gross rent[a]	$359.35	153.05	$393.31	175.47	$447.85	184.43
Central city	.777	.415	.702	.458	.651	.477
Number rooms	3.954	1.244	4.023	1.365	4.064	1.227
Number baths	1.253	.521	1.267	.517	1.292	.537
Bad street	.094	.292	.089	.285	.080	.271
New construction	.112	.315	.120	.325	.114	.318
Boom construction	.388	.487	.352	.478	.299	.458
Old construction	.310	.462	.251	.434	.236	.425
Inad. structure	.052	.235	.052	.239	.070	.285
Inad. public hall	.002	.040	.002	.040	.007	.085
Inad. heat	.234	.469	.231	.462	.216	.465
Inad. electricity	.001	.044	.000	.000	.002	.060
Inad. sewer	.113	.456	.093	.417	.114	.458
Inad. kitchen	.015	.123	.013	.112	.007	.083
1 or more inad.	.225	.418	.229	.420	.209	.407
1 or more severe	.084	.278	.072	.258	.084	.277
Number units	5.618	2.235	5.569	2.147	5.408	2.206
No. airconditioners	2.531	1.784	2.773	1.788	2.922	1.749
Characteristics of Renters						
Head black	.202	.401	.199	.399	.192	.394
Head Hispanic	.128	.334	.154	.361	.156	.363
Head female	.286	.452	.301	.459	.330	.470
Number children	.794	1.290	.762	1.234	.839	1.266
Head under 25	.219	.413	.215	.411	.165	.371
Head over 65	.074	.261	.079	.270	.054	.226
Hi school dropout	.302	.459	.286	.452	.280	.449
Beyond hi school	.398	.490	.396	.489	.424	.494
Subsidized	.008	.089	.011	.104	.023	.149
Income[a]	$24,026	17,415	$25,323	16,629	$24,028	15,268
N of cases	5221		5715		1344	

[a]Income and rent in constant 1986 CPl-XI dollars.

Table 9.4
Weighted Means and Standard Deviations of Quality and Renter Variables for Occupied Units, Seattle SMSA, 1976–1983

Variable	1976 Mean	1976 S.D.	1979 Mean	1979 S.D.	1983 Mean	1983 S.D.
Characteristics of Unit						
Gross rent	$329.47	141.86	$381.24	178.80	$404.35	167.01
Central city	.570	.495	.537	.499	.484	.500
Number rooms	3.902	1.507	3.996	1.656	4.069	1.577
Number baths	1.159	.437	1.186	.462	1.193	.458
Bad street	.080	.272	.064	.246	.047	.211
New construction	.042	.200	.084	.278	.079	.269
Boom construction	.464	.499	.428	.495	.385	.487
Old construction	.462	.499	.416	.493	.361	.481
Inad. structure	.031	.183	.033	.199	.022	.152
Inad. public hall	.002	.045	.002	.042	.004	.076
Inad. heat	.035	.249	.035	.251	.013	.144
Inad. electricity	.003	.075	.001	.380	.000	.000
Inad. sewer	.034	.252	.034	.254	.036	.264
Inad. kitchen	.018	.132	.018	.132	.010	.102
1 or more inad.	.054	.226	.051	.220	.037	.188
1 or more severe	.054	.226	.058	.233	.037	.189
Number units	5.492	2.182	5.508	2.166	5.508	2.160
No. airconditioners	.049	.410	.058	.443	.058	.459
Characteristics of Renters						
Head black	.057	.232	.054	.225	.065	.246
Head Hispanic	.016	.126	.020	.140	.018	.134
Head female	.391	.488	.383	.486	.418	.493
Number dhildren	.492	.984	.446	.907	.539	1.002
Head under 25	.230	.421	.232	.422	.173	.378
Head over 65	.136	.343	.127	.333	.103	.304
Hi school dropout	.190	.393	.155	.362	.156	.363
Beyond hi school	.481	.500	.506	.500	.513	.500
Subsidized	.082	.274	.075	.263	.079	.270
Income	$21,482	16,707	$23,516	16,308	$22,337	14,725
N of Cases		4230		5041		1580

mean values have been constant, or if changes in rent may be associated with changes in the mean values of size or quality of the housing unit. It should be noted that there has been a slight increase in the number of rooms per unit in all four SMSAs. Since there is at least anecdotal evidence that newly constructed rental units have smaller square footage per room, we cannot assume that this increase is actually an indication of increased space. Speculatively, some units may have been subdivided to increase the number of rooms while space remained constant. This information is not available in the AHS. Rental units overall are about half a room larger in Baltimore than in the other three cities, a statistically significant difference. This may help explain the lower levels of overcrowding in Baltimore relative to Chicago and Houston when measured by the number of persons per room.

Seattle and Houston show a slight increase of about 3 percent in the mean number of baths, whereas Baltimore was stable and Chicago has declined somewhat. The trend for newer units to have more than one bathroom may be responsible for this finding. As can be seen, the proportion of the stock that is newly constructed has continued to increase in Seattle and Houston, whereas it has declined in Baltimore and Chicago. In the former cities, the largest proportion of rental housing was built between 1950 and 1970, whereas in the latter SMSAs it predates 1950.[7] Chicago and Seattle show a slight increase in the mean number of units per building, whereas there was a slight decline in Baltimore and Houston.

A second amenity variable is the number of air conditioners. Here it can be seen that there has been a significant increase in the mean number of air conditioners for those two metropolitan areas in which they would be most necessary for climate control, Houston and Baltimore. The mean for Houston is about three-tenths of a unit larger in 1983 than in 1976, an increase of about 15 percent, and this cannot be discounted as a factor in the rising rents found in Houston. It may be that air conditioning is as essential in Houston as heat is in Chicago. As such, it may be less of an amenity or an indication of high quality in Houston than in a northern climate where air conditioning is truly optional.

The only measure of neighborhood quality in the AHS that is based on the observation of the interviewer rather than the subjective judgment of the tenant is whether boarded-up units are present on the street. The proportion of rental units that are located on a street with boarded-up units declined in all four SMSAs and ranged in 1983 from 5 percent in Seattle to 10 percent in Chicago. For the other indicators of substandard quality, only inadequate heat in Baltimore and Seattle shows a decline of as much as 2 percent.[8] At 7 percent, Seattle has by far the lowest percentage of housing that is substandard (inadequate or severely inadequate). Houston, by virtue of the high proportion of housing with inadequate heat, has the highest. If heat is excluded, Baltimore has the most substandard rental housing of the four SMSAs. The stability in the proportion of the inadequate and severely inadequate stock indicates that even where the total stock has declined, such as in the central cities of Baltimore and Chicago, the proportion of the remaining stock that is inadequate has declined only very slightly.

This finding further challenges the presumption that filtering will lead to an overall higher quality of housing by eliminating substandard units from the stock. We cannot determine from this data whether the units that were removed from the stock were not substandard or whether more housing has dilapidated to take the place of low-quality housing that has been removed. It is likely that both factors are at work.

One of the responses landlords may make to a declining ability of renters to pay the full cost of maintenance and repairs is to reduce the expenditure in these areas and allow housing to deteriorate.[9] In the extreme, the unprofitable property may be abandoned entirely and taken over by the city for back taxes.[10] The supply of substandard housing may thus be continually replenished. Urban renewal and highway construction may eliminate standard quality as well as dilapidated housing, especially in growing cities such as Houston and Seattle, but these factors would be less important during the period of these surveys than in the 1960s when major urban renewal and federal highway construction projects were underway. In any case, for the period of the study, we do not see a significant change in the quality of the rental housing stock, except in Seattle, which had the smallest percentage of substandard units initially.

The tables further provide mean values for the characteristics of renter heads and households. Of interest is the fact that the proportion of households headed by a person under the age of 25 has declined by a significant amount in all four metropolitan areas. This is reflective of the inability of younger would-be householders to afford housing, as well as of the aging of the population in general. The decline in the rate of household formation has already been noted. A catch-up period in which those who have delayed are anticipated to establish new independent households has been predicted by the Census Bureau (McGough and Casey, 1986), but will probably not occur as rapidly as expected in the face of continued high housing costs.

In the Baltimore and Chicago SMSAs the proportion of renter heads who are over 65 has also increased, while in Houston, Seattle, and central Chicago it has decreased. This is speculatively related in the latter cities to mechanisms such as migration, which affect the age structure. Seattle and Houston have experienced rapid growth through in-migration, which typically involves the younger working population.

In all four areas, the heads of renter households had higher mean levels of education in 1983 than in 1976. Half of all Seattle renter heads had education beyond high school. Forty percent of central Chicago renters are high school dropouts, a decline from 45 percent in 1976. The mean number of children has increased in Houston and Seattle and decreased in Chicago and Baltimore, but the level remains highest in central-city Chicago, where the mean is .89. This compares with a mean of .54 in Seattle, which, as might be expected, has the smallest mean household size of the areas studied.

In terms of income it is interesting to note that only in Baltimore did mean income not increase between 1976 and 1979 before falling in 1983, and only in Seattle did 1983 income exceed that of 1976. Although mean income of Seattle renters was 4 percent higher in 1983 than in 1976, it had fallen 5 percent from 1979 to 1983. Similarly, mean income of Houston renters, while unchanged when viewed over the entire eight-year period, had a shorter-term decline of 5 percent from 1979 to 1983. For the Chicago SMSA, mean income fell 4 percent over the eight-year period, but nearly 10 percent over the four-year period. Baltimore renters' mean income fell monotonically by 9 percent. These figures may indicate several trends, among them the strength of the economy prior to the recession of 1982. When examined in terms of the proportion of the population in poverty or vulnerable to homelessness, it should be recalled that this proportion was curvilinear in some areas over the years of the survey,[11] an indication that antipoverty programs may, in fact, have been having some success prior to the cuts that occurred in these programs in the early 1980s.

Overall, the decline or stagnation in incomes is most meaningfully considered relative to changes in rent. Mean rents in both the Houston and Seattle SMSAs increased by about 23 percent, while the increase was 14 percent in Chicago and 9 percent in Baltimore. Central-city Chicago rents increased by 12 percent, but incomes fell further than in the SMSA as a whole. Rents increased in each year of the survey except in Baltimore, where there was no change between 1976 and 1979. The entire 9-percent increase in Baltimore mean rents therefore occurred in the most recent four years of the survey.

HEDONIC EQUATIONS OF GROSS RENT

The purpose of the hedonic analysis is not only to explain, to the extent possible, the variation in rents within metropolitan areas, but also to see whether changes may have occurred in the rent-reducing or rent-increasing effect of positive and negative indicators of quality cross-sectionally over time. In the additive model, mean gross rent is equivalent to the sum of the coefficient of each variable times its mean value. It is thus possible to disaggregate the effect on gross rent of a change in price from that of a change in the mean value of a housing attribute. A second model adds the characteristics of renters to the equation. Renter characteristics have previously been employed in hedonic equations to measure the association between household or occupant characteristics and gross rent, all else held constant (Hanushek and Quigley, 1979:90-111). Such regressions allow us to examine differences in the rents paid by demographic subgroups, controlling for the size and quality of the unit, as well as for the income and education of the occupant.

BALTIMORE SMSA

In Baltimore, the variance in gross rent explained by Model 1 in Table 9.5 (excluding characteristics of the occupant) increases somewhat over time, from .43 to .47. The price of a room increased significantly, from $26 in 1976 to $39 in 1983. Because the mean number of rooms has also increased, the additive value of the number of rooms at mean value in 1983 is about $6.50 higher than it would have been had the mean number of rooms remained at their 1976 level.[12] Thus the far greater effect on gross rent is due to the increase in cost per room rather than the increase in the mean number of rooms per unit.

Baths have become less expensive and their mean number unchanged. The contribution of bathrooms to total rent has declined from 34 percent in 1976 to 24 percent in 1983. The cost coefficient of air conditioners has declined only slightly over the period, but since the mean number of air conditioners has significantly increased, the product of cost times number of units was larger in 1983 than in 1976. However, as a percentage of total rent, the addition of air conditioning at its mean value has increased little, from 10.5 to 10.7 percent of total rent.

Units within the central city of Baltimore were substantially less expensive relative to the SMSA as a whole, and units built between 1950 and 1970 command a premium for all three years. Perhaps surprisingly, newly constructed units were less costly by 1983, while old construction in Baltimore was not discounted by a statistically significant amount in any of the three years. The number of units in a building, which was positively related to gross rent in the two earlier time periods, had a nonsignificant negative association by 1983. Since most new construction has taken place outside of the central city, I speculate that once location is controlled for, new construction, which

Table 9.5
Regression of Gross Rent on Characteristics of Unit and Unit and Renter, Baltimore SMSA

Variable	Model One						Model Two					
	1976		1979		1983		1976		1979		1983	
	B	t	B	t	B	t	B	t	B	t	B	t
Constant	75.53	4.42***	85.54	5.20***	94.00	5.38***	112.06	6.71***	134.98	8.50***	149.15	9.18***
Central city	-37.99	-6.25***	-49.09	-7.66***	-57.12	-8.57***	-13.19	-2.17**	-14.02	-2.24**	-15.66	-2.45**
Rooms	25.87	12.97***	28.60	13.96***	39.07	16.16***	19.01	9.88***	22.39	11.90***	30.73	13.97***
Boom constru	15.16	1.38	22.56	2.37**	20.14	2.23**	-8.01	-.80	-7.27	-.86	-15.76	-2.00**
New constru	35.45	2.53**	-6.69	-.63	-50.26	-3.13***	20.72	1.63	11.45	.70	-5.07	-.36
Old constru	-5.86	-.48	-1.91	-.17	-11.94	-1.11	-32.25	-2.89***	-29.93	-3.05***	-52.28	-5.56***
Bad street	-19.13	-2.25**	-40.85	-4.62***	-44.67	-4.10***	-13.96	-1.79*	-18.11	-2.27**	-14.74	-1.56
Baths	97.56	12.98***	96.06	13.11***	76.00	9.40***	81.44	11.82***	80.02	12.20***	57.72	8.23***
Aircondition	19.83	9.90***	16.60	8.30***	18.59	9.34***	14.54	7.89***	13.12	7.39***	12.54	7.21***
No. units	4.42	2.89***	2.50	1.58	-.81	-.51	3.35	2.31**	.64	.45	-.88	-.62
Inad. electric	24.88	.65	-31.72	-.61	0.00	0.00	24.78	.72	-47.62	-1.04	0.00	0.00
Inad. heat	12.17	1.54	-5.88	-.66	22.55	2.15**	18.15	2.52**	-1.82	-.23	24.53	2.74***
Inad. hall	49.87	.78	-2.37	-.04	-74.64	-1.23	37.86	.67	-2.27	-.05	6.40	.12
Inad. sewer	-10.58	-1.23	-6.81	-.73	-.61	-.07	-7.51	-.96	-1.78	-.22	.39	.05
Inad. structu.	-1.56	-.19	7.60	1.00	8.44	.97	-2.69	-.35	2.79	.42	1.21	-.16
Inad. kitchen	-158.41	-6.69***	-156.32	-6.57***	-116.37	-2.81***	-141.06	-6.51***	-144.37	-6.87***	-105.22	-2.97***
Black							-8.23	-1.36	-29.96	-4.86***	-27.14	-4.34***
Income							.002	11.21***	.002	7.57***	.002	8.15***
Children							9.16	4.32***	11.51	5.04***	11.37	4.72***
Subsidized							-82.68	-11.23***	-117.47	-15.02***	-137.35	-16.62***
Head < 25							3.00	.43	6.26	.86	3.32	.39
Head > 65							4.75	.60	18.46	2.42**	14.98	1.95**
Female							5.25	1.00	5.22	.97	2.74	.50
High educ.							8.93	1.40	18.22	2.83***	20.78	3.28***
Dropout	.43		.42		.47		-20.66	-3.40***	-31.80	-5.18***	-16.88	-2.66***
R Squared							.55		.57		.62	
N of cases[a]	1690		1670		1591		1669		1651		1565	

[a] weighted by the population weight divided by mean weight   *=p < .1; **=p < .05; *** p= < .01;

makes up only about 4 percent of the stock in Baltimore, is not as spacious as older housing and may cost less. In spite of its high percentage of substandard housing, Baltimore also has a considerable proportion of well-maintained and gentrifying older housing which may successfully compete in price with new housing.

In terms of the indicators of substandard quality, it can be seen that living on a bad street and lacking complete kitchen facilities were significantly rent-reducing in all three periods. Having an inadequate kitchen reduced rent to a lesser extent in 1983 than in 1976 or 1979, while living on a street with boarded-up units reduced rent more in 1983 than in the earlier years. By 1983, however, lack of adequate heat was positively and significantly associated with gross rent. This finding remained stable within several different regression models.[13] It is supportive of the hypothesis that substandard quality was not associated with reduced rent to the extent that it had been in the past. Of the six measures of substandard quality, only an inadequate hallway had a larger negative coefficient in 1983 than in 1976, but it was not significant. When combined with the finding that the proportion of the housing stock that is of low quality has remained unchanged, these results challenge the idea that the increase in gross rent is attributable to increasing quality. Rather they suggest that poor quality has become increasingly irrelevant to the price of housing.

THE CHARACTERISTICS OF BALTIMORE RENTERS IN RELATION TO GROSS RENT

In a separate analysis (Model 2), the characteristics of renter households and household heads are examined, controlling for the quality and size of the unit. Race dummy variables have been used in hedonic regressions to measure racial discrimination. Schafer (1979), for example, states in a study of Boston housing that a positive coefficient for the race dummy variables "measures the extent of pure racial price discrimination in a unified housing market." He shows that dual or multiple housing submarkets exist in which the cost of amenities or inadequacies varies. In Boston, Schafer found that blacks paid more, both within the unified market and within the ghetto submarket.

In the Baltimore SMSA as a whole, blacks are shown to pay significantly less for housing. A negative coefficient is not, of course, a measure of the absence of pure racial price discrimination. It rather indicates that within the theoretically unified housing market, blacks pay less rent. Only by examining submarkets, as Schafer suggests, can it be determined whether the same housing attributes are more costly in the black ghetto than in white neighborhoods. Unfortunately, the AHS does not provide geographical information or racial composition of neighborhoods. It is possible, however, to estimate the same equations for low-income black and Hispanic renters. Examining each of the housing markets studied here for evidence of racial discrimination is beyond the scope of this study, but because racial discrimination is hypothesized to play a role in the growing percentage of homeless who are minority, equations are estimated for blacks and Hispanics for the Houston housing market.

One would expect that larger families would pay more rent because they would require more space.[14] Yet, even after controlling for size of the unit and income, households with children pay more rent in the Baltimore SMSA in all three years. This may indicate that landlords expect a premium from families that have children, perhaps due to anticipated increased maintenance and repair costs that might be associated with children. The logit model (see Table 5.3) indicated a significant positive relationship between presence of children and vulnerability to homelessness. Female-headed households in Baltimore have a positive but nonsignificant relationship to gross rent in all three years.

By 1979, elderly renters paid significantly higher rents, controlling for income and subsidies, as well as size, quality, and location. It is more difficult to speculate about the possible reasons for this. To the extent that elderly renters are female and women have been found to experience discrimination in the housing market (National Council of Negro Women, 1975), these higher rents may reflect such discrimination. Given that the proportion of renter heads who are over 65 has increased in Baltimore and Chicago and that these are also the two metropolitan areas in which the elderly pay higher rents, one may also speculate that within units or neighborhoods traditionally occupied by the elderly, increased demand has driven up the price for these units.

All else equal, higher-educated renters in Baltimore pay more for housing and less well educated renters pay less. This may be related to the higher value well-educated renters place on neighborhood characteristics and services, variables not well tapped in the AHS and hence in the models. Lastly, it is seen that the rent-reducing value of housing subsidies has increased in Baltimore. The mean proportion of subsidized units has also increased. The rent-reducing value of subsidies has more than kept pace with the increase in gross rent in Baltimore. This may be a factor in the lower per capita rates of homelessness found in Baltimore relative to other metropolitan areas where the value of subsidies has fallen relative to gross rent.

Table 9.6
Regression of Gross Rent on Characteristics of Unit and Unit and Renter, Chicago SMSA

Variable	Model One 1975 B	1975 t	1979 B	1979 t	1983 B	1983 t	Model Two 1975 B	1975 t	1979 B	1979 t	1983 B	1983 t
Constant	167.26	12.24***	251.63	18.44***	106.29	4.74***	144.81	11.19***	221.80	17.43***	76.55	3.77***
Central city	-40.19	-9.88***	-43.13	-9.85***	-75.85	-11.03***	-25.03	-6.46***	-16.04	-3.93***	-43.32	-6.86***
Rooms	27.14	21.23***	20.10	15.49***	34.74	14.05***	23.85	18.77***	16.61	13.62***	26.22	11.18***
Boom constru.	-15.55	-1.96**	-31.92	-4.82***	7.09	.76	-8.45	-1.16	-30.09	-5.12***	.83	.10
New constru.	3.59	.35	19.91	1.80*	18.10	.95	20.11	2.12**	9.66	.99	54.11	3.22***
Old constru.	-53.52	-6.39***	-49.60	-6.94***	32.62	3.24***	-56.33	-7.31***	-68.67	-10.66***	1.08	.21
Bad street	-31.49	-6.15***	-36.68	-7.38***	-61.65	-5.46***	-17.37	-3.55***	-17.68	-3.86***	-19.23	-2.29**
Baths	55.05	12.18***	61.97	11.51***	38.70	4.32***	45.95	11.03***	50.35	10.56***	23.12	2.93***
Air condition	39.09	23.60***	37.33	22.80***	40.59	16.50***	23.02	14.31***	24.44	16.21***	21.07	9.41***
No. units	6.46	5.98***	-1.20	-1.07	13.77	7.49***	7.42	7.30***	1.34	1.33	13.54	8.29***
Inad. electric	28.67	.91	1.17	.03	-53.06	-.66	27.77	.98	-.38	-.01	-47.81	-.68
Inad. heat	3.94	.64	1.73	.31	6.13	.57	7.28	1.28	-1.82	-.37	9.25	.99
Inad. hall	-35.26	-2.60***	-36.74	-1.84*	-27.27	-.90	-19.87	-1.60	-21.86	-1.26	9.99	.38
Inad. sewer	-8.69	-1.43	-13.18	-2.32**	5.40	.55	1.14	.21	-10.18	-2.18**	8.87	1.03
Inad. structu.	6.63	1.05	12.14	2.05**	-10.68	-1.11	3.20	.55	11.41	2.18**	-8.64	-1.13
Inad. kitchen	-53.67	-4.19***	-58.47	-4.32***	116.36	5.81***	-42.86	-3.64***	-68.66	-4.88***	94.61	5.40***
Hispanic							-24.68	-4.12***	-10.86	-1.84*	-19.75	-2.21**
Black							-6.40	-1.52	-12.54	-2.97***	-10.46	-1.58
Income							.002	16.59***	.002	17.66***	.004	20.73***
Children							4.50	3.58***	7.62	5.44***	14.53	6.11***
Subsidized							-141.44	-20.52***	-142.04	-22.35***	-153.14	-15.47***
Head < 25							1.72	.39	1.11	.24	5.26	.70
Head > 65							2.28	.49	.64	.14	47.46	6.42***
Female							13.21	3.86***	9.01	2.64***	25.58	4.88***
High educ.							33.75	8.60***	29.91	7.57***	26.07	4.27***
Dropout							-19.34	-5.01***	-20.49	-5.08***	-26.88	-4.18***
R Squared	.34		.33		.25		.46		.48		.45	
N of cases	5572		5257		3301		5446		5106		3261	

[a] weighted by the population weight divided by mean weight

CHICAGO SMSA

As Table 9.6 shows, in constant dollars the cost of a room increased more slowly over a somewhat longer period in Chicago than in Baltimore, from $27 to $35 dollars between 1975 and 1983. The percentage of total rent related to the number of rooms increased from 33 to 37 percent. The mean number of rooms remained constant, so that the increase in the percentage of mean gross rent that was due to the number of rooms was entirely the result of an increase in the cost per room. Similar to the findings for Baltimore, the price of bathrooms dropped and that of air conditioners remained quite stable. Thus these positive indicators of quality are not shown to be increasing rent. The contribution of air conditioning to total rent, for example, increased by less than 1 percent.

For the indicators of negative quality, the picture is quite different. In the first year of the survey, living on a bad street, having an inadequate kitchen, and having an inadequate public hallway were all significantly rent reducing. In 1979 these were joined by inadequate sewer, but there was also a significant positive relationship between inadequate structure and gross rent. By 1983, only living on a bad street was significantly rent reducing. Having an inadequate kitchen contributed positively and significantly to gross rent. Earlier I speculated that the loss of SROs, (which generally lack kitchen facilities) and the competition for the few that remain may have driven up the price of these units. This finding also remains stable across the several models that were run and when the characteristics of renters are included as in Model 2. For two other inadequacy measures, the coefficients had a positive though nonsignificant effect on rent in 1983. Finally, old construction was positively and significantly related to higher rent in the latter period, a complete turnaround from 1979. A greater number of units in the building is also strongly associated with higher rents in 1983, although this was not the case in 1979. Chicago is the only SMSA in which this relationship supports the hypothesis promoted by Gilderbloom and Appelbaum (1988). It may be the case that ownership of rental property is more concentrated in Chicago than elsewhere and that higher rents in larger buildings are promoted through this mechanism.

Chicago Renter Household Characteristics in Relation to Gross Rent

When the size and quality of the unit, as well as the income and education of the occupant, are controlled for, Hispanics in the Chicago SMSA are shown to pay less rent than whites in 1983, while for blacks, the coefficient is negative but nonsignificant. As in Baltimore, households with children pay higher rent in Chicago. Female heads of households, unlike those in Baltimore, also pay significantly higher rents, and the coefficients for both females and children have doubled over time. By 1983, female-headed households paid $26 more in gross rent than did male heads, and households with children paid about $15 more than households without children. The coefficients for the Chicago SMSA were by far the largest of the four, indicating that the disadvantages for women and children were more severe in Chicago than elsewhere. Elderly heads are shown to pay a significant premium in 1983, while this was not the case in earlier years. The income coefficient has also doubled over time, indicating that the elasticity of demand based on income has increased.[15] The positive relationship between income and rent has grown stronger, and this could indicate that lower income households are being driven out of the housing market.

Chicago Central City

As a comparison, and to determine if the multivariate analysis of the SMSA as a whole is obscuring a pattern unique to the central city, it is useful to examine the central city separately from the SMSA. In the interest of time and because central-city sample size was largest in Chicago in 1983, this analysis is only done for the central city of Chicago. Chicago central city had the highest proportion among cities of those vulnerable to homelessness and the greatest increase in this proportion over the course of the surveys. Comparison of the mean values for the quality variables (see Table 9.7) shows that while rents are lower in the central city than in the SMSA as a whole, number of rooms, number of bathrooms, and number of units are quite similar in the two analyses. The central city has a higher proportion of housing built before 1950 (78 percent versus 59 percent) and a higher proportion of inadequate housing.

In the Chicago central-city models shown in Table 9.8, the two dummy variables for inadequacy or severe inadequacy are used, in addition to living on a bad street, in place of the six separate indicators of quality. Recall that these dummy variables indicate the presence of any one of the six inadequacies. The regressions show that within the central city part of the reason that rent is less expensive than in the SMSA as a whole is that the cost per room has increased more moderately, from $25 to $32 dollars. Cost of baths has declined as in the SMSA as a whole, but the cost of air conditioners has increased by a significant amount. Unlike the SMSA as a whole, there was a significant premium attached to new construction and a reduction in rent for units built between 1950 and 1970. As for the entire

Table 9.7
Weighted Means and Standard Deviations of Quality and Renter Variables for
Occupied Units, Central City Chicago

variable	1975 Mean	1975 S.D.	1979 Mean	1979 S.D.	1983 Mean	1983 S.D.
Characteristics of Unit						
Gross rent	$306.59	147.90	$317.92	141.35	$341.89	154.05
Number rooms	4.053	1.555	4.105	1.674	4.092	1.449
Number baths	1.113	.415	1.086	.354	1.070	.318
Bad street	.179	.383	.226	.418	.150	.357
New construction	.020	.139	.007	.083	.008	.088
Boom construction	.169	.374	.161	.367	.164	.370
Old construction	.799	.401	.794	.404	.777	.417
1 or more inad.	.078	267	.090	.279	.085	.266
1 or more severe inad.	.080	.271	.083	.276	.075	.263
Number units	6.023	1.889	6.112	1.886	6.072	1.912
No. airconditioners	.577	.930	.546	.943	.585	.982
Characteristics of Renters						
Head black	.367	.482	.400	.490	.420	.494
Head female	.428	.495	.464	.499	.494	.500
Number children	.917	1.542	.877	1.422	.894	1.351
Head under 25	.121	.326	.104	.306	.100	.300
Head over 65	.169	.374	.168	.374	.159	.365
Hi school dropout	.449	.498	.427	.495	.400	.490
Beyond high school	.281	.450	.297	.457	.344	.475
Subsidized	.078	.268	.100	.300	.098	.298
Income	$18,951	15,970	$19,695	15,062	$17,083	14,126
N of Cases		3625		3260		2004

SMSA, higher rents are strongly associated with a greater number of units in the building. The central city contains both very large public housing with low rents and luxury buildings with high rents, but the balance appears to be tipped in favor of higher rents in larger buildings. For older construction (pre-1950), there was no statistically significant discount in 1983, although there had been in the earlier years of the survey.

In all three years, living on a street with boarded-up units reduced rent. In 1975, severely inadequate units in the central city were discounted by more than $50. In 1979, this discount was $69, and units that were inadequate were very close to being significantly discounted by about $13 (t=1.64). But, by 1983, neither inadequacies nor severe inadequacies were significantly rent reducing. Although the coefficient for inadequacy increased from $2 to $17, that for severe inadequacy decreased from $51 to $5.

Table 9.8
Regression of Gross Rent on Characteristics of Unit and Unit and Renter, Central City Chicago

Variable	Model One						Model Two					
	1975		1979		1983		1975		1979		1983	
	B	t	B	t	B	t	B	t	B	t	B	t
Constant	180.52	7.48***	233.55	11.76***	103.91	3.71***	152.87	6.84***	228.78	12.32***	136.53	5.51***
Rooms	25.42	16.20***	15.44	10.67***	31.54	12.71***	25.01	15.71***	14.90	10.87***	29.31	12.64***
Boom constru.	-93.55	-4.90***	-78.10	-6.37***	-30.47	-2.01*	-63.98	-3.69***	-69.31	-6.22***	-43.36	-3.38***
New constru	-44.36	-1.88*	-2.51	-.09	120.47	3.39***	-10.87	-.51	-1.40	-.06	76.50	2.49**
Old constru	-114.84	-6.05***	-66.07	-5.48***	-10.21	-.69	-111.98	-6.50***	-96.26	-8.78***	-67.89	-5.27***
Bad street	-27.13	-4.89***	-27.93	-5.29***	-45.13	-5.32***	-15.47	-2.90***	-11.09	-2.27***	-14.14	-1.92*
Baths	53.00	8.85***	53.77	7.60***	36.16	3.60***	41.84	7.56***	36.00	6.00***	15.47	1.78***
Aircondition	52.66	21.68***	52.04	21.23***	58.92	18.06***	28.92	11.78***	31.64	13.50***	28.86	9.62***
No. units	8.59	6.12***	1.69	1.21	9.56	4.67***	10.77	8.11***	5.34	4.22***	11.32	6.32***
Inadequate	-2.03	-.26	-12.53	-1.64	-16.91	-1.55	-4.04	-.56	-6.79	-1.00	-8.46	-.91
Severe inad.	-51.37	-4.44***	-69.08	-5.42***	-4.50	-.29	-36.77	-3.48***	-36.30	-3.75***	4.27	.32
Hispanic							-19.55	-2.77***	-10.46	-1.57	-29.83	-3.51***
Black							-.63	-.13	-10.72	-2.26*	-14.98	-2.40*
Income							.002	11.73***	.002	13.28***	.003	12.74***
Children							3.27	2.18*	7.32	4.55***	5.38	2.35**
Subsidized							-156.53	-18.99***	-151.48	-20.48***	-163.75	-16.92***
Head < 25							6.60	1.10	4.10	.64	14.12	1.63
Head > 65							-3.17	-.55	-2.44	-.42	-11.46	-1.46
Female							13.16	3.11***	10.34	2.47**	15.37	2.78***
High educ.							38.43	7.18***	33.61	6.47***	41.05	5.99***
Dropout							-15.47	-3.22***	-16.89	-3.47***	-8.09	-1.21
R Squared [a]	.27		.23		.27		.41		.42		.48	
N of cases	3726		3356		2004		3625		3260		1978	

[a] weighted by the population weight divided by mean weight   *=p < .1; **=p < .05; *** p= < .01;

It should be noted that the variance in gross rent explained by either of the Chicago models (R squared) is considerably less than that explained in Baltimore, Seattle, and Houston. It is perhaps the case in Chicago, where high-rise public housing abuts the most expensive real estate in the downtown area, that location as a quality variable is almost building—rather than neighborhood—specific. Many factors not explored in these regressions may be of more relevance to rent in Chicago than elsewhere. One can speculate that crime, litter, security, lighting, traffic noise, parking, access to shopping, lakeview, and so on, may be more critical in estimating the cost of rental housing in a city such as Chicago, which, of the areas studied, has the highest proportion of renters living in poverty.

Characteristics of Central Chicago Renters

Within the central city, both blacks and Hispanics are shown to pay significantly less rent than whites, all else held constant. This pattern has become stronger for both groups over time. As in the SMSA as a whole, females as well as households with children are seen to pay significantly more. Because central-city renter households are 42 percent black and 49 percent female-headed, one could speculate that once being female and having children are controlled for, the remaining effect of race is negative.

High-school dropouts do not pay significantly less rent in Chicago, as they do in other metropolitan areas and in the SMSA as a whole. Overall, the central Chicago findings are supportive of the greater vulnerability of women, children, and the less well educated to homelessness, not only because of their greater representation among the poor, but also because they have higher actual housing costs.

HOUSTON SMSA

Houston began the period of the survey with the highest mean rent of the four metropolitan areas and had the greatest growth in mean rent over the eight years covered by the survey.[16] Why this should be the case is clearly not related to substantial changes in the mean values of the low-quality variables. But as previously noted, Houston had the highest proportion of new construction (11 percent) among the metropolitan areas, and this factor undoubtedly did play a role in increasing rents.

As Table 9.3 indicated, there were changes in the mean number of air conditioners and the number of units in a building that may be large enough to have an effect on rent. The mean number of air conditioners increased from 2.5 to nearly 3.[17] Air conditioning was the single best predictor of gross rent in Houston, with correlation coefficients above .6. However, as Table 9.9 shows, the cost per air unit dropped considerably, so that the overall contribution to gross rent declined from 23 percent to 15 percent. This supports the suggestion made earlier that air conditioning in Houston is less an amenity than a necessity, and thus its rent-enhancing value may have declined. Air conditioning is likely to be as critical in Houston as heat is elsewhere. On the other hand, Houston does have 1,550 heating degree days per year, an indication that some form of heat is necessary.[18] Higher-quality units in Houston typically have central heating, and lack of heat or presence of only substandard heating such as space heaters is still an indication of lower quality. Inadequate heat was negatively and significantly associated with gross rent for all years. While the size of the negative coefficient increased, the percentage amount by which inadequate heat reduced rent declined over time relative to the dramatic increase in rent.

The cost of a room increased more in Houston than in the other areas studied, by nearly $20. The percentage of rent attributable to rooms (the mean number of rooms times the price coefficient) was 37 percent of gross rent in 1983 as opposed to 25 percent in 1976. The data do not allow much interpretation on whether this may reflect an increase in the quality of construction or in the size of rooms. The cost of bathrooms increased in Houston, as was not the case in Baltimore and Chicago.

Age of the structure follows a more predictable pattern in Houston than in the other two metropolitan areas. New construction consistently commands a premium, while old construction is consistently discounted, an indication perhaps that, unlike the case in Chicago, gentrification of older neighborhoods is not widespread in Houston. Units built during the boom period of 1950 to 1970 are not significantly different in price from those more than three years old at the time of the survey. It can be seen in Table 9.9 that Houston renters pay a premium for living in the central city, and that premium has increased significantly over time. Units in larger buildings are significantly less expensive in Houston, a challenge either to the hypothesis that increasing professionalization drives up rents or to the validity of this measure to test the hypothesis.

Informants have indicated that Houston has had an abundance of poorly constructed housing, which is gradually being eliminated (Ballinger interview, 1989), but this is not reflected in the level of structural

Table 9.9
Regression of Gross Rent on Characteristics of Unit and Unit and Renter, Houston SMSA

Variable	Model One						Model Two					
	1976		1979		1983		1976		1979		1983	
	B	t	B	t	B	t	B	t	B	t	B	t
Constant	81.37	8.35***	141.83	11.74***	88.46	3.52***	96.39	9.77***	155.85	12.40***	92.18	3.91***
Central city	4.26	1.24	16.80	3.93***	42.78	4.93***	11.80	3.57***	22.81	5.60***	47.90	5.71***
Rooms	22.72	16.57***	19.20	11.60***	41.14	10.46***	22.20	16.41***	15.09	9.38***	40.25	10.61***
Boom constru	13.24	3.20****	2.06	.41	3.54	.36	7.29	1.89*	-1.33	-.28	8.88	.99
New constru	30.33	5.76***	36.68	5.69***	53.29	4.00***	19.07	3.90***	28.14	4.72***	52.35	4.26***
Old constru	-23.25	-4.48***	-14.51	-2.14**	-21.40	-1.66*	-28.74	-6.65***	-18.25	-2.84***	-22.18	-3.90***
Bad street	-29.72	-5.93***	-41.66	-6.06***	-61.02	-4.28***	-13.24	-2.82***	-23.69	-3.70***	-19.62	-1.47
Baths	89.70	29.09***	83.92	20.04***	111.50	13.60***	76.64	26.52***	64.65	16.51***	96.60	12.59***
Air Condition	33.45	28.42***	32.27	21.58***	22.57	7.85***	25.39	22.01***	25.10	17.58***	15.04	5.62***
No. units	-.34	-.40	-6.09	-4.56***	-6.95	-3.06***	-.03	-.04	-6.37	-5.75***	-5.71	-2.69***
Inad. electric	-.34	-.01	0.00	0.00	-20.32	-.32	-7.60	-.25	0.00	0.00	-9.83	.86
Inad. heat	-24.50	-6.91***	-32.04	-6.04***	-36.59	-3.80***	-20.99	-6.40***	-31.69	-6.82***	-21.21	-3.19***
Inad. hall	13.65	.37	-86.06	-2.14**	-11.75	-.26	-4.20	-.13	-68.46	-1.88*	-25.17	-.61
Inad. sewer	-1.70	-.54	-10.85	-2.48**	14.00	1.69*	.38	.14	-5.79	-1.43	12.21	1.63
Inad. structu	-15.08	-2.02**	-10.29	-1.31	-30.75	-2.16**	-10.37	-1.81*	-1.48	-.20	-31.07	-2.41**
Inad. kitchen	-101.32	-8.39***	-102.08	-6.02***	-108.01	-2.48**	-80.25	-7.23***	-70.53	-4.50***	-71.20	-1.80*
Hispanic							-15.81	-3.49***	-5.71	-1.03	-20.61	-1.86*
Black							-42.13	-11.21***	-43.58	-8.99***	-64.27	-5.46***
Income							.001	12.86***	.002	17.44***	.002	6.25***
Children							4.01	3.38***	8.66	5.39***	7.96	2.50**
Subsidized							-90.47	-13.10***	-77.30	-9.83***	-118.51	-7.37***
Head < 25							-3.67	-1.11	6.40	1.46	1.13	.12
Head > 65							-1.93	-.36	-48.50	-7.07***	-39.71	-2.59***
Female							-6.25	-1.69*	10.24	2.55***	-9.26	-1.22
High educ.							22.51	6.91***	19.29	4.54***	27.02	3.12***
Dropout							-12.91	-3.59***	-8.96	-1.86*	-23.91	-2.52**
R Squared	.57		.37		.49		.64		.47		.58	
N of cases [a]	5234		5913		1344		5080		5715		1338	

[a] weighted by the population weight divided by mean weight   *p < .1; **p < .05; *** p ≤ .01;

inadequacies reported in the AHS. Poor quality continued to have a more stable rent-reducing effect in Houston, among all renters, than in Baltimore and Chicago. Having inadequate heat and living on a bad street were significantly rent reducing in all three time periods. By 1983, four of the seven indicators of substandard quality (inadequate heat, structure, kitchen, and street) were still significantly negative for all renters. The size of the coefficients also increased over time, so that their proportional effect on reducing a rising rent had eroded only modestly in some cases, and in others, not at all. Having an inadequate sewer however, which had been significantly negative in 1979, was significant and positive in 1983.

Characteristics of Houston Renters in Relation to Gross Rent

Households with children paid higher rents in Houston in all three years, but more in 1983 than in 1976. Elderly households paid less. In all cities we would expect an increased ability of the aged, relative to other age groups, to obtain subsidized housing, but this factor did not reduce the rent paid by the elderly in Chicago or Baltimore. However, only 5 percent of the renter population in Houston were over the age of 65, a decline from 7 percent in 1976. This may indicate a reduced demand for the type of rental housing typically occupied by the elderly.

Model 2 shows that by 1983, Hispanics, as well as blacks, paid less rent than whites in Houston, with blacks paying considerably less than Hispanics. To test whether or not this finding held up within submarkets, separate hedonic regressions were run for white, black, and Hispanic renters in the Houston SMSA.

According to James, McCummings, and Tynan (1984), Houston was much more highly segregated in both 1970 and 1980 than either Denver or Phoenix, cities that also had large Hispanic populations. During the decade, there was a significant increase in the concentration of blacks in central-city ghettos and in main black communities lying outside of the central city. Hispanics spread out and occupied more neighborhoods than blacks, but there was little integration with whites taking place. Seventy-four percent of Hispanic renters and 89 percent of black renters still lived in the central city of Houston in 1983.

It is possible that although blacks and Hispanics pay less rent than whites overall, within certain areas or for certain bundles of housing services they may pay more. Schafer (1979) demonstrated that in Boston, blacks received a discount relative to white neighborhoods for housing of low quality, but paid a premium in the ghetto for amenities such as air conditioning. In Boston, a nice house in the ghetto was more expensive for blacks than a comparable house was for whites in the white submarket.

Table 9.10 compares the weighted means and standard deviations for whites, blacks, and Hispanics in the Houston SMSA in 1976 and 1983. As can be seen, whites paid higher mean gross rents in both time periods, but blacks and Hispanics had much larger percentage increases in rents over the eight years. A 20-percent increase for whites can be compared with a 32-percent increase for Hispanics and a 38-percent increase for blacks. (Note that in chapter 7, median rents were shown to have increased even more for blacks.) This finding is important, since it indicates that the largest percentage changes in rent are occurring at the low end of the housing market. Hispanics are seen to live in somewhat smaller units in terms of number of rooms than blacks or whites, and both blacks and Hispanics have fewer bathrooms and air conditioners. Blacks and Hispanics are much more likely to live on a street with boarded-up buildings. Twelve percent of Hispanics and 23 percent of blacks lived on such a street in 1983 as compared with 4 percent of whites. Blacks and Hispanics have much higher incidences of inadequate heat and poor-quality structure, and few live in newly constructed units.

Table 9.11 compares the hedonic equations for non-Hispanic white, black, and Hispanic renters in the three time periods. By 1983, none of the indicators of poor quality, including living on a street with boarded-up units, were significantly rent reducing for blacks. In 1976, three indicators—bad street, inadequate kitchen, and inadequate heat—had been significant, and in 1979, four inadequacies—street, heat, sewer, and public hall—had been statistically significant in reducing rent. It might be argued that the coefficients have become more negative over time and that the reduction in sample size accounts for their failure to reach significance. However, with even smaller sample sizes, two of these low-quality variables reached significance for Hispanics.

For Hispanics, two low-quality variables were significant each year. By 1983, living on a street with boarded-up units began to discount rent for Hispanics, as it had since 1976 for all renters. Blacks paid a higher premium for living in the central city than did Hispanics. For whites, the number of rent-reducing inadequacies declined from four in 1976 and 1979 to two in 1983. Only inadequate heat and living on a bad street were contributing to a reduced rent by the later survey date.

Estimating the Cost of Housing Bundles over Time

Because the coefficients when multiplied by their mean values represent dollars in the additive model, it is possible to grossly es-

Table 9.10
Weighted Means and Standard Deviations of Quality and Renter Variables for Occupied Units for White, Black and Hispanic Renters, Houston SMSA

variable	Whites				Blacks				Hispanics			
	1976		1983		1976		1983		1976		1983	
	Mean	S.D.	Mean	S.D.	Mean	S.D.	Mean	S.D.	Mean	S.D.	Mean	S.D.
Gross rent	$403.56	154.70	$483.98	198.11	$266.43	108.35	$351.24	133.74	$286.50	113.21	$385.08	146.83
Central city	.720	.449	.555	.497	.913	.282	.891	.321	.798	.402	.741	.439
Number Rooms	3.981	1.210	4.097	1.268	4.020	1.352	4.058	1.134	3.789	1.176	3.969	1.244
Number Baths	1.322	.560	1.371	.588	1.118	.396	1.130	.370	1.126	.409	1.180	.467
Bad Street	.046	.209	.038	.191	.211	.408	.227	.429	.155	.362	.116	.321
New Construction	.141	.348	.157	.364	.062	.241	.016	.127	.041	.198	.054	.227
Boom Construction	.408	.492	.297	.457	.355	.479	.329	.471	.305	.461	.270	.445
Old Construction	.223	.416	.159	.366	.415	.493	.300	.459	.581	.494	.505	.501
Inad structure	.027	.170	.032	.201	.104	.328	.136	.380	.093	.308	.145	.388
Inad public hall	.001	.035	.004	.065	.001	.034	.010	.101	.004	.061	.014	.118
Inad heat	.149	.397	.124	.375	.337	.515	.338	.552	.482	.583	.461	.626
inad electricity	.000	.026	.003	.073	.001	.046	.000	.000	.004	.086	.000	.000
Inad sewer	.109	.450	.114	.460	.147	.514	.067	.362	.097	.419	.162	.528
Inad kitchen	.010	.098	.004	.065	.035	.183	.024	.152	.008	.090	.000	.000
Number units	5.946	2.282	5.635	2.295	4.956	2.079	5.179	2.019	4.701	2.063	4.898	1.897
No. Airconditioners	3.304	1.622	3.311	1.560	1.571	1.727	2.178	1.795	1.368	1.602	2.035	1.960
N of cases	3379		874		1097		265		658		204	

Table 9.11

Regression of Gross Rent on Characteristics of Unit for Whites, Blacks
and Hispanics, Houston SMSA, 1976–1983

Variable	NonHispanic White Renters 1976 B	1976 t	1983 B	1983 t	Black Renters 1976 B	1976 t	1983 B	1983 t	Hispanic Renters 1979 B	1979 t	1983 B	1983 t
constant	63.56	5.15***	59.43	1.83*	154.58	8.19***	161.91	3.36***	86.21	3.30***	212.46	3.61***
cencity	16.44	3.87***	71.93	6.44***	24.42	2.70**	46.45	2.22**	1.95	.25	16.41	.86
rooms	34.21	17.33***	52.34	10.03***	5.31	2.79**	29.11	4.16***	30.93	10.32***	23.29	2.97***
new const	23.14	3.78***	63.29	4.11***	24.42	1.51	87.34	1.71*	51.40	2.70**	-38.72	-.99
old const	-33.15	-4.99***	-14.61	-.85	-31.00	-3.30**	-55.95	-3.36***	-18.63	-1.23	-13.51	-.46
boom const	5.96	1.20	10.77	.87	7.81	.95	-37.55	-2.14**	10.22	.75	3.41	.14
bad street	-22.20	-2.51**	-50.22	-1.88*	-11.50	-1.87*	-15.24	-.87	-11.43	-1.32	-47.77	-1.95*
baths	93.46	24.53***	118.07	11.77***	44.62	6.60***	33.96	1.73*	34.34	4.39***	43.61	2.15**
aircondition	24.16	15.12***	15.99	4.21***	32.81	15.74***	26.84	5.24***	29.91	10.00***	32.97	4.94***
no. units	.73	.69	-8.87	-3.12**	-3.29	-2.12**	-4.23	-.95	3.51	1.66*	-4.87	-.84
inad heat	-34.19	-6.69***	-32.61	-2.17**	-11.94	-2.18**	-23.88	-1.55	-8.12	-1.36	-26.61	-1.82*
inad hall	-1.57	-.03	-54.84	-.72	18.71	.26	-29.80	-.45	12.41	.24	14.28	.22
inad elect	35.60	.51	-42.87	-.64	-52.57	-.78	0	0	1.52	-.04	0	0
inad sewer	.12	.03	18.32	1.69*	5.39	1.11	-14.72	-.81	-16.00	-2.15**	9.08	.61
inad struct	-20.12	-1.85*	-22.70	.88	3.20	.42	-27.18	-1.14	-11.40	-1.07	-17.00	-.83
inad kitch	-91.67	-4.80***	-93.63	-1.27	-72.47	-5.06***	-44.00	-.99	-79.07	-2.26**	0	0
R Squared	.54		.49		.46		.43		.53		.51	
N of cases[a]	3379		874		1097		265		658		204	

*=p <.1; **=p <.05; ***=p <.01;

[a] weighted by the population weight divided by mean weight

0 indicates no units with given inadequacies identified in that year.

205

timate the cost of specific housing bundles. Five housing bundles are
estimated for white, black, and Hispanic renters over two time periods. The first is a small central-city house built in the boom period,
1950 to 1970, in a slum (boarded-up units on the street), with no air
conditioning and with substandard heating. Table 9.12 shows that
blacks and whites would pay about the same for this bundle in 1976,
but by 1983 whites would pay considerably more.

The second bundle is a central-city multifamily unit with one air
conditioner, built before 1950, without central heating, and on a bad
street. The third bundle is a similar unit, but on a street without
boarded-up units. Here it can be seen that Hispanics would pay more
than black or white renters in the first time period, but by the second,
whites would pay more than either blacks or Hispanics. Blacks would
pay only slightly less for a unit on a street with boarded-up buildings,
while whites and Hispanics would pay considerably less. This is due
to the fact that blacks receive little reduction in rent, either absolutely
or relative to whites and Hispanics, for living on a bad street. Nearly
one-fourth of black renters lived on such a street in 1983. This finding
points out that although blacks are seen to pay less rent than whites
overall, the housing that is occupied by blacks may be relatively
expensive for its quality. Blacks were also found to pay a higher price
than whites for units with air conditioning.

The fourth and fifth bundles show that outside of the central city,
both blacks and Hispanics pay less than white renters for ostensibly
equivalent units. Because the coefficients for new construction and
living in a multiunit are negative for Hispanics, these renters are seen
to pay less (in constant 1986 dollars) for a modern suburban two-
bedroom with central air in a large complex in 1983 than they would
have paid in 1976. It is problematic to assume that we are dealing with
standard measures for variables such as rooms. The fact that
Hispanics show a decline in the cost of rooms between 1976 and 1983
and a negative, though nonsignificant, value for new construction
may be an indication that units occupied by Hispanics are declining
in square footage per room relative to older units.

The point to be made with these bundles of housing services is that,
in spite of the fact that minorities were shown to pay less than whites
in the Houston housing market as a whole, it is possible to describe
bundles in which they pay more. It is difficult to make any assumptions about discriminatory effects from these equations. Lower housing costs for minorities than for whites may indicate that whites are
willing to pay a premium to live separately from minorities and to pay
a higher premium for segregation from blacks than from Hispanics. It
is troubling, however, that the substandard housing disproportionately occupied by minorities is no longer relatively less expensive for

Table 9.12
Price Comparison of Housing Bundles for Houston SMSA: Non-Hispanic White,
Black, and Hispanic Renters, 1976 and 1983 in Constant 1986 CPI-XI Dollars

Renters	1976	1983
3 Room Detached, Central City, Built 1950–1970, One Bath, Bad Street, No Air, Inadequate Heat		
Hispanic Renters	$206	$271
Black Renters	$224	$253
White Renters	$226	$334
All Renters	$203	$272
4 Rooms, Central City, One Bath, in 50 Unit Building, Old Construction, Bad Street, Inadequate Heat, One Air Conditioner		
Hispanic Renters	$270	$268
Black Renters	$193	$253
White Renters	$250	$314
All Renters	$219	$248
Same Type Unit, Not On A Street With Boarded Up Units		
Hispanic Renters	$281	$320
Black Renters	$205	$268
White Renters	$272	$364
All Renters	$249	$309
6 Rooms Outside Central City, Built 1950–1970, 1 1/2 Baths, One Air Conditioner, Inadequate Public Hall, in 10 Unit Building		
Hispanic Renters	$400	$434
Black Renters	$290	$317
White Renters	$442	$466
All Renters	$412	$468
New 2 Bedroom (4 room) Outside Central City, 2 Bath, Central Air, in 50+ Unit Building		
Hispanic Renters	$481	$442
Black Renters	$391	$503
White Renters	$514	$580
All Renters	$513	$571

blacks. Instead, mean rents have risen for black households by nearly 40 percent in just eight years. This increase might be related to the increase of homelessness among blacks in Houston.

SEATTLE SMSA

It might be predicted that of the three metropolitan areas, Seattle would be the most comparable to Houston in that both are rapidly growing areas in which renters have experienced large increases in mean rent and have fairly stable mean incomes. However, the regressions for

Seattle shown in Table 9.13 present quite a different picture from those of Houston. First we notice that unlike the other metropolitan areas, there was no difference in mean rent between the central city and the suburbs. Secondly, the cost of a room was already much more expensive in Seattle in 1976 than in the other areas studied, and it changed little in the eight-year period, increasing from $49 to $53. The contribution of room price to total mean rent therefore dropped, from 58 percent to 53 percent, but still exceeded that of the other areas.

Similarly the price of bathrooms rose modestly but as a percent of total rent dropped slightly. New construction was no longer at a premium by 1983, but pre-1950 construction was still significantly discounted. Air conditioners had a very small impact on mean gross rent and they are not widely available in rental housing. In Seattle, as in Houston, there does seem to be some economy of scale at work. Units in larger buildings became significantly less expensive, a reversal from 1976 when they were slightly, but significantly, more expensive.

While living on a bad street was rent reducing in all three time periods, its impact on gross rent declined. In 1976 there were three additional negative quality indicators that were statistically significant. By 1979 only lack of a complete kitchen was significantly reducing rent. In 1983, units with incomplete kitchens were not significantly less expensive, but those with inadequate structures were. The coefficients of three of the five remaining quality variables, even though nonsignificant, had less of a rent-reducing effect over time. Thus we see quite a substantial change in the effect of quality variables over the eight-year period in Seattle. Because the overall level of substandard quality declined somewhat and was quite low to begin with, it cannot be claimed that increasing rents were not accompanied by increasing quality. It can be said that poor quality was not associated with lower rent to the same extent in 1983 that it was in 1976.

More so than in the other metropolitan areas studied, increased rents in Seattle appear to be a function of market demand. Vacancy rates are very low, as a result of a strong economy and intense in-migration. The cost of owned housing is rising rapidly. The substandard housing typically occupied by the poor does not exist to any great extent in Seattle, and what does exist is not much less expensive. This may help us understand why Seattle, in spite of its thriving economy, has a high rate of homelessness.

In Model 2, it is seen that blacks in 1983 paid significantly more for housing in the Seattle SMSA, while in 1976 they had paid significantly less. Is this a sign that in a tight housing market, blacks are more likely to be discriminated against? Neither Hispanic renters nor females paid significantly higher rents by 1983. Households with children, as in all the areas studied, paid an increased premium. In Seattle, high-

Table 9.13
Regression of Gross Rent on Characteristics of Unit and Unit and Renter, Seattle SMSA

Variable	Model One 1976 B	Model One 1976 t	Model One 1979 B	Model One 1979 t	Model One 1983 B	Model One 1983 t	Model Two 1976 B	Model Two 1976 t	Model Two 1979 B	Model Two 1979 t	Model Two 1983 B	Model Two 1983 t
Constant	66.54	4.62***	217.40	14.97***	168.97	7.88***	105.81	8.18***	190.92	13.76***	132.71	6.77***
Central city	-10.08	-2.79***	-5.78	-1.23	-5.75	-.79	-3.03	.94	1.38	.32	5.42	.83
Rooms	49.01	36.30***	41.94	26.99***	53.03	20.35***	41.84	32.13***	33.67	22.85***	48.08	19.84***
Boom const	30.04	3.12***	-14.88	-1.71*	-4.58	-.50	-15.40	-1.79*	-21.44	-2.75**	-14.35	-1.77*
New const	88.80	7.27***	43.19	4.02***	11.14	.84	27.60	2.54***	28.57	2.98***	7.17	.62
Old const	-30.87	-3.12***	-73.12	-7.99***	-40.33	-3.79***	-68.12	-7.67***	-74.39	-9.00***	-46.78	-5.02***
Bad street	-41.68	-6.89***	-52.44	-6.19***	-41.21	-2.79***	-20.66	-3.88***	-31.88	-4.22***	-21.94	-1.68*
Baths	62.84	14.79***	60.07	12.01***	69.22	9.13***	43.84	11.74***	42.26	9.39***	45.66	6.80***
Aircondition	15.37	3.86***	30.54	6.43***	24.98	3.64***	5.76	1.56	25.97	5.90***	18.62	3.11***
No. units	1.62	1.74*	-6.90	-5.84***	-7.69	-4.08***	2.08	2.41**	-4.26	-3.82***	-3.46	-2.03**
Inad electric	-31.52	-1.43	52.53	.95	0.00	0.00	-38.06	-2.00**	54.03	1.10	0.00	0.00
Inad heat	-4.59	-.70	-1.08	-.13	-7.00	-.33	-5.05	-.89	-.12	-.02	-7.02	-.37
Inad hall	45.74	1.26	-5.37	-.11	-20.66	-.51	56.79	1.81*	11.55	.26	12.63	.35
Inad sewer	-15.19	-2.34**	2.29	.28	-4.87	-.41	-13.62	-2.42**	10.07	1.39	-13.17	-1.28
Inad structu	-25.11	-2.76***	4.36	.41	-46.01	-2.22**	-31.56	-3.97***	1.47	.16	-44.83	-2.46**
Inad kitchen	-89.94	-6.33***	-110.29	-6.33***	-37.36	-1.13	-73.00	-5.92***	-92.26	-6.96***	-25.84	-.89
Hispanic							5.05	.45	4.28	.33	3.50	.17
Black							-14.62	-2.31**	-1.42	-.17	21.74	1.87*
Income							.002	18.65***	.003	18.95***	.002	10.68***
Children							5.33	3.12***	11.53	4.92***	8.90	2.80***
Subsidized							-130.63	-23.16***	-163.11	-21.45***	-161.05	-14.21***
Head <25							5.28	1.49	21.52	4.70***	5.78	.77
Head >65							4.60	.96	-2.90	-.45	6.32	.60
Female							9.51	3.04***	10.89	2.69***	-8.22	1.39
High educ							13.88	4.24***	18.55	4.44***	26.65	4.27***
Dropout							-18.10	-4.26***	-21.48	-3.63***	15.63	1.76**
R Squared	.44		.32		.46		.59		.47		.59	
N of cases [a]	4306		5145		1592		4230		5041		1580	

school dropouts also experienced a reversal since 1979 and in 1983 paid significantly higher rents than the omitted category of high-school graduates.

COMPARISON OF HOUSING COSTS ACROSS METROPOLITAN AREAS

The additive model allows us to compare the cost of housing bundles within metropolitan areas. Considering the variation in gross rent

Table 9.14

Price Comparison of Housing Bundles by SMSA for 1976 and 1983 in Constant 1986 CPI-XI Dollars

Metropolitan Area	1975–6	1983
2 Room Plus Bath, Central City, Old Construction,4 plex.		
Baltimore	$193	$178
Chicago	$202	$212
Houston	$197	$283
Seattle	$191	$275
5 Room Detached, Central City, Built 1950–1970, One Bath, Inadequate Heat		
Baltimore	$280	$351
Chicago	$306	$256
Houston	$278	$415
Seattle	$390	$486
4 Rooms Plus Bath in 4 Unit Building,Central City, Old Construction, Bad Street, Inadequate Heat		
Baltimore	$240	$232
Chicago	$236	$249
Houston	$188	$261
Seattle	$245	$325
Six Rooms Outside Central City, Built 1950–70,1 1/2 Baths, One Airconditioner, Inadequate Sewer, in 10 Unit Building		
Baltimore	$432	$475
Chicago	$473	$522
Houston	$400	$494
Seattle	$496	$553
New 2 Bedroom (4 Room) 2 Bath, Central Air, Suburban in 50+ Unit Building		
Baltimore	$529	$419
Chicago	$591	$600
Houston	$513	$571
Seattle	$550	$588

that is explained by these models, ranging in 1983 from .25 to .49, these estimations are crude at best. They do give some indication of the substantial variability across these areas in the cost of housing. Table 9.14 provides price comparisons for five different bundles of housing, three within and two outside of the central city. It can be seen that rents increased for all five bundles in Seattle and Houston, but less uniformly for Baltimore and Chicago.

This is consistent with the much higher percentage increase in gross rent in the former metropolitan areas. The table illustrates that within Chicago and Baltimore, there were some bundles of housing services that appear to have been less expensive (in constant dollars) in 1983 than they were in 1976. In these two areas however, the mean income of renters fell over the period, by 9 percent in Baltimore and 4 percent in Chicago, whereas in Houston mean renter income was unchanged and in Seattle it was up by 4 percent. These findings illustrate that changes in the rent to income ratio can result from declining incomes or from rising rents, or both, and that the salience of these factors will vary across metropolitan areas. The relationship between the extent of homelessness and the changes in income and rent across the central cities of the four metropolitan areas will be examined in the final chapter.

NOTES

1. It is also true that high rates of homeownership are a good indication of the deconcentration of ownership.

2. Heilbrun (1974:256) cites data from the U.S. Bureau of the Census showing a reduction by two-thirds between 1960 and 1970 in the proportion of units that lacked complete plumbing. Within central cities, 79 percent of units that lacked complete plumbing were occupied by renters rather than owners (ibid.:244).

3. This argument was made 15 years ago by Heilbrun (1974) and seems all the more relevant today.

4. These are cross-sectional changes. As noted in the methodology section, longitudinal analysis is possible with the AHS, but is greatly limited by the vastly reduced sample size in the most recent years of the survey.

5. Margaret Reid (1962:376-78) found that the income elasticity of the number of rooms per person was about +.5. Thus although space consumption goes up as income rises, the larger share of increased consumption must be accounted for by other factors, which Reid assumes to be quality.

6. The dummy and individual quality variables do not appear in the same regressions, but for convenience both are shown in the tables of means and standard deviations.

7. The omitted category is units built after 1970 and at least three years before the date of the survey.

8. The six inadequacy variables cannot be viewed as proportions of the stock that are inadequate because they are not dummy variables. Changes in these figures could occur as a unit changes from inadequate to severely inadequate or vice versa. The percentage of all units that had such inadequacies or severe inadequacies was provided in earlier tables. The proportion of the stock that has any inadequacy or severe inadequacy is represented by the dummy variables. Note that inadequate heat is included in Table 9.3 for Houston.

9. A large portion of the work of the United Housing Coalition in Detroit, in addition to helping tenants whose landlords fail to make repairs, is devoted to restoring utilities to households whose landlords have not paid the bills (Ted Phillips interview, 3/89).

10. Heilbrun (1974:258-61). Russell Baker (1989) reports that the city of New York owns more than 5,000 vacant buildings, some of which are occupied by squatters.

11. The proportion of the renter population below the poverty line was stable in Baltimore and Houston between 1976 and 1979 and fell in Seattle over this period. Only in Chicago did the proportion in poverty increase monotonically.

12. The cost of a room in 1983 ($39.07) times the mean number of rooms in 1983 (4.595) = $179.53; if cost was constant, $39.07 x the mean number of rooms in 1976 (4.427) = $172.96; the difference is $6.50.

13. Earlier models did not include age of the structure or the number of units.

14. The number of children was collinear (above .8) with total household members, which was dropped from the model.

15. An estimate of the income elasticity of demand for 1976 is .002 (the income coefficient) x $21,039 (mean income) divided by $338 (mean gross rent) = .124. For 1983, it is .004 x $19,991/384 = .208. This is a substantial increase and may be indicative of lower-income households being driven out of the market.

16. Seattle had the greatest increase (25 percent) in median gross rent in the central city, as is discussed in the final chapter.

17. Central air is treated as equivalent to one unit per room.

18. U.S. Bureau of the Census (1983). Heating degree days for Baltimore, Chicago, and Seattle are given in Table 3.6.

10

Conclusions

This study began with a number of hypotheses about the relationship between homelessness and the affordability of rental housing for the low-income population. Specifically, it has been demonstrated that in the four metropolitan areas and central cities studied, there has been an increase in the numbers of renter households with incomes below 125 percent of the poverty line, thus increasing demand for low cost housing, and there has been a concomitant decline in the availability of low-cost rental units. The housing squeeze that has resulted leads renters to pay increasing proportions of income to rent over time. The rent burden of many low-income renters has reached levels that one might predict are unsustainable for the long term.

In attempting to explain why the extent of homelessness varies widely across metropolitan areas, the hypothesis was made that the extent of homelessness would be associated with the extent of the mismatch between size and incomes of the low-income renter population and the availability of low-cost housing within those areas. The relative contribution that increased numbers of low-income households and decreased numbers of low-cost units have made to this housing squeeze, as well as the severity of the mismatch, was found to vary across metropolitan areas. Under the assumption that excessive rent burdens among the poor and those of low income result from lack of alternatives rather than through choice, the extent of the mismatch will be represented here by the size of the vulnerable population—those low-income households who pay in excess of 45 percent of their incomes to rent. How strongly is this mismatch associated with estimated levels of homelessness in these areas?

To reiterate, the relationship between homelessness and the renter population was described as follows:

$$\frac{\text{Homeless}}{\text{Total Pop.}} = \frac{\text{Renters}}{\text{Total Pop.}} \times \frac{\text{Low-Inc. Renters}}{\text{All Renters}} \times \frac{\text{Vulnerable}}{\text{Low-Inc. Renters}} \times \frac{\text{Homeless}}{\text{Vulnerable}}$$

Ideally, one would like to estimate two such equations, one for 1975-76 and one for 1983. Table 10.1 summarizes these relationships for two time periods in the four central cities. Note that a major shortcoming of the data is a lack of information about the extent of homelessness prior to 1983. While it would be desirable to compare changes in the proportion of renters, low-income renters, and vulnerable renters with changes in the proportion of homeless over time, the reliability of the scant data that exist on homelessness at the earlier time period does not warrant such a comparison. At the bottom of the table is shown the per capita rate of homelessness and the size of the estimated homeless population for the Rand McNally Metropolitan Areas[1] as estimated by HUD for 1983.

Assume for the moment that the data allow us to conclude that homelessness was an insignificant problem in 1975 and that the occupants of skid row at that time were by and large not homeless in the same sense that to be homeless means today. We would then want to account for differences in the rate of growth of homelessness that would have led, for example, to a nearly tenfold difference in per capita homelessness between Baltimore and Chicago by 1983. Such an assumption would be flawed, but because the extent of change is central to understanding why there has been a growth in homelessness over time, much of the discussion that follows will focus on the change in the three ratios that can be estimated.

If one considers the ratios for which data is available in Table 10.1, it is clear that of the four cities, Chicago has the most adverse indicators, which would be associated with a higher per capita rate of homelessness. Chicago has the highest proportion of households that are renters; a high proportion of low-income renters, equivalent to that of Baltimore; and by far the greatest percentage of low-income renters who are vulnerable. In the absence of any knowledge about the extent of homelessness in Chicago in 1975, we would predict, on the basis of this formula, that Chicago would have the highest per capita rate of homelessness.

It was hypothesized that homelessness within a city would be inversely related to the extent of homeownership. The percentage of central-city households that were homeowners increased over the period in all but Seattle, which had a 2-percentage point-decline but which remained the highest in percentage of all households that were

Table 10.1
Total Population, Number of Units, Renter Households, Low Income Renters, Vulnerable Renters, and Homeless Estimates for 4 Central Cities

Number	Baltimore		Chicago		Houston		Seattle	
	1976	1983	1975	1983	1976	1983	1976	1983
Total SMSA Population	2,027,100	2,224,400	6,797,400	6,891,800	2,243,200	3,354,100	1,406,700	1,643,300
Total Central City Population	751,400	740,800	2,953,100	2,808,300	1,271,700	1,401,400	508,100	520,700
Central City Households	268,600	273,300	1,069,900	1,045,900	463,000	531,500	222,800	240,300
Renters Households	146,700	143,200	667,100	634,200	253,500	292,000	103,500	117,200
Percent Renters	54.6	51.5	62.4	60.6	55.4	54.9	46.4	48.8
Median Rent	$291	$308	$293	$325	$347	$411	$285	$357
Percent Increase		5.6		10.9		18.4		25.3
Low Income Renters	57,000	57,370	207,360	250,430	41,320	65,410	22,010	28,610
Percent Low Income	38.9	40.1	31.1	39.5	16.3	22.4	21.3	24.4
Vulnerable Renters	29,810	28,770	134,180	175,050	25,650	40,790	12,750	17,290
Vulnerable as % Low Income	52.3	50.1	64.7	69.9	62.1	62.3	57.9	60.4
Vulerable as % All C.C. Households	11.1	10.5	12.5	16.7	5.5	7.7	5.7	7.2
Very Vulnerable	21,690	22,270	93,930	126,020	18,630	33,200	8170	12,670
Very Vul. as % All C.C. Households	8.1	8.1	8.8	13.3	4.0	6.2	3.7	5.3
Severly Vulnerable	15,230	18,420	49,780	110,900	15,250	29,610	4670	8300
Severe Vul. as % All C.C. Households	5.7	6.7	4.7	10.9	3.3	5.6	2.1	3.5
1983 Homeless Estimate	750		20,300		7500		3250	
Rate Per 10,000		3		28		22		20

Sources: Annual Housing Survey, 1975, 1976 and 1983; [a] HUD 1984

homeowners. It was followed by Baltimore, Houston, and Chicago. Sixty-one percent of central Chicago households rented in 1983.

The population of renter households who had low incomes increased significantly in Seattle, Houston, and Chicago. In Baltimore, which already had the highest percentage of renters (40 percent) who were below 125 percent of the poverty line, there was only a slight increase. The percentage increase was particularly large in Chicago, 27 percent, and Houston, 37 percent.

There were also divergent changes in the percentage of all low-income renters who were vulnerable—who paid more than 45 percent of income to rent. While the vulnerable among Baltimore renters had declined somewhat since 1976 to about half of all low-income renters, in Chicago 70 percent of low-income renters were vulnerable in 1983, an increase of five percentage points from 1975. In Houston, although there was a large increase in low-income renters, both in numbers and in percent of all renters, there was no change in the percentage of all low-income renters who were vulnerable. Although with an N of only 4 cities, multivariate analysis could not tell us a great deal, the zero order correlation coefficient between the per capita rate of homelessness and the percent of all low-income renters who are vulnerable is .98 for these 4 cities.

That the percentage of all Baltimore low-income renters who were vulnerable actually declined somewhat over the eight-year period, from 52 to 50 percent, is in part attributable to less dramatic changes in rent. While all four cities showed an increase in median gross rent that exceeded the rate of inflation, Baltimore had the lowest percentage increase in median gross rent between 1976 and 1983. Its 6 percent increase compares with 11 percent in Chicago, 18 percent in Houston, and 25 percent in Seattle.[2]

RENT AND HOMELESSNESS IN BALTIMORE

Perhaps, in spite of the high percentage of Baltimore renters who have low incomes, it is the stability in the numbers of low-income and vulnerable renters that is contributing to Baltimore's unexpectedly low per capita rate of homelessness. This stability was facilitated by relatively small increases in rent.

Baltimore also had the greatest percentage increase in homeowners among the four cities, lending support to the proposed relationship between rents and the cost of homeownership. Where homeownership is "affordable," the cost of owned housing may act as a ceiling on rents, since there will be a lower point at which owning is more economical than renting. The fall in median income of Baltimore renters may represent a case of higher-income renters becoming homeowners, and leaving behind a group of renters who are relatively poorer than in the past. We see that there was a slight growth in Baltimore in the number and percentage of households who were severely vulnerable.

Baltimore was also distinguished by having the highest percentage of vulnerable households headed by a female (75 percent). The proportion of the homeless in Baltimore who are women far exceeds the national average of 19 percent as found by Cohen and Burt (1989). Thirty-four to 36 percent of the homeless in Baltimore were found to be women (Cowan, Breakey, and Fischer, 1987; Institute of Medicine, 1988).

That levels of homelessness were not higher in Baltimore may be due in part to high levels of doubling up. Eight percent of vulnerable Baltimore renters and five percent of severely vulnerable renters had subfamilies in 1983, higher levels than those seen elsewhere except among low-income Hispanic renters in Houston. The number of public and subsidized housing units is higher in Baltimore than in Chicago. Because it is illegal to house subfamilies in such units, we can expect that there is considerable underreporting on subfamilies in these units.

Baltimore also has a network of nonprofit agencies, such as the Women's Housing Coalition, that have been in place for a number of years, working to help at-risk families avoid homelessness. The director of the coalition reports that it is generally possible to locate housing in the city for persons who are evicted or who otherwise lose their residence. The quality of such housing, as might be expected from the fact that 20 percent of Baltimore's rental housing stock is substandard, is not high (Melvin interview, 1989). The continued availability in Baltimore of relatively inexpensive poor-quality housing, the traditional home of the poor, would also lead us to predict that homelessness in Baltimore would not be as extensive as in other cities where more inexpensive substandard housing has been demolished. That the numbers of vulnerable remained fairly constant over the period would speculatively have allowed agencies and programs to deal more effectively with those who were at risk. The growth of homelessness may have been temporarily stalled in Baltimore by the stability of poverty. But, as might be expected from the growth in the severely vulnerable population to 1983, a substantial increase in the numbers of homeless in Baltimore was found by Cowan, Breakey, and Fischer, in 1987,[3] and reports from shelter operators showed a continued increased demand through 1989 (Action for the Homeless, 1989).

CHICAGO

For Chicago, in addition to the 11 percent rise in gross rent, there was an 11 percent decline in median income of all renters between 1975 and 1983 (see Table 6.1). The percentage of all renters who were low income increased from 31 to nearly 40 percent. Of these, the great majority were vulnerable, being unable to find housing that consumed less than 45 percent of income. More than half of low-income renters were very vulnerable, paying more than 60 percent of income to rent. The most rapidly increasing group in Chicago were the severely vulnerable. The number of these households more than doubled and by 1983 made up nearly 11 percent of all central-city households.

It can be seen that there were about five times as many of these severely vulnerable households as there were homeless individuals on any given night in Chicago in 1983. Since the time of the survey, there has been a tripling in the number of shelter beds in Chicago, from 891 to 2,542, and the publicly funded budget for shelter and drop-in services expanded from $277,000 in 1982 to $6.7 million in 1987 (Sosin, Colson, and Grossman, 1988). The number of shelter beds now equals the lower bound estimate of the homeless made by Rossi,Fisher, and Willis, (1986). Yet shelter operators in Chicago report turning away as many as half again the numbers who are sheltered because of lack of space (Sosin, Colson, and Grossman, 1988:236-37). Coupled with the substantial evidence that many of the homeless do not seek public shelter at all but stay in abandoned buildings, cars, or the like (Mc-Kinsey, 1989; Dockett, 1989), these factors lead me to question the accuracy of Rossi's estimates for Chicago.

Blacks were seen to be disproportionately represented among those vulnerable to homelessness in Chicago, as well as among those literally homeless, to an extent that they were not in Baltimore. The extended black family, which has been shown to be more likely than white families to provide help in time of crisis (La Gory et al., 1989), may help prevent the percentage of homeless who are black from rising even further. While there were fewer reported subfamilies in Chicago than in Baltimore, levels of overcrowding in terms of persons per room were higher in Chicago than in the other cities. That the majority of the vulnerable, but not the homeless, are women suggests that extended family networks are providing shelter and that these households may not identify additional members as subfamilies. It is likely that women, more than men, will go to extraordinary lengths to avoid homelessness. This is both mandated by the greater physical vulnerability of women and, perhaps, facilitated by a greater number of sources of social support among women than among men.

It cannot be stressed enough that to become homeless represents an almost unfathomable loss, not only of a physical address, space, privacy, and safety, but also of virtually all of one's worldly possessions, basic needs, and external identity. At a shelter in Detroit I was shown a room in which were piled brown plastic bags labeled with magic marker. Each homeless shelter resident was allowed one bag, no larger than approximately 24 inches square, in which to store everything he or she owned. Little beyond a change of clothing could be kept. Personal mementos were of necessity discarded in favor of more practical items. Each tampon and diaper had to be requested from a dispensary. No personal items could be left in the rooms during the day. That the homeless are frequently seen to be wearing layers of clothing or coats out of season is most likely due to having no place to store these things. Interviews with shelter operators have invariably confirmed the extreme demoralization associated with homelessness.

The extent of this trauma should tell us that homelessness is truly an end state; those who have reached it have first tried to avoid it by any means possible. The literal homeless are likely to represent a small portion of the population that verges on homelessness. We may expect that some people drift in and out of literal homelessness as their private living situations are lost and recreated.

The figures for Chicago indicate that the size of the at-risk population increased rapidly in just a few years. Economic vulnerability may be exacerbated by continuing residential segregation, which is more pronounced in Chicago than in virtually any other city (Massey and Denton, 1988). The evidence is suggestive that racial segregation and discrimination in housing play a role in the disproportionate representation of blacks among both the homeless and the population at risk.

HOUSTON

Despite a vacancy rate more than twice as high as that of the other cities, Houston median gross rent increased both at a faster rate and to a higher level. Overall, Houston renters had a 5 percent increase in median income with which to offset the 18 percent increase in gross rent. However, among low-income black and Hispanic households, rent increases were much higher. The per capita incomes of low-income black and Hispanic households actually fell over the period, while rents of blacks increased by 41 percent and Hispanics by 27 percent in just eight years. Whereas the rent burdens of low-income blacks and Hispanics had been about the same in 1976, by 1983 55 percent of these black households as compared with 35 percent of Hispanic households paid more than 60 percent of income to rent.

Hispanics were three times as likely to be overcrowded as blacks. These findings help explain why blacks are disproportionately represented among the homeless of Houston, while Hispanics are not. Although the two groups each make up about 19 percent of the Houston population, both a recent and a previous survey of the homeless have found blacks to be three to four times as likely as Hispanics to be homeless (McKinsay, 1989; Andrade, 1988).

While the percentage of all low-income Houston renters who were vulnerable remained constant at 62 percent, there was a near doubling in the numbers of households who were very vulnerable or severely vulnerable. A higher percentage of vulnerable renters were severely vulnerable in Houston than elsewhere. Eighty-one percent of vulnerable renters spent more than 60 percent of their incomes on rent, while nearly 75 percent of the vulnerable had less than $50 dollars per person remaining after rent is paid.

These 29,610 severely vulnerable households, representing 94,152 individuals (when multiplied by mean household size) in 1983, can be compared with the estimate of 108,000 individuals, including those doubled up, that a 1989 survey of the homeless in Houston found to be literally or on the verge of homelessness[4] (Resource Group Inc., 1989). Severely vulnerable renters composed about 6 percent of all central-city households in Houston.

That homelessness is as significant a problem as it is in Houston is proposed to be related to several factors in addition to rapidly increasing rent. Unlike Baltimore, Houston does not appear to have a strong network of nonprofit agencies working in housing, and as was pointed out earlier, the city has been less than aggressive in pursuing its fair share of federal housing dollars or in attempting to make up for the decline in federal dollars with local housing initiatives (Gilderbloom, Rosentraub, and Bullard, 1987). Racial discrimination in housing and the confinement of minorities to central-city submarkets (Feagin, 1988) were also proposed as factors contributing to homelessness in Houston.

SEATTLE

Although the decline in the percentage of homeowners is now a nationwide trend, this decline was already taking place in Seattle between 1976 and 1983. Seattle, the most economically healthy of the four cities (see Tables 3.5 and 3.6), had a smaller percentage of renter households than Houston, but a larger percentage of these renters had low incomes. About 44 percent of low-income households paid more than 60 percent of income to rent, and 29 percent were severely vulnerable. Thus, while the numbers and percentages of low-income renters were relatively small, among those who have less than 125 percent of poverty income a higher percentage were vulnerable than in Baltimore.

Median per capita income of Seattle renters was somewhat smaller than in Houston but grew by nearly 8 percent between 1976 and 1983. As noted earlier, rents in Seattle rose by 25 percent beyond the rate of inflation in just eight years. In the last chapter we saw that, while the quality of housing had improved over time in Seattle as it had not elsewhere, the association between poor quality and lower rent was not as strong as it had been in the past.

Seattle policymakers have speculated about the reasons for rising housing costs. Increased construction cost has largely been ruled out as a factor in the most recent rise in rent. Land costs are speculated to have risen, while interest rates are known to have had an effect over the period of study. Interest rates climbed to between 11 and 14 percent between 1980 and 1984, after remaining between 8.5 and 9.5 from 1970 to 1980. At the same time, inflation fell, leading to a net interest rate (mortgage interest rate minus inflation) that rose from 3 percent in 1981 to 8 percent in 1984.[5] These rates are passed on to renters. Of course, inflation in mortgage rates occurred across the country. To the extent that the housing stock was newly built and subject to high financing rates in Seattle and Houston, as opposed to Baltimore and Chicago, we would expect interest rates to have had a greater impact on rent in the former cities than in the latter.

Units in buildings with a large number of apartments were not more expensive in Seattle relative to smaller units, disputing the hypothesis that growing professionalization and concentration of ownership, as measured by the number of units in a complex, should be associated with higher rents (Gilderbloom and Appelbaum, 1987). To estimate what would constitute a "just" market rent—one offering a reasonable rate of return on investment—one would want to know the true profit margin for units in a large as opposed to a small apartment building. It is quite conceivable that the economies of scale inherent in a large complex should have allowed rents in buildings with many units to be much less than in single or duplex units.[6] The very modest reduction in gross rent associated with more units per building as seen in Seattle does not disprove the hypothesis that professionalization leads to higher relative rents. Further research is needed to test this.

It was seen in Seattle that a very low vacancy rate, coupled with rapid population growth and high ownership costs, led to a competitive market in which more renters competed for a limited stock, thus driving up prices. Sternlieb (1989:66) notes that as buying power declines relative to housing costs, "increased competition for units at the bottom rung of the ladder ... only intensifies the problems faced by those with the fewest resources." Increases in both rent and homelessness are easier to understand in Seattle in terms of "normal" market functions than in Houston, where rents and vacancies increased simultaneously.

The Seattle housing market has been characterized by an increasing bipolarization. Market analysis indicates that most of the new single-family homes that have been constructed in the last several years have been bigger, better-quality homes for those at the upper end of the housing market. For the low-income household, the trend has been increasingly toward multifamily units and mobile homes (Washington State Department of Community Development, 1989:39).[7] There is no evidence that the decline in the proportion of all single-family rental units is being driven by a preference on the part of renters for multi-family units. Instead, these trends are evidence of a growing two-tiered tenure system in which the advantages of ownership have increased, but ownership has become increasingly more difficult for low-income households to attain. Chevan (1989) notes that the difference in the probability of homeownership for a poor, unmarried, childless non-white male as opposed to a married, middle-class white male with children has more than doubled since 1940. The differences between renter and owner-occupied property in cost, quality, and density suggest that housing tenure is a growing part of "an overall pattern of structural inequality" (Dreier, 1982). Much of these differences have been attributed to the enormous unearned increment in housing value benefiting homeowners that occurred as a result of inflation in the post-1970 period, as well as to the tax policies that so clearly favor ownership over renting.

FEDERAL REDISTRIBUTIVE POLICIES

This brings us to the hypothesis that both the demand for and the supply of housing have been affected by federal policies. Only a small proportion of housing in the United States is socially owned. As Marcuse (1989:69) notes, "If housing is provided only in proportion to the profits to be made from its provision, those having too little money to buy adequate housing will be ill-housed regardless of how efficiently the market is organized." Federal policies have increased the proportion of the poor who, with reduced income from federal sources, are forced to compete on the open market for housing. But the impact of federal policies extends well beyond the controversy over housing as a right versus housing as a commodity. Federal redistributive programs, providing unlimited tax deductions for mortgage interest and property taxes to owners, make it profitable for the affluent to "overconsume" housing relative to needs. As owned housing is increasingly built at the high end of the market, the amount of tax expenditure or tax forgiveness has increased. At the same time, direct subsidies for low-income housing have been severely cut. Subsidies for low-income housing are subject to far greater scrutiny, as part of the annual federal budget review process, than are the subsidies that homeowners are able to deduct from their taxes (Dolbeare, 1989). Thus little public attention has been directed to the increasing inequity that has occurred over time in this subsidization.

Table 10.2 shows that federal expenditures for housing are heavily biased toward tax benefits for owners. In 1988, federal outlays for low-income housing assistance were only about one-fourth of the amount of tax forgiveness to owners. The National Low Income Housing Coalition estimates the regressivity of federal housing expenditures, including tax subsidies and housing programs, in Figure 10.1.[8]

For the low-income household, without substantial income that could be offset with tax deductions, the more serious disadvantages in being unable to own are the inability to stabilize housing costs and to accumulate transferable wealth. We have seen that the proportion of income being spent on rent by these renters has risen dramatically and may be unprecedentedly high by historical standards. In terms of residual income remaining after rent, such rent-to-income ratios are sufficient to create and to maintain de facto poverty among those who are 125 percent above the poverty line.

Homeownership is the main source of wealth accumulation for most families (Kain and Quigley, 1975). To the extent that the ability to become a homeowner may be increasingly tied to the tenure status of one's parents, tenure status may be viewed as a stratification mechanism promoting inequality from one generation to the next (Henretta, 1984). Such stratification is supported by the tax system.

It should not be considered an irony that the economy has improved while poverty has deepened.[9] The Reagan decade can stand as a giant social experiment testing the validity of "trickle-down" economics. Social programs were cut or eliminated under the (some would say) disingenuous assumption that they would be unnecessary in an era of economic expansion and lowered inflation. The results are quite striking in their failure to have lifted people out of poverty. In addition to the severe cuts in housing funds, the low-income population was adversely affected by cuts in federal social welfare programs, further decreasing their ability to afford market rate housing.

The anomaly of an expanding economy accompanied by deepening poverty is illustrated by the unemployment rate and emergency shel-

Table 10.2
Federal Spending for Housing in Billions of Dollars, 1976–1989

Year	Appropriations	Outlays	Tax expenditures
1976	$19.5	$3.2	11.2
1977	28.6	3.0	10.2
1978	32.3	3.7	14.7
1979	24.8	4.4	19.4
1980	27.9	5.6	26.5
1981	26.9	7.8	33.4
1982	14.6	8.7	35.6
1983	10.5	10.0	35.1
1984	12.7	11.3	37.9
1985	26.9	25.3	40.6
1986	11.6	12.4	48.5
1987	9.9	12.7	53.5
1988	9.7	13.9	53.9
1989 estimate	10.0	15.3	53.2

Source: Center for Budget and Policy Priorities, 1989

ter turnaways (number of persons unserved when shelters are filled beyond capacity) for Seattle. As unemployment returned to a more moderate level of 6 percent from a high of 9.8 percent in 1982, the number of shelter programs increased sixfold, and the number of persons who had to be turned away from homeless shelters showed an unrelenting increase of 167 percent. Families with children were more than twice as likely to be turned away from shelters as were single adults (Seattle King County Emergency Shelter Update, 1986).

Seattle was the clearest case among the four of a city battling to offset the loss of federal dollars through local programs, and losing the struggle. While these programs appear to have held the growth of homelessness to a moderate level, Seattle continues to have a serious problem of homelessness. Housing all of its low-income citizens and finding permanent solutions to homelessness have proved to be too expensive for even this prosperous and progressive city. For cities with very large poverty populations, such as Baltimore and Chicago, this is likely to be an insurmountable task. Figure 10.2 shows that as a percent of all renters who were severely vulnerable to homelessness, Chicago and Baltimore have the more serious problem.

Paul Peterson (1986) has identified housing as one of the critical areas in which the federal government should not disengage itself from responsibility as part of the "new federalism." It is the only level of

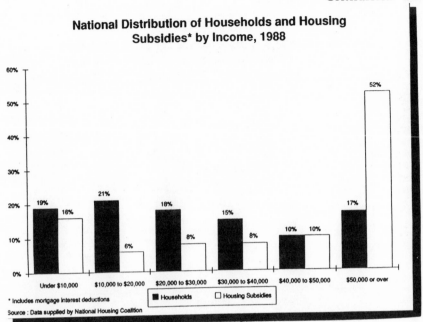

National Distribution of Households and Housing Subsidies* by Income, 1988

* Includes mortgage interest deductions

Source : Data supplied by National Housing Coalition

■ Households ☐ Housing Subsidies

Figure 10.1

government, he believes, that has the resources and the legitimate authority to provide housing on a massive and equitable scale. Most other Western industrialized countries promote "tenure-neutral" housing policies in which renters and owners are on a more even par (Gilderbloom and Appelbaum, 1987). In the United States, renters are in effect punished financially for their inability to become home owners.

This study began with the premise that housing problems and homelessness were structurally based. Ideally, they would be addressed with structural solutions. It has been argued (Marcuse, 1989) that focus on responding to the housing needs of special groups, such as the homeless, can divert attention from structural changes that are needed to address the more general issue of inequities in housing and other social goods. But, as some with many years of experience in trying to affect these broader social changes have found, tying housing reform to theory-based changes may be unrealistic in an era of fiscal and political conservatism. In the long run, practical, policy-specific approaches may do more to advance the cause of housing as a basic human right (Dolbeare, 1989).

It is to be hoped that the severity of the homeless problem and the discomfort that it has created will stimulate interest once again in developing a national housing policy. Public opinion polls show that voters, even though often misunderstanding the reasons for homeless-

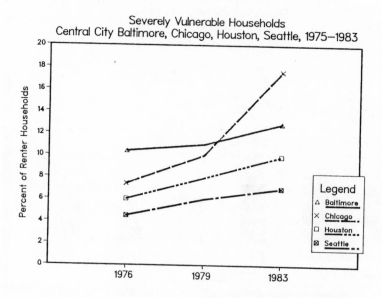

Figure 10.2

ness, are willing to pay higher taxes to eliminate homelessness[10] and favor permanent rather than temporary solutions. Yet, the federal government has not responded with renewed commitment to permanent housing.

The President's Commission on Housing had indicated in 1982 that a major shift from construction of public units and subsidization of developers to direct (nonentitlement) housing allowances was about to occur. Instead the former programs were drastically cut, and appropriations for the allowance program did not begin to compensate for the loss.

The ongoing disclosures of mismanagement and fraud at HUD are a testimony to the dangers of leaving social obligations unregulated in the hands of the private sector. The past failures of federal housing programs indicate that new approaches are in order. We can learn from successful housing programs in Europe and even perhaps from some Third World approaches to housing the poor, such as "sites and services," which would allow low-income households to contribute "sweat equity" to build or rehabilitate housing. Gilderbloom and Appelbaum (1987) favor more emphasis on limited equity cooperatives that would provide at least some of the benefits of ownership to the poor.

We can also act on the basis of considerable research that has already been done on the effectiveness of housing allowances, providing direct income subsidies to participants to secure their own housing on the open market, and subsidizing the supply side, particularly nonprofit and cooperative ventures, for building affordable housing.

HOUSING ALLOWANCES

A massive social experiment, reportedly the largest, longest and most expensive study ever undertaken (Lowry, 1983), was carried out by HUD beginning in the early 1970s on the impact and effectiveness of both demand- and supply-side housing subsidies. Part of the research agenda was to provide all eligible renter and owner households in two mid-sized communities with cash payments to help them with their housing costs and to encourage them to purchase better-quality housing. The results of this study showed that participation in the housing allowance program increased the percentage of participants living in standard quality housing from 50 to 80 percent and decreased the average housing expenditure from 50 to 30 percent of income. Although the allowances augmented the average income of renters by about 25 percent, renters increased their housing consumption by only about 8 percent. Four-fifths of the allowance, since it was not stipulated exclusively for housing, was spent on nonhousing consumption (Lowry, 1983). This finding is clearly supportive of the hypothesis that excessive rent burdens are involuntary. Given the choice, people will devote a smaller percentage of increased income to housing, even as they improve the space and quality of their environments.

The housing allowance experiment had good public support in the communities in which it was conducted. It had no appreciable effect on rents charged, and its cost was about half that of providing public housing, although of course it was not as targeted to the direct consumption of housing. The program was found to have little effect on other federal housing goals, such as neighborhood improvement, racial integration, increasing access to home ownership or stabilizing the construction industry (ibid.:28). About 20 percent of those living in substandard housing who enrolled failed to make mandatory repairs or move to a standard-quality unit and were therefore ineligible for payments. Nevertheless, the housing allowance program was judged to be a worthy component of a national entitlement program. It was estimated that about one-fifth of all households nationally would be eligible for such a program under the guidelines used in the experiment and that about 10 percent, including the neediest households, would participate.

A successful housing voucher program would depend on a reevaluation of the fair market rents on which these subsidies are currently based. The deputy commissioner of New York City's Department of Housing Preservation and Development notes that giving housing vouchers to the homeless in New York "is like giving out food stamps when all the shelves in the grocery store are empty," because fair market rents "bear little relationship to reality" (*New York Times*, Dec. 4, 1989).

SUPPLY-SIDE SUBSIDIES

Demand-side housing allowances alone might be inadequate in tight rental markets or insufficient to raise the overall quality of housing. Apgar (1989:62), in noting a "surprisingly persistent housing quality problem," concludes that an appropriate mix of demand and supply programs will not be possible "unless policy analysts have available good empirical data on the causes and extent of current housing affordability and housing quality problems" (ibid.:38).

It is hoped that the present study has made a contribution to that debate. The findings not only support Apgar's contention that there has been a stall in the decline of substandard housing since 1974, but also show that the relative contributions of income and rent to housing affordability vary widely across metropolitan areas. In a housing market such as Baltimore's, where a large percentage of the stock is substandard, income subsidies alone will, in all likelihood, only allow recipients to purchase low-quality housing. Supply-side subsidies to upgrade the existing stock would be cost-effective. In Seattle, where the housing stock is of reasonably high quality, income subsidies will not affect the shortage of housing, particularly for larger units needed by families. In a highly segregated city like Chicago, income subsidies alone are unlikely to make much headway toward racial integration if discrimination continues to limit blacks to housing in predominantly black neighborhoods.

In some large cities, as much as half of the stock of public housing has been removed from the market and remains boarded up, awaiting demolition. Often this has been the result of the inadequacy of operating budgets to meet repair costs and the subsequent decline in the quality of housing. In other cases, such as in metropolitan Detroit and Baltimore, the proximity of public units to expanding downtown development has made the location a politically unpopular site for housing the poor. This housing has been labeled as "unredeemable." In many cases, however, it is structurally sound, and renovation would be far less expensive than the cost of new construction.[11] Rehabilitation of such units could provide an almost immediate source of housing for homeless and precariously housed families.

CONCLUSION

The goal of the Housing Act of 1949, to provide a decent home and a suitable living environment for every American, was a good one. Forty years later, however, we are in many respects further from meeting that goal. The majority of Americans are well housed, but the inequity of distribution in housing has worsened dramatically in the last decade. For the low-income renter, devoting an ever-increasing percentage of income to rent virtually rules out the possibility of saving for a down payment for a home. Thus renting is likely to become a permanent state rather than a life-cycle transitional state for low-income renters. Ability to own a home will become increasingly tied to the tenure of one's parents. To the extent that low-income renter households are far more likely to be minority and female-headed than are the households of owners, we can see that tenure may be increasingly stratified by race and sex as well as class.

Pragmatic economic considerations should tell us that such inequities will engender social costs that are too high to bear. These costs should be evident when we see that in all four SMSAs, renter households with children, which had been less likely to be at risk of homelessness in 1975-76, were significantly more likely to be at risk in 1983. The long-term impact of raising increasing numbers of children in severely deprived environments, whether substandard and overcrowded housing in run-down neighborhoods or homeless shelters and welfare hotels, is likely to be far greater than the cost of guaranteeing a right to housing. Shelter operators and school officials report physical and emotional problems are nearly universal among homeless children. The scars of homelessness for these children may never be mended.

It is apparently easy to be mystified by homelessness.[12] Perhaps it is out of fear that we seek to find personal characteristics that would clearly distinguish the poor and the homeless from ourselves. A number of researchers have found that the majority of the homeless are still single "disaffiliated" males, with histories of substance abuse and institutional placement (Piliavin, Sosin, and Westerfelt, 1987; Rossi, 1989), but their level of deprivation is far more serious than that of the skid row inhabitants of even a decade ago.

I have argued that our societal standards of acceptable living conditions for the poor have become eroded. Nevertheless, I do

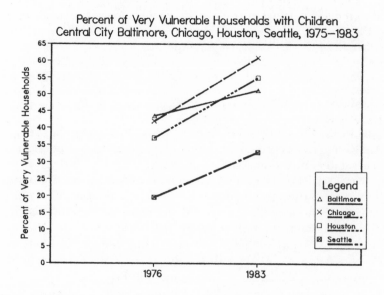

Figure 10.3

not believe that a majority of Americans are indifferent about home-lessness. Before we allow homelessness to become a permanent component of our society, we must weigh both the direct and the hidden costs of a continuing failure to provide a right to housing. An enlightened public policy would recognize that lack of decent, safe, and affordable housing is tied to much more than the growth of homelessness. Efforts to combat such social problems as drug use and crime are hopeless if the living environments of the poor are themselves without hope. The provision of such housing should be the very cornerstone of a social welfare policy. As a society, we can and must do better.

NOTES

1. As pointed out in the first chapter, the RMA incorporates most of the population, but not all of the area of the SMSA. Thus it might be thought of as a midrange category between a central city and an SMSA. Since this RMA measurement is not available for the AHS data, central cities, where the majority of vulnerable are concentrated, are shown for comparison.

2. It should be borne in mind that considerable changes have taken place in locational rents since the AHS data were collected in 1983. Seattle, for instance, had a 35 percent increase in rent between 1983 and 1988, while in

Houston, as noted earlier, median rent fell after 1983 and has just recently returned to the level of that year (Seattle's 1989 Housing Assistance Plan; Smith, 1988). The comparison being made here is between 1983 rents and 1983 estimates of homelessness as reported by HUD in 1984.

3. Cowan, Breakey, and Fischer (1986) estimated that about 1,200 persons per night were homeless in the city of Baltimore in 1986. While this figure was generally supportive of HUD's earlier estimate, it does lead to a per capita rate of at least 5 per 10,000 for the RMA and about 16 per 10,000 if just the central-city population were considered.

4. The at-risk population included those who were currently housed with others, that is, doubled up, and who stated that they would have to leave in less than a year but didn't know where they would go.

5. The average annual increase in the Composite Construction Cost Index reported by the Department of Commerce was 9.7 percent from 1974 to 1980 and 2.9 percent from 1981 to 1986 (*Construction Review*, [March-April 1986, p. 57], as cited in *Washington State Housing Needs and Market Trends: An Overview*, Washington State Department of Community Development, March 1989).

6. Marx noted that the concentration of capital and returns to constant capital would favor economies of scale—"one hundred small offices cost incomparably more than one large one" (Capital, III: 358). Such economies should allow landlords to charge lower rents and yet make higher profits. If large complexes appeal to a different constituency than do single-family homes or duplexes, however, lower rents for multi-family units may not lead to a competitive price reduction among single-family rental units.

7. Similarly, LeGates and Murphy (1982) found a 30 percent increase between 1970 and 1979 in the size of new single-family homes.

8. One proposal that would both address the inequities in the current redistributive system and also generate federal money to support low income housing in a time of fiscal constraint, would be to cap the amount of mortgage interest and property taxes that are deductible, and to limit these deductions to the principal residence, as is done in most of Western Europe. The majority of homeowners would not be adversely affected by such a cap, but the savings in federal tax expenditure could be sufficient to mount an low income housing entitlement program.

9. I use the phrase "poverty deepening" to describe the concentration of poverty at the lowest levels of income rather than to describe an increase in the overall rate of poverty.

10. The *New York Times* (June 29, 1989) reports that 59 percent of those polled by NYT/CBS-TV indicated their willingness to pay $100 or more in additional taxes to help eliminate homelessness.

11. Ted Phillips interview. United Housing Coalition of Detroit. A housing consultant hired to evaluate the soundness of boarded-up Detroit public housing concluded that the solid brick structures, scheduled for demolition, would in many cases require only cosmetic repairs and in others could be cost-effectively rehabilitated.

12. The National Coalition for the Homeless (1986) did a study of newspaper coverage of homeless issues and discovered that less than 10 percent of the articles discussed housing in reference to homelessness (cited in Marcuse, 1989).

Appendixes

APPENDIX A
HOUSING QUALITY STANDARDS: INADEQUATE UNITS

HUD suggests two standards of housing quality, "inadequate" and "severely inadequate." Possession of any one of the following defects renders a housing unit as "inadequate":

1) Lack or share some or all plumbing facilities. This requires a unit to have hot and cold piped water, a flush toilet, and a bathtub or shower all inside the structure and designed for the exclusive use of the unit.

2) Lack or share some or all kitchen facilities. A unit must have an installed sink with piped water, a range or cookstove, and a mechanical refrigerator inside the structure for the exclusive use of the occupants of the unit.

3) Contain three of six signs of inadequate maintenance, a)leaky roof, b) open cracks or holes in interior walls and ceiling, c) holes in interior floors, d) either peeling paint or broken plaster over one square foot of an interior wall; e)evidence of rats or mice in the last 90 days, and f) a leaky basement;

4) Contain three of four public hall deficiencies including a)no light fixtures or no working light fixtures in public halls, b)loose, broken, or missing steps on common stairways;c) railings that are loose, or missing entirely; and d) no elevator in building for units two or more floors from main building entrance, in a four or more story building;

5) Have inadequate heating equipment or equipment breakdown of six consecutive hours or longer, three or more times last winter; inadequate units are heated primarily by room heaters without flue or vent which burn gas, oil, or kerosene;

6) Have three selected electrical defects or no electricity. The defects, all of which must be present, are a)a room with no working wall outlet; b) blown fuses or tripped circuit breakers three or more times in the last 90 days, and c) exposed wiring;

7) Have inadequate provision for sewage disposal and breakdown of the facilities. Adequate means of sewage disposal include a public sewer, septic tank, cesspool, or chemical toilet. Facilities must be in the structure. Breakdown of a flush toilet for six consecutive hours or longer, three or more times during the last 90 days.

APPENDIX B
HOUSING QUALITY STANDARDS: SEVERELY INADEQUATE UNITS

Possession of any one of the following defects renders a housing unit as "severely inadequate":

1) Lack or share some or all plumbing facilities. This requires a unit to have hot and cold piped water, a flush toilet, and a bathtub or shower all inside the structure and designed for the exclusive use of the unit.

2) Contain five of six signs of inadequate maintenance, a) leaky roof, b) open cracks or holes in interior walls and ceiling, c) holes in interior floors, d) either peeling paint or broken plaster over one square foot of an interior wall; e) evidence of rats or mice in the last 90 days, and f) a leaky basement;

3) Contain four of four measured public hall deficiencies including a) no light fixtures or no working light fixtures in public halls, b) loose, broken, or missing steps on common stairways; c) stair railings that are loose, or missing entirely; and d) no elevator in building for units two or more floors from main building entrance, in a four or more story building;

4) Have heating equipment breakdown of six consecutive hours or longer, three or more times last winter;

5) Have three selected electrical defects or no electricity. The defects, all of which must be present, are a) a room with no working wall outlet; b) blown fuses or tripped circuit breakers three or more times in the last 90 days, and c) exposed wiring;

6) Have inadequate provision for sewage disposal. Adequate means of sewage disposal include a public sewer, septic tank, cesspool, or chemical toilet. Facilities must be in the structure.

Appendix C
Hedonic Regression of Gross Rent and Log of Gross Rent, Chicago Central City Hispanics, 1975–1983

Variable	1975 Model 1[a]		1975 Model 2[b]		1979 Model 1		1979 Model 2		1983 Model 1		1983 Model 2	
	B	t	B	t	B	t	B	t	Beta	t	Beta	t
constant	121.64	5.65***	5.02	59.84***	300.72	7.68***	5.66	38.65***	249.64	4.47***	5.54	29.14***
rooms	26.26	10.34***	.10	9.97***	17.55	7.49***	.06	6.96***	29.98	6.63***	.10	6.18***
baths	-2.34	-.85	-.02	-1.58	7.44	2.30**	.02	1.29	-3.39	-.40	-.03	-.90
street	-27.07	-3.02***	-.10	-2.88***	-29.12	-3.77***	-.11	-3.73***	-15.75	-1.07	-.03	-.53
inad hall	.59	.03	-.00	-.02	-1.77	-.07	-.01	-.08	0[c]	0	0	0
inad heat	17.12	1.16	.07	1.26	2.00	.23	.02	.56	19.57	1.29	.05	1.04
inad sewer	-15.99	-2.02**	-.09	-2.82***	21.76	1.26	.09	1.25	-13.35	-1.06	-.05	-1.22
inad struct	.74	.07	.00	.10	-3.85	-.45	-.01	-.16	3.53	.28	.01	.32
inad kitch	-9.88	-.41	-.12	-1.32	-10.48	-.60	-.00	-.02	4.19	.09	-.09	-.56
boom con	66.167	3.16***	.24	2.92***	4.13	.10	.03	.18	-95.19	-1.82*	-.40	-2.24**
old con	0	0[d]	0	0	-91.21	-2.83***	-.28	-2.33***	-117.92	-2.79***	-.36	-2.53***
new con	183.81	6.28***	.50	4.35***	0[d]	0	0	0	19.73	.31	-.38	-1.76*
aircondition	10.82	2.24**	.04	2.26**	5.97	.98	.02	.97	34.64	3.80***	.11	3.65***
num. units	11.13	3.04***	.04	2.98***	-.60	-.17	-.00	-.35	12.41	2.39**	.04	2.00**
R Squared	.37		.35		.21		.18		.27		.24	
N of cases	364		364		429		429		285		285	

[a] Model 1 dependent=gross rent [b] Model 2 dependent=semilog of gross rent.

[c] No cases identified [d] Tolerance limits reached.

Appendix C
Hedonic Regression of Gross Rent and Log of Gross Rent, Chicago Central City Blacks, 1975–1983

Variable	1975 Model 1[a] B	t	1975 Model 2[b] B	t	1979 Model 1 B	t	1979 Model 2 B	t	1983 Model 1 Beta	t	1983 Model 2 Beta	t
constant	303.97	6.73***	5.58	39.35***	307.75	12.43***	5.58	37.42***	135.97	3.89***	5.12	36.73***
rooms	25.11	9.36***	.09	10.87***	9.76	5.13***	.04	5.34***	28.14	8.19***	.08	5.80***
baths	-.96	-.03	-.01	-1.54	5.93	2.10**	.00	.33	-2.57	-.52	-.02	-1.16
street	-18.57	-2.63***	-.05	-2.33**	-12.78	-1.86*	-.03	-1.10	-24.83	-2.52**	-.11	-2.79***
inad hall	-36.43	-2.40**	-.13	-2.63***	-15.80	-.71	-.07	-.87	-9.04	-.36	-.04	-.36
inad heat	11.43	1.37	.06	2.44**	10.73	1.32	.06	1.81*	16.02	1.36	.04	.68
inad sewer	-3.99	-.42	-.01	-.33	-6.94	-.80	-.03	-.97	4.81	.35	-.01	-.22
inad struct	4.64	.53	.02	.83	2.85	.34	.02	.68	-.42	-.04	.01	.36
inad kitch	-42.15	-1.91**	-.25	-3.58***	-55.36	-2.32**	-.17	-1.85*	-42.23	-1.12	-.25	-1.68*
boom con	-162.69	-4.25***	-.61	-5.06***	-74.01	-4.43***	-.35	-5.62***	21.30	1.08	.04	.54
old con	-110.33	-2.89***	-.30	-2.48**	-12.65	-.79	.06	1.05	78.07	4.07***	.39	5.08***
new con	-102.70	-2.46**	-.43	-3.25***	-21.32	-.49	-.13	-.81	6.33	.28	-.05	-.20
aircondition	38.22	7.67***	.15	9.75***	34.35	7.61***	.12	7.01***	46.79	9.18***	.17	8.13***
num. units	-3.92	-1.24	-.02	-1.94*	-15.51	-5.45***	-.06	-5.37***	-3.72	-.93	-.03	-2.04**
R Squared	.19		.30		.17		.23		.25		.26	
N of cases	1389		1341		846		1389		1341		846	

Appendix D
Comparison of the CPI and the CPI-XI Poverty Line (in constant 1986 dollars)

Household Member	CPI Poverty Line	CPI-XI	CPI-XI 125% of Poverty
One Person 65 and Over	5255	4780	5975
One Person Under 65	5701	5186	6483
Two Persons, Head Over 65	6630	6031	7539
Two Person,Head Under 65	7372	6709	8383
Three Persons	8737	7948	9935
Four Persons	11,203	10,191	12,739
Five Persons	13,259	12,061	15,076
Six Persons	14,986	13,633	17,041
Seven Persons	17,049	15,509	19,386
Eight Persons	18,791	17,094	21,368
Nine or More Persons	22,487	20,456	25,570

Appendix E
Key to the Variables Used in the Analysis

Variable	Definition	Coding
	Characteristics of Unit	
Cencity	unit is inside central city	1-yes
Rooms	Number of rooms in unit	continuous
Baths	Number of Baths	1=.75 2=1 3=1.25 4=1.5 5=2 6 thru 10=3
Bad street	Boarded up units on street as observed by interviewer	1=yes
NewCon	Built since last survey (less than 4 years old)	1=yes
BoomCon	Built between 1950 and 1970	1=yes
OldCon	Built before 1950	1=yes
Inad structu	Structure is inadequate as Defined in Appendices A and B	1=inad 2=severe
Inad pubhall	Public hallway is inadequate as defined in Appendices A and B	1=inad 2=severe
Inad heat	Heat is inadequate as defined in Appendices A and B	1=inad 2=severe
Inad electricity	Electricity is inadequate as defined in Appendices A and B	1=inad 2=Severe
Inad plumb	Plumbing is inadequate as defined in Appendices A and B	1=inad 2=severe
Inad sewer	Sewer is inadequate as defined in Appendices A and B	1=inad 2=Severe
Inad kitch	Lacks a complete kitchen	1=yes
1 or more inad	Unit has one or more inadequacies	1=yes
1 or more severe	Unit has one or more severe inadequacies	1=yes
Number units	Number of units in building	1=3=1 4=2 5=3 6=4 etc.
Aircondition	Number of room airconditions	continuous. If central, number=rooms
	Characteristics of Household	
White	Head of household is white	1=yes
Black	Head of household is black	1=yes
Hispanic	Head of Household is Hispanic	1-yes
Female	Head of household is female	1=yes
Single	Head is currently unmarried	1=yes

240

Variable	Definition	Coding
	Characteristics of Household	
Tothm	Total household members	continuous
Largefam	More than 5 members	percent of total
Subfam	Presence of subfamily	1=yes
Children	Number of Children	continuous
Agehd	age of head	continuous
<25	Head Under 25	1=yes
>65	Head Over 65	1=yes
Dropout	Head did not complete high school	1=yes
Highed	Head went beyond high school	1=yes
Subsid	Unit is subsidized	1=yes
Public	Unit is public housing	1=yes
Welfare	Household receives public assistance	1=yes
Pprroom	Number of persons/room	continuous
Crowd	More than one person per room	1=yes
Employed	Head is employed	1=yes
Income	Total Household Income in constant 1986 dollars	Continuous
Percap	Percapita income=Above income/total household members	continuos
Poor	Below the CPI-XI poverty line	1=yes
Vulnerable	Below 125% of CPI-XI poverty line and pay more than 45 % income to rent	1=yes
VeryVul	Below 125% of poverty and pay>60% income to rent	1=yes
SevereVul	Have less than $50.00 per person per month in residual income	1=yes
Povgap	Amount that income falls below poverty line	continuous
Gross Rent	Total gross rent in constant 1986 dollars	continuous
Rentinc	Rent to income ratio	continuous
Resid	Monthly income minus gross rent	continuous

241

Bibliography

Aaron, Henry. Rationale for a Housing Policy, in J. Paul Mitchell (ed.), *Federal Housing Policy and Programs*. New Brunswick, N.J.: Rutgers Center for Urban Policy Research, 1985.

Aldrich, J. and Nelson, F. *Linear Probability, Logit and Probit Models*. Beverly Hills, Calif: Sage Publications, 1984.

Andrade, Sally. *Living in the Grey Zone: Health Care Needs* of Homeless Persons. Austin, Texas: Texas Department of Human Services, 1988.

Annual Housing Survey. SMSA file [Machine-readable data file] conducted by the Bureau of the Census for the Department of Housing and Urban Development. Washington, D.C: The Bureau, 1975, 1976, 1979, 1983.

Apgar, William. The Leaky Boat, in Peter Salins (ed.), *Housing America's Poor*. Chapel Hill: University of North Carolina Press, 1987.

Apgar, William. Recent Trends in Housing Quality and Affordability: A Reassessment, in S. Rosenberry and C. Hartman (eds.), *Housing Issues of the 1990's*. New York: Praeger Publishers, 1989.

Apgar, William, and Brown, James. The State of the Nation's Housing, Joint Center for Housing Studies of Harvard University, 1988.

Appelbaum, Richard. Testimony on HUD's Report to the Secretary on the Homeless and Emergency Shelters, in J. Erickson and C. Wilhelm (eds.), *Housing the Homeless*. New Brunswick, N.J.: Center for Urban Policy Research, 1988.

Bachrach, Leona. Homeless Women: A Context for Health Planning. *The Milbank Quarterly*, Vol. 65, No. 3:371-396, 1987.

Bahr, Howard, and Caplow, Theodore. *Old Men Drunk and Sober*. New York: New York University Press, 1974.

Baker, Russell. "Housing Shortage Prompts Squatters to Rehabilitate Buildings". *Christian Science Monitor*, 6/12/89.

Ballinger, A. University of Houston Center for Public Policy, telephone interview, May 1989.

Bane, Mary Jo, and Ellwood, David. Slipping into and out of Poverty: The Dynamics of Spells. *Journal of Human Resources*, September, 1986.

Bane, Mary Jo, and Jargowsky, Paul. Urban Poverty and the Underclass Issue: Basic Questions. Paper prepared for the APPAM Research Conference, Washington, D.C., October, 1987.

Bardy, Frank. New York City Housing Authority. Interview, November, 1988.

Bassuk, Ellen, Rubin, Lenore, and Lauriat, Alison. Characteristics of Sheltered Homeless Families. *American Journal of Public Health*, Vol. 78:1097-1111, September, 1986.

Bawden, D. Lee, and Palmer, John. Social Policy: Challenging the Welfare State, in John Palmer and Isabel Sawhill (eds.), *The Reagan Record*. Cambridge, Mass: Ballinger Publishers, 1984.

Berger, M., and Blomquist, G. Income, Opportunities and the Quality of Life of Urban Residents, in M. McGeary and L. Lynn (eds.), *Urban Change and Poverty*. Washington, D.C.: National Academy Press, 1988.

Berman, Richard. The Housing Crisis: Responses to New Federalism. *Journal of Housing*, November/December, 1982.

Bingham, R., Green, R., and White, S. (eds.), *The Homeless in Contemporary Society*. Newbury Park, Calif.: Sage Publications, 1987.

Birch, Eugenie (ed.), *The Unsheltered Woman*. New Brunswick, N.J.: Center for Urban Policy Research, 1985.

Birch, Eugenie. Women and Shelter: Needs and Issues, in S. Rosenberry and C. Hartman (eds.), *Housing Issues of the 1990's*. New York: Praeger Publishers, 1989.

Blake, Gerald, and Abbott, Martin. Homelessness in the Pacific Northwest, in J. Momeni (ed.), *Homelessness in the United States*, Vol. 1. New York: Greenwood Press, 1989.

Blank, Rebecca, and Rosen, Henry. Recent Trends in Housing Conditions among the Urban Poor. National Bureau of Economic Research, Inc., *Working Paper No. 2886*, 1989.

Blonston, Gary. "Money Gap is Growing Ever Wider." *St. Paul Pioneer Press Dispatch*, p. 1G, 2/21/89.

Bluestone, Barry, and Harrison, Bennett. The Great American Job Machine: The Proliferation of Low Wage Employment in the U.S. Economy. Study prepared for U.S. Congress Joint Economic Committee, Washington, D.C., December, 1986.

Bogue, Donald. *Skid Row*. Chicago: University of Chicago Community and Family Study Center, 1963.

Bratt, Rachel. The Housing Payments Program: Its Possible Effect on Minorities, Poor. *Journal of Housing*, July/August:108-110, 1983.

Bratt, Rachel. Public Housing: The Controversy and Contribution, in R. Bratt, C. Hartman and A. Meyerson, *Critical Perspectives on Housing*. Philadelphia: Temple University Press, 1986.

Brown, L., and Rosengren, E. (eds.), *The Merger Boom*. Proceedings of a Conference sponsored by the Federal Reserve Bank of Boston, October, 1987.

Brueggeman, William. The Rental Housing Situation: Implications for Policy and Research, in J. Weicher, K. Villani, and E. Roistacher (eds.), *Rental Housing: Is there a Crisis?* Washington, D.C.: Urban Institute Press, 1981.

Burt, Martha, and Cohen, Barbara. *America's Homeless: Numbers, Charac-teristics and the Programs that Serve Them.* Washington, D.C.: Urban Institute Press, 1989.

Cain and Scott, Inc. Cain and Scott Apartment Vacancy Report. Seattle, 1989.

Carliner, Michael. Homelessness: A Housing Problem? in R. Bingham, R. Green and S. White (eds.), *The Homeless in Contemporary Society.* Newbury Park, Calif: Sage Publications, 1987.

Center on Budget and Policy Priorities. Poverty Rate and Household Income Stagnate as Rich-Poor Gap Hits Post War High. Washington, D.C., October 20, 1989.

Chevan, Albert. The Growth of Homeownership 1940-1980. *Demography*, Vol. 26, No. 2:249-266, 1989.

Chicago Coalition for the Homeless. When You Don't Have Anything: A Street Survey of Homeless People in Chicago. Chicago: Chicago Coalition for the Homeless, 1983.

Chicago Coalition for the Homeless. Youth Homelessness in Chicago. Position Paper, 1985.

Clark, A. L. Health Care Needs of Homeless Women in Baltimore. Un-published paper, University of Maryland, College Park, 1985.

Clay, Phillip. *At Risk of Loss: The Endangered Future of Low Income Rental Housing Resources.* Neighborhood Reinvestment Corporation, Washing-ton, D.C.: 1987.

Cleghorn, Steven. Director, Transitional Housing of Baltimore, Maryland. Interview, March, 1989.

Cohen, Barbara, and Burt, Martha. Demographic Characteristics of the Home-less Derived from a New National Survey. Paper presented at the Population Association of America Annual Meeting, Baltimore, 1989.

Collier, Ellie. Coalition for the Homeless, Houston, Texas. Telephone inter-view, May, 1989.

Courant, Paul. Racial Prejudice in a Search Model of the Urban Housing Market. *Journal of Urban Economics*, Vol. 5:329-345, 1978.

Cowan, D., Breakey, W., and Fischer, P. The Methodology of Counting the Homeless. Proceedings of the American Statistical Association Survey Research Section, 1987.

Danziger, Sheldon. Antipoverty Policy and Welfare Reform. Paper prepared for the Rockefeller Foundation Conference on Welfare Reform, Williams-burg, Virginia, February, 1988.

Danziger, Sheldon, and Weinberg, Daniel (eds.), *Fighting Poverty: What Works and What Doesn't.* Cambridge: Harvard University Press, 1986.

Dearborn, Phillip. Fiscal Conditions in Large American Cities, in M. Mc-Geary and L. Lynn (eds.), *Urban Change and Poverty.* Washington, D.C, National Academy Press, 1988.

Dinkins, David, and Wackstein, Nancy. Addressing Homelessness. *Social Policy*, Fall:50-53, 1986.

Dockett, Kathleen. *Street Homeless People in the District of Columbia.* Wash-ington D.C.: University of the District of Columbia, 1989.

Dolbeare, Cushing. How the Tax System Subsidizes Housing for the Affluent, in R. Bratt, C. Hartman, and A. Meyerson (eds.), *Critical Perspectives on Housing*. Philadelphia: Temple University Press, 1986.

Dolbeare, Cushing. The Low Income Housing Crisis, in C. Hartman, (ed.), *America's Housing Crisis: What is to be Done?* Boston: Routledge and Kegen Paul, 1983.

Dolbeare, Cushing, personal communication, October, 1989.

Downs, Anthony. *Rental Housing in the 1980's.* Washington, D.C.: Brookings Institution, 1983.

Dreier, Peter. The Status of Tenants in the United States, *Social Problems*, Vol. 30, No. 2:179-198, 1982.

Dreier, Peter. Community-Based Housing: A Progressive Approach to A New Federal Policy, *Social Policy*, Vol. 18, no. 2:18-22, 1987.

Easterlin, Richard. *Birth and Fortune: The Impact of Numbers on Personal Welfare.* New York: Basic Books, 1980.

Ellwood, David. *Poor Support.* New York: Basic Books, 1988.

Engle, Robert, and Marshall, Robert. A Microeconometric Analysis of Vacant Housing Units, in Ronald E. Greison (ed.), *The Urban Economy and Housing.* Lexington, Mass: Lexington Books, 1983.

Erickson, Jon, and Wilhelm, Charles (eds.), *Housing the Homeless.* New Brunswick, N.J.: Center for Urban Policy Research, 1988.

Fabricant, Michael. The Political Economy of Homelessness. *Catalyst*, No. 21:11-28, 1987.

Farley, Reynolds. Unpublished figures calculated from the 1987-1988 Current Population Survey, 1989.

Farley, Reynolds. Is There a Crisis in Rental Housing? Unpublished paper, University of Michigan, 1983.

Farley, Reynolds, and Allen, Walter. *The Color Line and the Quality of Life in America.* New York: Russell Sage Foundation, 1987.

Feagin, Joe. *Houston: Free Enterprise City.* New Brunswick, N. J.: Rutgers University Press, 1988.

First, Richard, Roth, Dee, and Arewa, Bobbie. Homelessness: Understanding the Dimensions of the Problem for Minorities. *Social Work*, Vol. 33, No. 22:120-124, 1988.

Freeman, Richard, and Hall, Brian. Permanent Homelessness in America? *Population Research and Policy Review*, Vol. 6:3-27,1987.

Furstenburg, George, Harrison, Bennett, and Horowitz, Ann (eds.). *Patterns of Racial Discrimination: Housing.* Lexington, Mass: D.C. Heath, 1974.

Gans, Herbert. *The Urban Villagers.* New York: Free Press, 1962.

Garfinkel, Irwin, and McLanahan, Sara. The Feminization of Poverty: Nature, Causes and a Partial Cure, Institute for Research on Poverty Discussion Paper, No. 776, University of Wisconsin - Madison, 1985.

Garfinkel, Irwin, and McLanahan, Sara. *Single Mothers and Their Children.* Washington D.C.: Urban Institute Press, 1986.

Gilderbloom, John and Appelbaum, Richard. *Rethinking Rental Housing.* Philadelphia: Temple University Press, 1988.

Gilderbloom, J., Rosentraub, M., and Bullard, R. Financing, Designing and Locating Housing and Transportation Services for the Disabled and Elderly. Houston: University of Houston Center for Public Policy, 1987.

Glickman, Norman. *The Urban Impacts of Federal Policies*. Baltimore: Johns Hopkins University Press, 1980.

Gonzales, Representative Henry. Letter to the Editor. *Washington Post*, November 1, 1988.

Gove, Walter, and Hughes, Michael. *Overcrowding in the Household*. New York, Academic Press, 1983.

Hadden, Louise, and Leger, Mireille. *Codebook for the Annual Housing Survey Data Base*. Cambridge, Mass.: Abt Associates, 1988.

Hagen, Jan. The Heterogeneity of Homelessness. *Social Casework*, Vol. 68:451-455, October, 1987.

Hanushek, Eric, and Quigley, John. The Dynamics of the Housing Market: A Stock Adjustment Model of Housing Consumption. *Journal of Urban Economics*, Vol. 6, No. 1:90-111, January, 1979.

Harrigan, Michael, and Haugen, Steven. The Declining Middle Class Thesis: A Sensitivity Approach. *Monthly Labor Review*, Vol. 11, No. 5, May, 1988.

Hartman, Chester. *Housing and Social Policy*. Englewood Cliffs, N.J.: Prentice Hall, 1975.

Hartman, Chester. Testimony on the HUD "Report to the Secretary on the Homeless and Emergency Shelters," in J. Erickson and C. Wilhelm (eds.), *Housing the Homeless*. New Brunswick, N.J.: Center for Urban Policy Research, 1988.

Harvey, David. *Social Justice and the City*. Baltimore: Johns Hopkins University Press, 1973.

Haveman, Robert. The Changed Face of Poverty: A Call for New Policies. *Focus*, Vol. 11 No. 2. Institute for Research on Poverty, Madison: University of Wisconsin, Summer 1988.

Hayes, R. Allen. *The Federal Government and Urban Housing: Ideology and Change in Public Policy*. Albany: State University of New York Press, 1985.

Health and Welfare Council of Central Maryland. *Report to the Greater Baltimore Shelter Network on Homelessness in Central Maryland*. Baltimore: Maryland Department of Human Resources, 1983.

Health and Welfare Council of Central Maryland. *Where Do You Go From Nowhere?* Baltimore: Maryland Department of Human Resources, 1986.

Heilbrun, James. *Urban Economics and Public Policy*. New York: St. Martin's Press, 1974.

Henretta, J. Parental Status and Child's Homeownership. *American Sociological Review*, Vol. 49:131-140, 1984.

Hirschl, Thomas. Homelessness in New York State: A Demographic and Socioeconomic Analysis, in Jamshid Momeni (ed.), *Homelessness in the United States*. Westport, Conn.: Greenwood Press, 1988.

Hoch, Charles. A Brief History of the Homeless Problem in the United States, in R. Bingham, R. Green and S. White (eds.), *The Homeless in Contemporary Society*. Newbury Park, Calif: Sage Publications, 1987.

Hoch, Charles, and Slayton, Robert. *New Homeless and Old*. Philadelphia: Temple University Press, 1989.

Hollingsworth, J. Rogers. The Structural Basis for Income Equality and Economic Productivity: A Cross National Perspective. Institute for Research on Poverty Discussion Paper No. 578, University of Wisconsin-Madison 1979.

Hombs, Mary Ellen, and Snyder, Mitch. *Homelessness in America: A Forced March to Nowhere*. Washington, D.C.: Community for Creative Nonviolence, 1982.

Hope, Marjorie, and Young, James. The Politics of Displacement, in John Erickson and Charles Wilhelm (eds.), *Housing the Homeless*. New Brunswick, N.J.: Rutgers Center for Urban Policy Research, 1988.

Howenstine, E. Jay. *Housing Vouchers: A Comparative International Analysis*. New Brunswick, N.J.: Rutgers Center for Urban Policy Research, 1986.

Institute of Medicine. *Homelessness, Health and Human Needs*. Washington, D.C.: National Academy Press, 1988.

Irby, Iredia. "Attaining the Housing Goal?" Unpublished paper, Office of Economic Affairs. Washington, D.C.: U.S. Department of Housing and Urban Development, 1986.

James, Franklin, McCummings, Betty, and Tynan, Eileen. *Minorities in the Sunbelt*. New Brunswick, N.J., Rutgers Center for Urban Policy Research, 1984.

Joe, Tom. "Shredding an Already Tattered Safety Net," in John Weicher (ed.), *Maintaining the Safety Net: Income Redistribution Programs in the Reagan Administration*. Washington: American Enterprise Institute for Public Policy Research, 1986.

Johnson, Bruce (ed.), *Resolving the Housing Crisis*. San Francisco: Pacific Institute for Public Policy Research, 1982.

Kain, John, and Quigley, John. *Housing Markets and Racial Discrimination: A Microeconomic Analysis*. New York: National Bureau of Economic Research, 1975.

Kasarda, John. Jobs, Migration and Emerging Urban Mismatches, in M. McGeary and L. Lynn (eds.), *Urban Change and Poverty*. Washington, D.C.: National Academy Press, 1988.

Kasinitz, Phillip. Gentrification and Homelessness: the Single Room Occupant and the Inner City Revival, *Urban and Social Change Review*. Vol. 17:9-14, Winter, 1984.

Kearns, Kevin. Urban Squatting: Social Activism in the Housing Sector. *Social Policy*, Sept./Oct.:22-29, 1980.

Kelley, E. N. How to get Your Manager to Raise Rents. *Journal of Property Management*, March/April, 1975.

King, A., and Mieskowski, P. Racial Discrimination, Segregation and the Price of Housing, *Journal of Political Economy*, 81: 590–606, 1973.

Kivisto, Peter. Homelessness in the Frostbelt: The Case of Illinois, in J. Momeni (ed.), *Homelessness in the United States*. New York: Greenwood Press, 1989.

Kolata, Gina. Twins of the Street: Homelessness and Addiction., *New York Times*, p. 1, 5/23/89.

Kolata, Gina. Homeless Drug Addicts: Studies in 'Lost Dreams.' *New York Times*, p. 1, 5/30/89.

Kondratas, S. Anna. A Strategy for Helping America's Homeless, in R. Bingham, R. Green and S. White (eds.), *The Homeless in Contemporary Society*. Newbury Park, California: Sage Publications, 1987.

Kozel, Jonathan. The Homeless. Parts I and II, *The New Yorker*, January 18 and 25, 1988.

La Gory, M., Ritchey, F., O'Donoghue, T., and Mullis, J. Homelessness in Alabama: A Variety of People and Experiences, in J. Momeni (ed.), *Homelessness in the United States*. New York: Greenwood Press, 1989.

Lamb, H. Richard, Deinstitutionalization and the Homeless Mentally Ill, in J. Erickson and C. Wilhelm (eds.), *Housing the Homeless*. New Brunswick, N. J.: Center for Urban Policy Research, 1986.

Lee, Barrett. Residential Mobility in Skid Row: Disaffiliation, Powerlessness and Decision-Making. *Demography*, Vol. 15, No. 3:285-300, 1978.

Lee, Barrett. Stability and Change in an Urban Homeless Population. Paper presented to the Population Association of America Annual Meeting, New Orleans, April, 1988.

LeGates, Richard and Murphy, Karen. Austerity, Shelter and Social Conflict in the United States. *International Journal of Urban and Regional Research*, Vol. 5:2:254-275, 1982.

Leichter, H.M and Rodgers, H. R. *American Public Policy in a Comparative Context*. New York: McGraw-Hill, 1984.

Leonard, Paul, Dolbeare, Cushing, and Lazere, Edward. *A Place to Call Home: The Crisis in Housing for the Poor*. Washington, D.C.: Center on Budget and Policy Priorities, and Low Income Housing Information Service, 1989.

Levy, Frank. *Dollars and Dreams, The Changing American Income Distribution*. New York: Basic Books, 1987.

Lewin, A. C. *Housing Cooperatives in Developing Countries: A Manual for Self Help in Low Cost Housing Schemes*. New York: John Wiley and Sons, 1981.

Liebow, Elliot. *Tally's Corner*. Boston: Little Brown and Company, 1967.

Liebow, Elliot. Interview. Rockville, Md., April, 1989.

Lowry, Ira. Rental Housing in the 1970's: Searching for the Crisis, in J. Weicher, K. Villani, and E. Roistacher (eds.), *Rental Housing: Is There a Crisis?* Washington, D.C.: The Urban Institute Press, 1981.

Lowry, Ira. (ed.), The Rand Corporation, *Experimenting with Housing Allowances, The Final Report of the Housing Assistance Supply Experiment*. Cambridge, Mass.: Oelgeschlager, Gunn and Hain, Publishers, 1983.

Lowry, Ira. Where Should the Poor Live, in Peter Salins (ed.), *Housing America's Poor*. Chapel Hill: University of North Carolina Press, 1987.

Luby, Sister Mary Anne, Director of Rachel's Place, Washington, D. C. Interview, October 1989.

Lundqvist, Lennar. *Housing Policy and Equality: A Comparative Study of Tenure Conversions and Their Effects*. London: Croom Helm, 1986.

McGough, D., and Casey, C. National Supply of and Demand for Rental Housing in the United States. Unpublished report, Washington D.C.: Department of Housing and Urban Development, 1986.

McGuire, Chester. *International Housing Policies*. Lexington, Mass: D.C. Heath and Company, 1981.

McIntire, Jim. Institute for Public Policy and Management, University of Washington - Seattle. Telephone interview. May, 1989.

McKinley, Blackburn, and Bloom, David. Earnings and Income Inequality in the United States. *Population and Development Review*, Vol. 13, No.4:575-612, December, 1987.

McKinsey and Company, Inc. Addressing the Problem of Homelessness in Houston and Harris County. Steering Committee Report, Houston: Coalition for the Homeless of Houston/Harris County, December, 1989.

McLanahan, S., Garfinkel, I., and Watson, D. Family Structure, Poverty and the Underclass, in M. McGeary, and L. Lynn, (eds.), *Urban Change and Poverty*. Washington, D.C.: National Academy Press, 1988.

Marcuse, Peter. The Pitfalls of Specialism: Special Groups and the General Problem of Housing in S. Rosenberry and C. Hartman, (eds.), *Housing Issues of the 1990's*. New York: Praeger Publishing, 1989.

Marin, Peter. How We Help and Harm the Homeless. *Utne Reader*, January/February:36-47, 1988.

Marriott, Michael. The 12 Worst Drug Bazaars: New York's Continuing Blight. *New York Times*, p.1 6/1/89.

Marx, Karl. *Capital*. Chicago: Chester Kerr and Company, 1909.

Massey, Douglas and Bickford, Adam. The Effect of Public Housing on Black Segregation in U.S. Metropolitan Areas. Paper presented to the Population Association of America Annual Meetings, New Orleans, April, 1988.

Massey, Douglas, and Denton, Nancy. Suburbanization and Segregation in the U.S. Metro Areas. *American Journal of Sociology*, Vol. 94, No. 3:592-626, Nov., 1988.

Mead, Lawrence. *Beyond Entitlement: The Social Obligations of Citizenship*. New York: Free Press, 1986.

Meehan, Eugene. The Evolution of Public Housing Policy, in J. Paul Mitchell (ed.), *Federal Housing Policy and Programs*. New Brunswick, N.J.: Rutgers Center for Urban Policy Research, 1985.

Meehan, Eugene. Is There a Future for Public Housing? *Journal of Housing*, May/June: 73-76, 1983.

Melvin, Carol. Executive Director, Women's Housing Coalition, Baltimore, Maryland, interview, March, 1989.

Merrill, Sally. *Hedonic Indices as a Measure of Housing Quality: The Housing Allowance Demand Experiment*. Cambridge, Mass: Abt Associates, 1980.

Meyers, D., and Baillargeon, K. Deriving Place Specific Measure of the Rental Housing Crisis from the 1980 Census: An Application from Texas. *Journal of Urban Affairs*, Vol. 7, No. 3: 63-74, 1985.

Michelman, Frank. The Right to Housing, in Norman Dorsen (ed.), *The Rights of Americans - What They are - What They Should be*. New York: Pantheon Press, 1971.

Michigan Housing Coalition. Out in the Cold: Homeless in Michigan. Lansing, Mich.: Michigan Housing Coalition, 1988.

Milgram, Grace, and Bury, Robert. Existing Housing Resources vs Need. Congressional Research Service Report for Congress, No.87-81 E, Washington, D.C.: Congressional Research Service, 1987.

Miller, Ronald. *The Demolition of Skid Row*. Lexington, Mass: D.C. Heath, 1982.

Mitchell, J. Paul (ed.). *Federal Housing Policy and Programs*. New Brunswick, N.J.: Rutgers Center for Urban Policy Research, 1985.

Moon, Marilyn, and Sawhill, Isabel. Family Incomes: Gainers and Losers, in John Palmer and Isabel Sawhill (eds.), *The Reagan Record*. Cambridge, Mass.: Ballinger Publishing Company, 1984.

Moss, Harold. Community for Creative Nonviolence, Washington, D.C. Interview, March, 1989.

Moynihan, Daniel Patrick. Letter to the Editor. *New York Times*, 5/22/89.

Murray, Charles. *Losing Ground*. New York: Basic Books, 1984.

National Coalition for the Homeless Newsletter. March 1989.

National Council of Negro Women. *Women and Housing - A Report on Sex Discrimination in Five American Cities*. Washington D.C.: U.S. Department of Housing and Urban Development, 1975.

Newman, Sandra, and Schnare, Ann. HUD and HHS Shelter Assistance: Two Approaches to Housing the Poor. *Journal of Housing*, January/February:22-32, 1986.

Newman, Sandra, and Schnare, Ann. *Subsidizing Shelter: The Relationship between Welfare and Housing*. Washington, D.C.: Urban Institute Press, 1988.

New York State Department of Social Services. Homelessness in New York State. Albany, New York: NYSDSS, 1984.

Office of the Special Assistant for Human Resource Development, Doubled-Up Households in the District of Columbia, Washington, D.C.: Office of the Mayor, 1989.

Ozanne, Larry. Double Vision in the Rental Housing Market and a Prescription for Correcting it, in J. Weicher, K. Villani and E. Roistacher (eds.), *Rental Housing: Is there a Crisis?* Washington, D.C.: Urban Institute Press, 1981.

Palmer, John, and Sawhill, Isabel (eds.). *The Reagan Record*. Cambridge, Mass: Ballinger Publishers, 1984.

Peroff, Kathleen. Who are the Homeless and How Many are There? in R. Bingham, R. Green, and S. White (eds.). *The Homeless in Contemporary Society*. Newbury Park, Calif: Sage Publications, 1987.

Peterson, Paul. *When Federalism Works*. Washington, D.C.: The Brookings Institution, 1986.

Phillips, Michael, DeChillo, Neal, Kronenfeld, Daniel, and Middleton-Jeter, Verona. Homeless Families: Services Make a Difference. *Social Casework*, Vol. 69, No. 1:48-53, Jan., 1988.

Phillips, Ted. Executive Director, United Housing Coalition, Detroit, Mich. Interview, February, 1989.

Piliavin, Irving, Sosin, Michael, and Westerfelt, Herb. Conditions Contributing to Long-Term Homelessness: An Exploratory Study. Institute for Research on Poverty Discussion Paper, No. 853. University of Wisconsin - Madison, 1987.

Piven, Francis Fox and Cloward, Richard. *Regulating the Poor*. New York: Vintage Books, 1971.

Piven, Francis Fox, and Cloward, Richard. *Poor People's Movements*. New York: Vintage Books, 1977.

Posa, Peggy. Executive Director, Coalition on Temporary Shelter, Detroit Michigan. Interview, April, 1989.

President's Commission on Housing, *Interim Report*. Washington D.C.: G.P.O., October 30, 1981.

Quigley, John. What Have We Learned About Urban Housing Markets? in Peter Mieszkowski and Mahlon Straszheim (eds.), *Current Issues in Urban Economics*. Baltimore: Johns Hopkins University Press, 1979.

Redburn, F. Stevens, and Buss, Terry. *Responding to America's Homeless: Public Policy Alternatives*. New York: Praeger Publishers, 1987.

Reid, Margaret. *Housing and Income*. Chicago: University of Chicago Press, 1962.

Resource Group, Inc., Don Baumann, Director, Homelessness in Houston, Harris County and the Gulf Coast United Way Service Delivery Areas, Preliminary Draft, December, 1989.

Rimer, Sara. *New York Times*, 7/3/89.

Rivlin, Leanne. A New Look at the Homeless. *Social Policy*, Spring:3-10, 1986.

Rodgers, Harrell. *The Cost of Human Neglect*. New York: M.E. Sharpe, Inc., 1982.

Rodgers, Harrell. *Poor Women, Poor Families: the Economic Plight of America's Female Headed Households*. Armonk, New York: M.E. Sharpe, Inc. 1986.

Roistacher, Elizabeth. A Modest Proposal: Housing Vouchers as Refundable Tax Credits, in Peter Salins (ed.), *Housing America's Poor*. Chapel Hill: University of North Carolina Press, 1987.

Rossi, Peter. No Good Applied Social Research Goes Unpunished. *Society*, November/December: 74-79, 1987.

Rossi, Peter. Minorities and Homelessness, in G. Sandefur and M. Tienda (eds.), *Divided Opportunities: Minorities, Society and Social Policy*. New York, Plenum Press, 1988.

Rossi, Peter. *Down and Out in America: The Origins of Homelessness*. Chicago: University of Chicago Press, 1989.

Rossi, Peter, Fisher, Gene and Willis, Georgianna. *The Condition of the Homeless in Chicago*. Amherst, Mass: Social and Demographic Research Institute, 1986.

Roth, Dee, Bean, Jerry, Lust, Nancy, and Saveanu, Traian. *Homelessness in Ohio*. Columbus, Ohio: Ohio Dept. of Mental Health, 1985.

Salins, Peter (ed.), *Housing America's Poor*. Chapel Hill: University of North Carolina Press, 1987.

Sanjek, Roger. Federal Housing Programs and Their Impact on Homelessness, in Jon Erickson and Charles Wilhelm (eds.), *Housing the Homeless*. New Brunswick, N.J.: Center for Urban Policy Research, 1986.

Schafer, Robert. Racial Discrimination in the Boston Housing Market. *Journal of Urban Economics*, Vol. 6:176-196, 1979.

Schill, Michael, and Nathan, Richard. *Revitalizing America's Cities: Neighborhood Reinvestment and Displacement.* Albany, New York: State University of New York Press, 1983.

Schiller, Bradley, R. *The Economics of Poverty and Discrimination.* Englewood Cliffs N.J.: Prentice Hall, 1973, 1980.

Schmalz, Jeffrey. Miami Police Want to Control Homeless by Arresting Them. P. 1, *New York Times*, 11/9/88.

Schmidt, William. Bold Plans for Curing Sick Housing. *New York Times*, 10/9/88.

Schultze, Charles W. *The Public Use of Private Interest.* Washington, D.C.: The Brookings Institution, 1977.

Seattle Housing Development Consortium. Nonprofit Housing in Seattle, information sheet, 1988.

Seattle Human Services Strategic Planning Office. *Status of Homelessness in the City of Seattle.* Seattle: Seattle Human Services Strategic Planning Office, 1989.

Seattle-King County Emergency Shelter Study Update. *Homeless Revisited.* Seattle: King County Housing and Community Development Division, 1986.

Seattle's 1989 Housing Assistance Plan. Seattle: Department of Community Development, Housing Division, 1988.

Seattle 1989-90 Overall Housing Development Plan. Seattle Housing Levy Program, Seattle: Seattle Housing Authority, 1988.

Seattle Office of Policy Planning. *Seattle Displacement Study.* Seattle: Seattle Office of Policy Planning, 1979.

Sexton, Patricia Cayo. The Life of the Homeless. *Dissent*, Vol. 30:79-84, Winter, 1983.

Shapiro, Issac, and Greenstein, Robert. Holes in the Safety Nets: Poverty Programs and Policies in the States: A National Overview. Washington, D.C.: Center on Budget and Policy Priorities, 1988.

Shelton, Beth Anne, Rodriguez, Nestor, Feagin, Joe, Bullard, Robert, Thomas, Robert. *Houston: Growth and Decline in a Sunbelt Boomtown.* Philadelphia: Temple University Press, 1989.

Simon, John. General Manager of the New York Housing Authority testifying on behalf of the Large Public Housing Authorities before the House Committee on Banking, Finance, and Urban Affairs, Subcommittee on Housing and Community Development *Hearings on the Housing Act of 1985*, pp. 775-782, Washington, D.C.: G.P.O., 1984.

Shlay, Anne. *Where the Money Flow: Lending Patterns in the Washington, D.C-Maryland - Virginia SMSA's.* Chicago: The Woodstock Institute, 1985.

Shlay, Anne. Maintaining the Divided City: Residential Lending Patterns in the Baltimore SMSA. A Report to the Maryland Alliance for Responsible Investment. Baltimore: Johns Hopkins University, 1987.

Shlay, Anne. Credit on Color: the Impact of Segregation and Racial Transition on Housing Credit Flows in the Chicago SMSA form 1980-1983. Chicago: Fair Housing Alliance, 1987.

Slitor, Richard. Rationale of the Present Tax Benefits for Homeowners, in J. Paul Mitchell (ed.), *Federal Housing Policy and Programs*. New Brunswick, N.J.: Rutgers Center for Urban Policy Research, 1985.

Smith, Barton. The Houston Housing Market, 1986 Update. University of Houston Center for Public Policy. Houston: Horne Financial Corporation, 1986.

Smith, Barton. The Houston Housing Market, Preparing for the Good Times. University of Houston Center for Public Policy, May, 1988.

Smolensky, Eugene, Danziger, Sheldon, and Gottschalk, Peter. The Declining Significance of Age in the U.S: Trends in the Well-Being of Children and the Elderly Since 1939. Institute for Research on Poverty Discussion Paper No. 839. University of Wisconsin - Madison, 1987.

Snow, David, Anderson, Leon and Baker, Suzanne G. The Myth of Pervasive Mental Illness Among the Homeless. *Social Problems*, Vol. 33:413-415: June, 1986.

Sosin, Michael, Colson, Paul and Grossman, Susan. *Homelessness in Chicago, Poverty and Pathology, Social Institutions and Social Change*. Chicago, The Chicago Community Trust, 1988.

Stegman, Michael. *The Dynamics of Rental Housing in New York City*. New Brunswick, New Jersey: Rutgers Center for Urban Policy Research, 1982.

Stegman, Michael. New Financing Programs for Housing, in Eugenie Birch (ed.) *The Unsheltered Woman*. Piscataway, N.J.: Rutgers Center for Urban Policy Research, 1985.

Steinbruck, Erna, Director of Carpenter's Shelter for Men, Women and Children, Alexandria, Va. Interview, October, 1989.

Stern, Mark. The Emergence of the Homeless as a Public Problem. *Social Service Review*, Vol. 58:291-301, June, 1984.

Sternlieb, George. The Future of Rental Housing, in J. Weicher, K. Villani, and E. Roistacher (eds.), *Rental Housing: Is There a Crisis? Washington, D.C.: Urban Institute Press, 1981.*

Sternlieb, George. Recent Trends in Housing Quality and Affordability, Comment, in S. Rosenberry and C. Hartman (eds.), *Housing Issues of the 1990's*. New York: Praeger Publishers, 1989.

Sternlieb, George, and Listokin, David. A Review of National Housing Policy, in Peter Salins (ed.), *Housing America's Poor*. Chapel Hill: University of North Carolina Press, 1987.

Stone, Michael. Shelter Poverty in Boston; Problem and Program, in S. Rosenberry and C.Hartman (eds.), *Housing Issues of the 1990's*. New York: Praeger Publishers, 1989.

Struever, Carl. Public/Private Partnerships: The Federal Withdrawal. *Journal of Housing*, May/June:72-75, 1982.

Struyk, Raymond. *A New System for Public Housing*. Washington, D.C.: The Urban Institute Press, 1980.

Struyk, Raymond, Marshall, Sue, and Ozanne, Larry. *Housing Policies for the Urban Poor*. Washington, D.C.: The Urban Institute Press, 1978.

Struyk, Raymond, Mayer, Neil, and Tuccillo, John. *Federal Housing Policy at President Reagan's Midterm*. Washington, D.C.: The Urban Institute Press, 1983.

Struyk, Raymond, and Blake, Jennifer. Selecting Tenants: The Law, Markets and PHA Practices. *Journal of Housing*, January/February:8-12, 1983.

Sunley, Emil. Housing Tax Preferences: Options for Reform, in J. Weicher, K. Villani, and E. Roistacher (eds.), *Rental Housing: Is there a Crisis?* Washington, D.C.: The Urban Institute Press, 1981.

Szanton, Peter. Baltimore 2000. A Report to the Morris Goldseker Foundation, Baltimore, 1986.

Townsend, Peter. *Poverty in the United Kingdom: A Survey of Households, Resources and Standards of Living*. Berkeley: University of California Press, 1979.

Turner, Margery, and Struyk, Raymond. *Urban Housing in the 1980's: Markets and Policies*. Washington, D.C.: The Urban Institute Press, 1984.

Turpin, Roland. An Open Letter on Public Housing. *Journal of Housing*, January/February:6-7, 1982.

United Community Services of Metropolitan Detroit staff report. Homeless Persons in the Metropolitan Detroit Area. Detroit: United Community Services, May, 1984.

U.S. Bureau of the Census. *U.S. Summary, General Social and Economic Characteristics*. Washington, D.C.: G.P.O. 1980.

U.S. Bureau of the Census. *Annual Housing Survey*. SMSA and National files, published volumes, 1973-1983, and SMSA File Technical Documentation/prepared by Data Access and Use Staff, Data Users Services Division. Washington, D.C.: The Bureau, 1975, 1976, 1979, 1983.

U.S. Bureau of the Census. *City and County Data Book*. Washington D.C.: G.P.O., 1980, 1983, 1987.

U.S. Bureau of the Census. Current Housing Report, *Housing Characteristics for Selected Metropolitan Areas*. Washington, D.C.: G.P.O., 1976, 1979, 1983.

U.S. Bureau of the Census. Current Population Reports, *Money Income and Poverty Status of Families and Persons in the United States: 1986*. Series P-60, No. 157. Washington D.C.: G.P.O., 1987.

U.S. Bureau of the Census. *United States Population Estimates by Age, Sex and Race: 1980 to 1987*. Current Population Reports, Series P-25, No. 1022. Washington, D.C.: G.P.O., 1988a.

U.S. Bureau of the Census. *Poverty in the United States, 1986*, Current Population Series P-60, No. 160. Washington, D.C.: G.P.O., 1988b

U.S. Bureau of the Census. Memoranda on Shelter/Street Night Enumeration Proposal for the 1990 Census, 1988c.

U.S. Bureau of the Census. *Statistical Abstract of the United States*. Washington, D.C.: G.P.O., 1982, 1988d.

U.S. Conference of Mayors. The Growth of Hunger, Homelessness and Poverty in America's Cities in 1985, a 25 City Survey. Washington, D.C.: U.S. Conference of Mayors, 1986.

U.S. Conference of Mayors. A Status Report on Homeless Families in American Cities, a 29 City Survey, Washington, D.C.: U.S. Conference of Mayors, 1987.

U.S. Congressional Budget Office. *Trends in Family Income, 1970-1986*. Washington, D.C.: G.P.O., 1988.

U.S. Department of Housing and Urban Development. The Extent of Homelessness in America: A Report to the Secretary on the Homeless and Emergency Shelters. Washington, D.C.: G.P.O.,1984.

U.S. Department of Labor. *Geographic Profile of Employment and Unemployment*. Washington, D.C.: G.P.O., 1987

U.S. Senate. Subcommittee on Children Youth and Families, Children, Youth and Families: 1983, Washington, D.C.: G.P.O., 1984.

United Way of Central Baltimore. Central Maryland Megatrends. Baltimore: United Way, 1987.

Van Vliet, Willem. (ed.). *Housing Markets and Policies under Fiscal Authority*. New York: Greenwood Press, 1987.

Villani, Kevin. Finding the Money to Finance Low Cost Housing, in Peter Salins (ed.), *Housing America's Poor*. Chapel Hill: University of North Carolina Press, 1987.

Von Hingle, Kim. King County (Seattle) Housing and Economic Development Commission, interview, May, 1989.

Waldrop, Judith. Houston on the Rebound. *American Demographics*, February, 1987.

Washington State Department of Community Development. Washington State Housing Needs and Market Trends: An Overview. Seattle, March, 1989.

Weicher, John. Urban Housing Policy, in Peter Mieszkowski and Mahlon Straszheim (eds.), *Current Issues in Urban Economics*. Baltimore: Johns Hopkins University Press, 1979.

Weicher, John. Halfway to a Housing Allowance, in J. Weicher (ed.), *Maintaining the Safety Net*. Washington, D.C.: American Enterprise Institute for Public Policy Research, 1986.

Weicher, John. Private Production: Has the Rising Tide Lifted All Boats? in Peter Salins (ed.) *Housing America's Poor*. Chapel Hill: University of North Carolina Press, 1987.

Weicher, J., Villani, K., and Roistacher, E. (eds.), *Rental Housing: Is There a Crisis?* Washington, D.C.: The Urban Institute Press, 1981.

Wilkerson, Isabel. "Growth of the Very Poor is Focus of New Studies." *New York Times*, November 20, 1987.

Wilson, Franklin. *Residential Consumption, Economic Opportunity and Race*. New York: Academic Press, 1979.

Wilson, William Julius. *The Truly Disadvantaged*. Chicago: University of Chicago Press, 1987.

Wolch, Jennifer, and Akita, Andrea. Hear No Evil, See No Evil: The Federal Response to Homelessness and its Implications for American Cities. Paper prepared for the Association of American Geographers Urban Geography Specialty Group Policy Review Committee Task Force on Homelessness, UCLA, 1987.

Word, David. *Population Estimates by Race and Hispanic Origin for States, Metropolitan Areas, and Selected Counties, 1980 to 1985*. U. S. Department of Commerce, Bureau of the Census. Current Population Reports, P-25, No. 1040-Rd-1. Washington, D.C.: G.P.O., 1989.

Wright, James. *Health and Homelessness.* Amherst, Mass: The Social and Demographic Research Institute, 1985.

Wright, James. The Worthy and Unworthy Homeless. *Society,* Vol. 25, No. 25: 64-69. July, 1988.

Wright, James, and Lam, Julie. Homelessness and the Low- income Housing Supply. *Social Policy,* Vol. 17:48-53, 1987.

Yezer, Anthony. Housing Quality: Comment, in S. Rosenberry and C. Hartman (eds.), *Housing Issues of the 1990's.* New York: Praeger Publishers, 1989.

Yinger, John. Prejudice and Discrimination in the Urban Housing Market, in Peter Mieszkowski and Mahlon Straszheim, (eds.), *Current Issues in Urban Economics.* Baltimore: Johns Hopkins University Press, 1979.

Index

About the Author

Karin Ringheim is a post-doctoral fellow at the Center for Demography and Ecology, a lecturer in the Department of Sociology, and an affiliate of the Institute for Research on Poverty at the University of Wisconsin, Madison.

She received her Ph.D. in Sociology from the University of Wisconsin and has a Master's degree in Public Health from the University of Minnesota.